Building a Linux Internet

George Eckel
Chris Hare

New Riders

New Riders Publishing, Indianapolis, Indiana

Building a Linux Internet Server

By George Eckel and Chris Hare

Published by:
New Riders Publishing
201 West 103rd Street
Indianapolis, IN 46290 USA

Printed in the United States of America 1 2 3 4 5 6 7 8 9 0

Library of Congress Cataloging-in-Publication Data

```
Hare, R. Christopher E., 1962-
   Building a Linux Internet server / R. Christopher E. haare, George
Eckel.
      p.   cm.
   Includes index.
   ISBN 1-56205-525-9
   1. Client/server computing.  2. Linux.  3. Internet (Computer
network)   I. Eckel, George, 1954-   .  II. Title.
QA76.9.C55H36  1995
004.6'7--dc20                                      95-38424
                                                      CIP
```

Warning and Disclaimer

This book is designed to provide information about the Internet. Every effort has been made to make this book as complete and as accurate as possible, but no warranty or fitness is implied.

The information is provided on an "as is" basis. The authors and New Riders Publishing shall have neither liability nor responsibility to any person or entity with respect to any loss or damages arising from the information contained in this book or from the use of the disks or programs that may accompany it.

Publisher	Don Fowley
Associate Publisher	Tim Huddleston
Marketing Manager	Ray Robinson
Acquisitions Manager	Jim LeValley
Managing Editor	Tad Ringo

Product Development Specialist
Emmett Dulaney

Software Specialist
Steve Weiss

Production Editor
Amy Bezek

Copy Editor
Phil Worthington

Associate Marketing Manager
Tamara Apple

Acquisitions Coordinator
Tracy Turgeson

Publisher's Assistant
Karen Opal

Cover Designer
Karen Ruggles

Cover Illustrator
Jerry Blank

Book Designer
Sandra Schroeder

Production Team Supervisor
Laurie Casey

Graphic Image Specialists
Dennis Clay Hager
Jason Hand
Clint Lahnen
Dennis Sheehan

Production Analysts
Angela Bannan
Bobbi Satterfield
Mary Beth Wakefield

Production Team
Kim Cofer
Kevin Foltz
Aleata Howard
Erika Millen
Regina Rexrode
Erich J. Richter
Christine Tyner
Karen Walsh
Robert Wolf

Indexer
Brad Herriman

About the Authors

George Eckel has worked on a number of books for Macmillan Publishing, including *Memory Management for All of Us*, *Inside Windows NT*, and *Inside UNIX*. As a professional writer, George has worked as a consultant for Hewlett-Packard, Sun Microsystems, Informix, AT&T, Time-Warner, and Silicon Graphics, Inc. Presently, he is a part of the core team that developed and demonstrated the world's first interactive television system. George is now working on the Japanese (NTT) implementation of interactive television, and running a consulting business for companies setting up services on the Internet. You can reach him at geckel@warp.engr.sgi.com, or 510-820-5243.

George is the father to three children—Madeline, Nathalie, and Genevieve—and happy husband of Shirlee, whose patience and support helped make this book possible.

Chris Hare is the Operations Manager for a Canadian national Internet service provider, i*internet. He started working in computer-based technology in 1986, after studying Health Sciences. Since that time, he has worked in programming, system administration, quality assurance, training, network management, consulting, and technical management positions.

Chris became the first SCO Authorized Training instructor in Canada in 1988, and has taught Unix courses all over the world for his previous employers and for SCO. As a professional writer, Chris has authored almost 20 articles for *Sys Admin* magazine and has coauthored several books for New Riders Publishing, including *Inside UNIX*, *Internet Firewalls and Network Security*, and the yet-to-be-released *Unix Professional Reference*.

Chris lives in Ottawa, Canada with his wife, Terri, and their children, Meagan and Matthew.

Trademark Acknowledgments

All terms mentioned in this book that are known to be trademarks or service marks have been appropriately capitalized. New Riders Publishing cannot attest to the accuracy of this information. Use of a term in this book should not be regarded as affecting the validity of any trademark or service mark.

Dedication

In memorium for Nancy M. Eckel...
For all the lovely memories...
All the lovely times...
Until we are together again...

Acknowledgments

Chris Hare would like to take the opportunity to thank a few people. First off, to George Eckel for such a wonderful manuscript to work with. Next, to Emmett Dulaney and the staff at New Riders for their encouragement. They are wonderful people as always.

A heartfelt thank you goes to Sohail Khan of Computers and More in Kanata, Ontario for assistance in providing some much-needed computing and network hardware to duplicate and test the various components of this book on the Linux Operating System.

Finally, thanks to wife Terri for supporting me in yet another authoring project. The 3 a.m. mornings are almost becoming habit for her (and me). Nevertheless, these projects wouldn't be possible but for her encouragement.

Contents at a Glance

Table of Contents

Building a Linux Internet Server

To say that the Internet has become a "hot" topic is an understatement. It has bubbled out of the confines of computer user groups and become the common fare of individuals connecting through one of many Internet service providers, and workers in many corporations that use networked computers. Certainly, when you go into a bookstore and look at the computer section, you are greeted with a wall of Internet user books. But the Internet is also showing up outside of computer sections in bookstores, magazines, and newspapers; it is appearing on the front page of newspapers.

The Internet has grown up with computer professionals. Its origins are in research and educational institutions, and its advocates and creative contributors, by in large, have been software engineers.

The number of Internet users has suddenly, this year, reached a critical mass. The number of users has grown to over 30 million. Businesses have opened their collective conscience to the presence of the Internet (and its 30 million potential consumers). They link the Internet to the "Information Superhighway" (a slogan that has permeated commercials and tabloids for the past several years). The Information Superhighway has become part of everyone's vocabulary, not just the vocabulary of software engineers. Everyone has been sold on the excitement of the Information Superhighway, usually without a clue what it means. But the talk has created a public appetite for it, and businesses are happy to oblige if there is a potential for profit.

With the number of Internet users growing at roughly 5 percent per month, with the awakening of businesses and the general public to the excitement and profit potential of the Information Superhighway, with the new multimedia Internet browsers that are capable of providing compelling presentations that allow users to navigate and retrieve information by pointing and clicking on pictures and words instead of through arcane commands, and with the lower cost and higher home penetration of computer hardware, use of the Internet is exploding.

The landscape of the Internet is about to change. Internet providers up to now have been specialized businesses, unfamiliar to the general public, or government-funded institutions, such as NCSA. The Internet has been shrouded in its own jargon, such as T1, PPP, SLIP, T3, TCP/IP, and ISDN. The wraps

are about to be taken off of the Internet, and this jargon is about to be obliterated by a user-oriented vocabulary that will make the process of connecting to the Internet as conceptually easy as getting electric service in your home. All a user will need to say is, "I want to be connected to the Internet." WWW clients will be standard so that users will not have to define the type of connection they need. And users will also ask, "How much for the service?" This is the question that means money to companies participating in the Internet.

Just recently Pacific Bell announced that it is going to flood California with Internet sites and offer Internet services at competitive prices: between $20 and $30 per month.

Toting $9.25 billion in annual revenues, and a familiarity with the public, Pacific Bell, along with other businesses that seize the opportunity, will popularize the Internet suddenly and dramatically.

Telephone companies have an obvious interest in the Internet. MCI has announced that they now offer a mall of stores, called marketplaceMCI.

Stores include Dun & Bradstreet Information Services, Hammacher Schlemmer & Co., OfficeMax Inc., Intercontinental Florist, National Wildlife Galleries, Doneckers, Aetna Life & Casualty, Amtrak, Borders Ind. bookstore, Healthrider, and Timberland. The variety of "stores" shows how wide an appeal the Internet has.

The Internet began as a non-commercial venue only, because the major network providers were government-funded. Commerce has slowly crept into Internet space, however. This year, for the first time, there are more commercial services than educational and research institution services combined. This trend will continue. There will be a shaking out

The Pacific Bell WWW site.

period as companies try to find the best way to become known by a world of users. The complexion of the Internet will become less freeware-oriented and more purchase-oriented (although there will always remain a fierce minority of users, large in number, who will continue to provide freeware). But businesses that persist will find the Internet market rich; it is a terrific place for servicing customer relations, distributing marketing information, and consummating product sales. As authentication software becomes available by the end of 1995 (and more bulletproof in 1996), secure money transactions will allow businesses and users to use the Internet in a way they have not been able to before. Just this month, a bank has introduced full service banking over the Internet.

The marketplaceMCI
WWW site.

How This Book Is Organized

As a business owner, it is important to understand the basic mechanics and the business applications of the Internet. As a system administrator, it is important to understand the tasks you need to complete to create Internet services. This book is divided into three parts.

*Doneckers in
marketplaceMCI.*

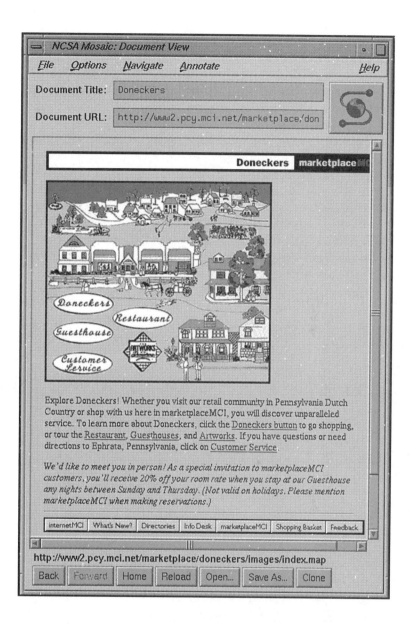

Part One: Using the Internet for Business

Chapters 1–3 are for general consumption. They introduce you to the Internet and describe how businesses can take advantage of it.

Part Two: Getting Connected to the Internet

Chapters 4–8 discuss the connection choices you have when hooking up to the Internet, the equipment you need, the cost of the enterprise, and the security software and machinery needed to secure your local area network.

Part Three: Setting Up and Managing Internet Services

The remaining chapters describe in detail how to offer and manage a variety of services, including an FTP service, a freeWAIS service, a Gopher service, or a World Wide Web service running under the Linux Operating System, a freely available implementation of Unix for the Intel PC platform.

Business owners should read, at least, the first part of the book. The last two parts of the book are relatively technical. They assume a basic knowledge of Unix and networking. If you are a system administrator interested in offering an Internet service, you can show the first part of the book to business officials in your company to introduce them to the Internet and foster their enthusiasm for it. You can then use the last two parts of the book to implement their Internet wishes.

All of the information in this book is, of course, time stamped. Writing about moving targets is never easy. You might get frustrated if you find that software discussed in this book has been revised, or that some Internet addresses no longer exist; such are the vagaries of the Internet, and the hazards of writing about it. But this is the time to get fascinated by the Internet. So often you may have remorsed, "If only I had known then what I know now and gotten in on the ground floor..." This year, 1995, is such a time; it is the ground floor of an opportunity. The Information Superhighway will rocket into the 21st century as surely as TV has become a part of our lives. Hop aboard, fasten your seatbelt, and brace yourself for a detonation of revelations and possibilities.

New Riders Publishing

The staff of New Riders Publishing is committed to bringing you the very best in computer reference material. Each New Riders book is the result of months of work by authors and staff who research and refine the information contained within its covers.

As part of this commitment to you, the NRP reader, New Riders invites your input. Please let us know if you enjoy this book, if you have trouble with the information and examples presented, or if you have a suggestion for the next edition.

If you have a question or comment about any New Riders book, there are several ways to contact New Riders Publishing. We will respond to as many readers as we can. Your name, address, or phone number will never become part of a mailing list or be used for any purpose other than to help us continue to bring you the best books possible. You can write us at the following address:

> New Riders Publishing
> Attn: Associate Publisher
> 201 W. 103rd Street
> Indianapolis, IN 46290

If you prefer, you can fax New Riders Publishing at (317) 581-4670. You can send e-mail to New Riders at the following Internet address:

edulaney@newriders.mcp.com

NRP is an imprint of Macmillan Computer Publishing. To obtain a catalog or information, or to purchase any Macmillan Computer Publishing book, call (800) 428-5331.

Thank you for selecting *Building a Linux Internet Server*!

I

Using the Internet for Business

1

What Is the Internet?

People wax philosophical when they try to define the Internet. Is the Internet a group of machines, or is it something for which people use machines? Is it an ideology? Or is it a combination of all three?

Stated most simply, the Internet is a global network of computers. Whereas a LAN consists of computers networked within a building or organization, the Internet consists of all the separate networks linked together throughout the world. Linking one network to another, to another, and to another, gives each Internet user on the global network the ability to communicate with machines as remote as the most remote local network. Today, for example, you can connect to a computer in Antarctica.

Boarding the Internet for the first time is exciting. Usually, people think of interacting with computers on a local scale. You might pass e-mail messages to someone down the hall, or coordinate schedules between a group of workers in your company.

The Internet provides gateways to the entire world. Clicking on one hypertext link might take you to a university in Egypt, and the next click might take you to Taiwan! Sending a letter that distance is one thing, but retrieving the information from literally around the world in seconds puts a world of information and people as close as your keyboard.

Just as you have to adjust the scope of your thinking when you switch from a single to a networked computer, you must adjust the scope of your thinking when you connect to a network of computers around the world. Once, you could share ideas and exchange documents with only the people down the hall; now, you can communicate with people several civilizations away. The Internet forces you to think globally. Crossing national boundaries with such ease makes working on the Internet revolutionary and presents unique opportunities for business.

A Revolution in Communications

The Internet is a fascinating development in the communication of ideas. Ever since Gutenberg, using media to disseminate knowledge has been expensive. Printing presses that can print thousands of newspapers per day are great—but can you afford one? Radio can reach hundreds of thousands of people. Television can reach millions of people. Great! But when was the last time you examined the cost of creating a radio or television station? You never have because you know the cost is prohibitive. Undeniably, these are all great communication mediums—but most people have no access to them.

The largest audience most people can reach has been limited to the number of Xerox copies they can afford. Now, however, the Internet enables you to reach millions of people. The Internet provides an inexpensive means of communication for anyone who has a computer and some basic skills.

A Short History of the Internet

The history of the Internet is interesting in its own right, and is included in this chapter because its metamorphosis impacts the way business can use it. Initially, because the Internet's founders were government institutions, such as the National Science Foundation, the Internet was staunchly antiadvertising and antibusiness. Today, however, that bias has been virtually reversed; business sites on the Internet now outnumber educational and research sites combined.

The Internet was born nearly thirty years ago as a Department of Defense experiment. At the time, the Department of Defense had several networks, including ARPAnet and various radio and satellite networks.

ARPAnet (Advanced Research Projects Agency) was an experimental network created to support Department of Defense research. Because the military designed it, they had their own, perhaps odd, set of requirements for the network. The network had to function, for example, even if part of it were knocked out—actually a nice design requirement because towns and cities occasionally experience power failures. The military, however, had to consider other implications, such as bombs blasting away parts of the network. Network communications needed to be able to continue even under such extreme conditions.

These design requirements reduce the number of hardware communication principles to one: communication occurs between two computers. That's it. The source computer puts its message in an envelope, called an Internet Protocol (IP) packet, addresses it, and sends it on its way. It is the target computer's job to figure out if the message is addressed to it, and if it is, to decode the IP packet.

The model for communication processing was, therefore, a decentralized model. It was impossible to base the Internet on one central processing router. That fact facilitated connections between computers because the DoD's design requirements stated that the Internet should continue to work even if part of it, any part, were knocked out. Every computer had to be able to talk to any other computer on a network, and to know whether a message was destined for it.

Getting different makes of computers across the world to talk to one another is no simple trick. The protocol that makes it possible is TCP/IP. TCP/IP came packaged in the Berkeley distribution of Unix. As freeware, TCP/IP (and Berkeley Unix) was on just about every workstation, and became the de facto protocol of network communications.

 n o t e The Organization for International Standardization (ISO) labored for years to develop a different networking standard. Manufacturers, however, did not have time to wait for a sanctioned standard. Customers wanted computers that could communicate. To respond to market pressure, manufacturers had to implement what worked: TCP/IP.

ISO finally created a standard called the Open Systems Interconnect (ISO/OSI) protocol suite. The United States government has decided that its networks should be able to use ISO/OSI. The fact is, however, that very few networks are ISO/OSI-based. The present system works without ISO/OSI, so switching to it faces a natural resistance—especially because using it offers no advantage. ISO/OSI is more complicated and less mature than IP. Although it offers some features that IP doesn't, it is less efficient.

During the effort to develop an IP standard, local networking matured. Ethernet LANs became available for desktop workstations around 1983. Because IP software was already on most machines (due to the freeware release of Berkeley Unix), people wanted to connect their local network to ARPAnet to participate on a national network and benefit from national information resources. A national network would enable anyone, anywhere, to communicate if they had IP software.

Companies, usually governmental and educational, using LANs, wanted to tie into ARPAnet so that everyone in their LAN could benefit from ARPAnet resources. Other institutions were using ARPAnet protocols, namely, IP and a suite of related protocols, to develop their own networks, so that they, too, could tie into ARPAnet. One of these networks was NSFNET.

The National Science Foundation (NSF), a government agency, had five supercomputers located in remote sites that they wanted to join with a network. NSF originally wanted to use ARPAnet to make the network, but staffing and bureaucratic problems prevented the use of ARPAnet. Instead, NSF created its own network, NSFNET.

NSFNET used 56 Kbps lines, considered very fast at the time, to connect the supercomputers. After people discovered what NSF had to offer, everyone wanted to get in on NSFNET.

Because of their high cost, supercomputers were available only to government agencies; agencies usually working on weapons development. The prospect of using supercomputers made NSFNET quite attractive. But how could other networks connect to NSFNET? ARPAnet was not the solution.

Running dedicated telephone lines from NSFNET to each university would cost a fortune, because the cost of such connections increases with each mile of wire laid. The solution to the problem formed the connection scheme used today (see fig. 1.1). Regional networks were created, each of which was connected to a supercomputer, and the regional networks were connected with the 56 Kbps lines.

Anyone in one region, therefore, could communicate with anyone in another region. This daisy chain connection scheme dramatically reduced the required miles of dedicated telephone lines, prevented NSFNET from becoming the hub of the Internet, and additionally, had the beneficial byproduct of connecting many regional networks into one large network that users could use to share resources. Because most networks were based in academia or research foundations, the prospect of

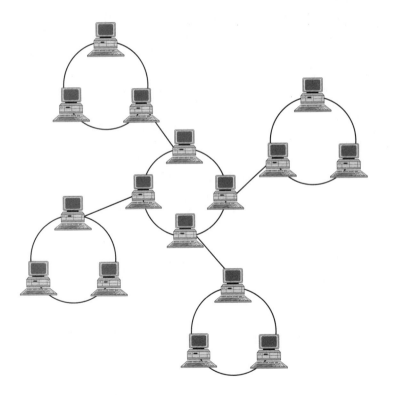

Figure 1.1

Network scheme of NSFNET.

easily sharing ideas across time zones excited network users. After all, ideas are their business. A network of this scale fostered discussion, debate, and research (the media for the flow of ideas) among many of the brightest minds of the age.

Connecting a nation of universities sparked worldwide collaborations. Internet traffic increased until the resources were overwhelmed. In 1987, IBM, MCI, and Merit Network Inc., which controlled Michigan's educational network, received a contract to manage and upgrade the network. Technology flourished between 1983 and 1987, and replacing the 1983 technology with faster telephone lines and faster computers was the obvious choice.

Because NSF was a government agency, it was inappropriate for NSF to support business use of the Internet. Other local networks that supported use of the Internet as a business tool, such as UUNET, grew. Those local networks then joined NSFNET and the rest of the Internet, which provided businesses with a friendly environment in which to join the Internet and have the same connection possibilities as anyone on NSFNET. Although the roots of the Internet are not related to business, the Internet continues to embrace businesses as valuable information and service providers.

The technology of the Internet continues to improve invisibly. You never read e-mail messages that report that the Internet will be down tomorrow for six hours. The Internet never shuts down, thanks to its decentralized nature. Servers might shut down for replacement or software upgrades, and services you seek might be temporarily unavailable, but the network as a whole continues without interruption. Not a war in the Middle East, not a revolution in Russia, not a bomb in the World Trade Center terminates Internet services.

Today, the Internet is reliable and robust. It connects people to people and people to information half a world away. It is an amazing repository of information available not only to government officials or graduate students at Princeton and Yale, but to anyone who has access to a computer linked to the Internet. It is a great equalizer; it empowers anyone who cares to use it. It has fulfilled the dreams of its originators: to connect a world of people and ideas. In so doing, it has reduced forever our dependence on large institutions, such as newspapers, television, and libraries, for information dissemination.

The Internet is the foundation from which the dream of an information superhighway springs—the tool that enables a world of people to talk.

Internationalization of the Internet

Originally, foreign countries stipulated the use of their own protocols rather than TCP/IP. They often felt that IP was bad because it was not home-grown. Using a protocol other than TCP/IP made foreign networks incompatible with the Internet.

The Scandinavian countries were an exception. They used IP from the beginning and are well-integrated into the Internet community. In 1989, however, most European countries began to switch to TCP/IP. An organization, Reseaux IP Europeans (RIPE), began to coordinate the integration of IP and the Internet in Europe. Presently, 25 percent of Internet hosts are European. Almost every European country (the old Eastern-block countries to a much lesser extent) participates in the Internet.

European participation continues to grow because of the attraction of the West's research and scientific resources. Since of the fall of the Iron Curtain, Eastern-block companies are now eager to participate in the Internet. With the price of technology falling, even third-world countries can afford Internet technology, with which they can add to their technological and educational resources.

The lack of a technologically sophisticated telephone provider currently restricts Internet expansion in some countries. Data rates often are limited to voice-speed, 9,600 bps, which reduces the kind of information that can be transmitted. Images, video, and audio are impractical to transmit in that environment. The only practical data to transmit is binary or text.

In Asia, the most technologically advanced countries participate on the Internet (for example, Japan, Hong Kong, Korea, Taiwan, India, Indonesia, and Malaysia). Australia and New Zealand are connected to the Internet. Even Antarctica is on the Internet.

Only a few countries in Africa, including Egypt, Zaire, and South Africa, participate on the Internet.

The United States ranks as the largest user of the Internet, but that will shift as technology becomes cheaper.

Who Governs the Internet?

Because the Internet is decentralized, it does not have a ruling body. No one is elected as president, board chairman, or CEO of the Internet. Some official organizations, however, do have a strong voice in Internet affairs.

 note Because the Internet consists of many connected networks, each network can have a president and a set of rules governing conduct on its local network. No one body, however, rules over all the connected networks.

The *Internet Society* (ISOC) is a nonprofit organization whose members volunteer time to promote global communication through the Internet. The ISOC has a council of elders that provides technical direction and management for the Internet, called the *Internet Architecture Board* (IAB). The IAB allocates resources, such as Internet addresses, and supports standards. Allocating resources does not mean the IAB actually tells companies their Internet addresses; rather, the IAB makes rules for the allocation of addresses. They worry, for example, about issues such as what to do about running out of unique Internet addresses. If the IAB considers a new standard important, it adopts it and broadcasts it over the Internet.

Another formal Internet organization is the *Internet Engineering Task Force* (IETF). The volunteers who form the membership of this organization discuss Internet operational and technical problems. IETF creates work groups for large or difficult problems, such as figuring out how networks should cooperate during Internet problems, or what the meaning of the bits should be in Internet packets. Such work groups often make recommendations to Internet users or to the IAB for canonization as an Internet standard.

A third organization important to the operation of the Internet is InterNIC. This body actually has little to do with governing the Internet. You apply to the InterNIC for a permanent Internet address. InterNIC also is a great resource for answering questions about the Internet. To receive an index of Internet documents, send e-mail to `mailserv@is.internic.net`; leave the subject field empty and send only the following words as the body of your e-mail letter:

```
send index
```

The mail server automatically processes your request by e-mailing you an index of Internet topics.

Although these organizations are the closest the Internet has to governing bodies, they have no teeth. Local networks can choose whether or not to follow the edicts of IAB. If they do not follow IAB recommendations, no one comes along and cuts their telephone lines; they can still participate in the Internet. If, however, their local network does damage to the network, their network will find itself alone, without global connections. Normally, local networks work within the boundaries of IAB standards and bring up their problems with the ITEF. Whether those problems bring about change is another matter.

In actuality, individual Internet users govern Internet usage as much as any of the formal Internet organizations. Formal organizations can prescribe Internet law, but they do not have a police department to enforce their policies. Users, however, often act like vigilantes to discourage use of the Internet that they consider inappropriate. The penance, for example, for sending e-mail to the wrong newsgroup can range from nasty e-mails to service requests that cripple your server. In the jargon of the Internet, this penance is called *flaming*.

Who Pays for the Internet?

You don't send your monthly check to a centralized Internet corporation. Nor does a government agency that has a long name starting out, "Department of ...," subsidize the Internet.

The majority of Internet providers are businesses in and of themselves. They survive by collecting Internet subscription fees from customers. Local networks connect to one another through business deals. They arrive at agreements that allow each to improve their businesses. As an individual, educational, or corporate Internet subscriber, you pay Internet service providers for connecting to the Internet, and the phone company for the lines that connect the networked computers.

What You Find on the Internet

Even the briefest of visits to the Internet should convince you that the wealth of information on the Internet is staggering. In part, the fun of the Internet is that you can go from document to document, down a rich path of interesting topics, knowing that you had ten other choices of interesting topics to read for every one topic you did read.

Joining the Internet are major companies, such as IBM, Silicon Graphics, and EXXON; small companies, such as Grant's Flowers; universities, national research centers, libraries, newspapers, the stock market, and, of course, a multitude of individuals.

The subject matter discussed on the Internet knows no limit. Any wild and weird topic you might imagine probably belongs to a discussion group somewhere on the Internet. Subject matter ranges from technical topics, to folk art, to J.R.R. Tolkien, to insects. The Internet is an encyclopedia of topics.

What Can You Do on the Internet?

You can do a wide variety of things on the Internet. The following is a list of the most common:

→ Exchange e-mail

→ Browse documents

→ Download and upload data

→ Download and upload software programs

→ Participate in discussion groups

→ Offer information and services

Rather than writing and faxing a letter to someone, why not e-mail the letter so that it arrives immediately? Or, if your company is researching the chemical makeup of exotic plants for potential medical uses, why not climb onto the Internet and search (and retrieve) research data from other institutions first? Perhaps your company produces cars; why not start (or participate in) a newsgroup that discusses cars so that you can establish your company in the minds of potential customers? Further, why not aid your company's customer support department by making available (through the Internet) answers to commonly asked questions?

As you can see, the number of topics and uses of the Internet knows few boundaries.

Summary

This chapter gave you background information about the Internet. We looked at the evolution of the Internet, and the organizations (and users) that have and will chart the course for the Internet's development.

Now that you understand in a general way how the Internet evolved, who governs the Internet, who uses the Internet, and what is on the Internet, it's time to look at how businesses, specifically, can benefit from participating on the Internet.

2

Business and the Internet

The challenges that businesses face today are similar to the challenges they have faced in the past: reduce costs, increase market share, reduce time to market, improve profitability, and become recognized as an industry leader. Although these goals remain constant, technology has blurred country borders and reduced oceans to phone-call distances. As a result, the number of competitors for your business has grown steadily over the years, from the business down the street, to the business in the next town, to businesses around the world.

Today, not only do you have to outsell every Tom, Dick, and Sally, you have to compete against Japanese, German, and Taiwanese Toms, Dicks, and Sallys.

Working within the scope of a global economy requires new approaches to marketing. Marketing to a global community requires a lot of money or great ingenuity. The Internet is used in 137 countries. It can give your company the global presence it needs to compete in the global market place.

The Internet is at a pivotal point in its development. Before 1994, fast computers were somewhat expensive, an easy-to-use graphical interface to the Internet was not available, and the preponderance of Internet sites were educational or research institutions. Today, 486 and Pentium computers are fast enough to handle the new graphical interfaces that make Internet access so much easier. With over 2 million servers on the Internet and over 20 million users, businesses are finally seeing that the Internet represents a large market. And as new businesses offer services on the Internet, more people are attracted to the Internet. Participation in the Internet is exploding.

Businesspeople know that you approach advertising in the local newspaper differently from advertising on television and differently again on radio. Each medium has its own idiosyncrasies. You would not run the audio portion of a TV commercial on radio, for example, nor would you videotape two people recording a radio commercial, show it as a television commercial, and expect to motivate many people. If you don't understand the idiosyncrasies of the medium, your message, more often than not, will fall on deaf ears.

The Internet is a new medium. It's important to know what makes it tick, what tools it provides to motivate users, and what works and what does not.

Who Is Using the Internet?

Successful businesspeople know the customer. They understand how the product or service fits the customer's needs.

More than 30 million people and 5 million services are now connected to the Internet. Roughly 1,133,000 services are at educational sites, 175,000 services at military sites, and the remaining 1,300,000 services at business and personal sites.

Internet traffic is growing at a monthly rate of 6 percent. In January, 1988, Internet traffic consisted of 85 million packets. In December, 1994, Internet traffic had grown to more than 86 billion packets—an increase of *1000 percent* in 7 years.

 note For more Internet statistics, ftp to `nic.merit.edu`.

Profile of PC and Online Services' Penetration into Homes

If the primary audience for your service or product is people at home, you need to know how many people have access to the Internet in their homes. This section provides some statistics.

The Internet Business Center made the following statistics available. You can find this data, collected from the 10th Annual Software Publishing Association conference, at the following address:

`http://tig.com/IBC/statistics.html`

➜ 33 percent of U.S. households currently have PCs.

- Estimates place PCs in 60 percent of U.S. households by 1998.

- 12 percent of households have modems.

- 6 percent of households subscribe to online services, such as CompuServe and America Online.

- 20 percent of online subscribers use more than one online service.

- The average user logs in to an online service 11 times per month.

- America Online has the highest trial rate.

- The average length of an online session is 25 minutes.

- CompuServe has 2.3 million subscribers, Prodigy more than 2 million subscribers, and America Online more than 1 million subscribers.

- Delphi has 100,000 subscribers; the Imagination Network has 509,000 subscribers; Ziffnet has 230,000 subscribers.

Profile of Internet Usage

Before you plunk down any advertising money, one key question is, "How many people might see my advertisement?" This section helps answer that question.

The Internet Business Center made the following statistics available; the data was collected from the 10th Annual Software Publishing Association conference.

- There are more than 71,000 private and public sites.

- There are more than 4.8 million servers providing services.

- There are an estimated 30 million Internet users.

- There are more than 1,400 WWW sites.

- There are Internet sites in 137 countries.

Profiling the Typical Internet User

Before you advertise on the Internet, you need to get to know Mr. John Q. Average. This section helps you do just that.

The Internet Business Center made the following statistics available. The statistics were compiled from the First World Wide Web User Survey prepared by the Graphics, Visualization, & Usability Center of the College of Computing at the Georgia Institute of Technology in January, 1994.

 note The Georgia Institute of Technology's goal is to conduct a user survey twice a year. To see the most recently updated statistics, use the following URL:

`http://www.cc.gatech.edu/gvc/user_surveys`

Table 2.1 lists the percentage of Internet users by specified group, and it does so based on several different forms of measurement, such as age, educational background, and so forth.

For more information concerning these figures, and for more Internet user statistics, look at `http://www.UMich.edu/~sgupta/conres.html`.

Table 2.1 Distribution of Internet Users

Specified Group	Percentage of Internet Users
Age	
Under 20	17%
21–25	29%
26–30	27%
31–35	8%
36–40	11%
41–50	6%
Over 50	2%
Educational Background	
Bachelor's degree	34%
Master's degree	23%
Some college experience	19%
Location	
North America	72%
Europe	23%
Australia	3%
Occupation	
Technical professionals	27%
Students	26%
Researchers	14%
Managers	7%
Gender	
Male	90%
Female	10%

Specified Group	Percentage of Internet Users
Affiliation	
Educational institution	51%
Commercial institution	31%
Government institution	7%
Marital Status	
Single	53%
Married	43%
Children in Household	
0	70%
1	11%
2	12%
3+	7%

Looking at Internet Trends

Before you commit major time and money to a project, you want to know that the Internet isn't going to disappear overnight. This section provides some statistics concerning the growth of the Internet.

The Internet Business Center made the following statistics available. The data was collected from the 10th Annual Software Publishing Association conference.

→ The Internet is experiencing explosive growth: the number of Internet users is growing between 6 and 10 percent *per month*.

→ The cost of subscribing to the Internet is declining.

→ Many major businesses—226 of the 490 largest companies—already have a presence on the Internet.

→ Networks grew 163 percent on the Internet in the United States in 1994.

→ The startup cost for a WWW service can be less than $20,000.

→ 39 percent of all communication companies are already on the Internet.

→ 24 percent of information technology firms are already on the Internet.

→ 27 percent of servers are sponsored by educational institutions (and have an .edu extension).

→ 24 percent of servers are sponsored by businesses (and have a .com extension).

→ By early 1996, encrypting credit card transactions will be possible.

→ 94 percent of Internet users are male; most have technical degrees.

These demographics are changing radically. The bell curve of the age range is skewed toward the younger ages because of the penetration of the Internet into the educational community. You can expect these students to continue to use the Internet as they grow older, and therefore, see a consequent gradual rise in the age of the average user.

The gender of the average Internet user is heavily male. As businesses continue to jump on the Internet bandwagon, however, they bring with them large numbers of female users. That statistic will moderate considerably.

Until recently, the interface to the Internet has been text-based. Text-based interfaces are never very user-friendly. Consequently, the statistic describing the occupation of the average user is presently skewed toward people in technical occupations, where, in addition, access to the Internet is most common. The advent of graphical user interfaces has made finding and retrieving information on the Internet much more user-friendly. These interfaces open the door for more and more less technically inclined people to use the Internet.

The growth of the Internet is phenomenal. While the number of educational users grows slowly, the bulk of new users consists of individuals and corporate personnel. In 1994, for the first time ever, the number of business sites on the Internet exceeded educational and research institutions combined. As more businesses become a part of the Internet, the demography of Internet users will shift toward a user profile that more closely matches working people rather than students. This shift also will happen because more and more students have been exposed to the Internet and, after they graduate, will carry that experience into the businesses with which they work. And as more and more businesses expose employees of all ages to the Internet, many will want to access the Internet from home so that they can connect to their company's e-mail system, or because they develop an interest in any of the other services on the Internet.

Business Uses of the Internet

Now that you know what the Internet is and who uses it, you might wonder how your business can take advantage of it. This section gives you some ideas along those lines (although you will undoubtedly think of many more).

Two groups benefit from Internet services—people inside your company and people outside your company. Internal employees might not necessarily reside in the same building, or even in the same state. Although a company that sits in one building can use a local network for distributing company information, companies that have satellite offices generally rely on the Internet. So "internal" uses for the Internet does not necessarily entail everyone sitting under the same roof.

Internal Uses of the Internet

Although company networks have been around for a while, often their use is relegated to e-mail. Here are some additional ideas for how you can use a network:

→ Use the network as the central source of all company information. Use WWW or Gopher services, for example, to present company newsletters, stock quotes, announcements, press releases, competitors' actions, organizational charts, orientation materials, company goal statements, product or service information, sales successes, promotions, employee successes, and company ethics. Gopher and WWW are particularly effective means of conveying such information. Gopher and WWW clients can start at a home page and provide access to any of these topics.

→ Network tools can help tie together all parts of your organization. If your company resides in more than one building, or if your company is divided into different departments, a situation can arise in which the left hand does not know what the right hand is up to. By using the network as a central source of information, each department or company satellite can stay up-to-date on what the others are doing and help foster cooperation or even friendly competition.

→ Put time cards (if you use them in your business) into electronic form by creating a WWW (HTML) version of them. Constructing a simple form that employees fill out enables you to automate time-card data processing.

→ Make available all standard documents, logos, trademarks, style templates, and forms that employees might use. Consider using a WAIS service to help employees find such documents. WAIS is a tool that can help you locate documents. For more information concerning this tool, see Chapter 13, "Setting Up a freeWAIS Service."

→ Make available to all employees in all company locations and departments any company-created software. You might want both a WAIS service to help people find the software, and an FTP service to help people actually download it.

→ Place an employee directory on the network. You might use a WAIS service to help employees find employee names and locations.

→ Use a WWW or Gopher client to publish internal employment opportunities with job descriptions.

→ Use WAIS, WWW, or Gopher services to publish product or service-specific information. Often employees in an organization have specialized knowledge about your services or products because they created them. Often others pound these people's doors when they need that information. Putting their information on a service can save them from having to explain the same topic over and over.

→ Increase your customer base. A user base of more than 30 million people can offer people who are interested in your products or services. As with any marketing project, however, you have to be adept at reaching appropriate prospects for your product or service. Sending e-mail to 20 million people is not exactly the way to go. We discuss some of the marketing techniques you can use to ply your trade within the boundaries of Internet etiquette.

→ Seek product reviews. Before your company makes major investments, someone on the Internet very likely has used the product your company plans to buy. Get your consumer report by asking for product reviews.

→ Get expert help. Many Internet participants are university professors, and corporate professionals—often at the top of their field. The Internet encourages friendly discussions. You might find answers for your hardest questions without paying a consulting fee!

→ Test-market your new products. Some users are willing to answer surveys. You can do product analysis by asking Internet users for input. You also can ask for feedback about products already on the market.

→ Recruit employees on the Internet. On your company's home page, you can have job offerings at your company as one of the topics. Internet Business Services, (408-524-2975) rick@ar.com, posts resumes. Also, USENET newsgroups, such as misc.jobs.offered or misc.jobs.resumes, are convenient places to post job listings and review candidates.

→ Transfer documents economically. Transferring documents on the Internet saves your company the postal charges. Courier companies make their profit from delivering mail overnight. You can use the Internet to deliver your documents in seconds, not days. And if a transmission gets damaged, you can just resend it.

Offering External Internet Services

The following services are geared for people outside your company.

→ Publish product or service announcements. On a home page, using a Gopher or WWW service, you might have a "Hot News" selection that takes people to new product or service announcements. You also want another selection that lets people find all services and products your company offers.

→ Use the Internet to offer customer support. You can put updated versions of your product manuals on a WAIS and WWW or Gopher service—perhaps manuals designed to be multimedia documents rather than just copies of hard documentation. Such services can reduce the load on technical support personnel. These services also reduce the ever-more-expensive costs of producing and shipping manuals.

→ Publish other, related information, such as press releases, product reviews, price guides, and special offers. It's the old trick of putting a clock on your building. Even though your company's business is not telling people the time, people often look at your store front if you have a clock on it. If you can offer information of general interest, perhaps a car buying guide if your company provides car parts, you can attract the attention of people who might then turn and look at your services.

→ Offer software updates or patches over the Internet. This service requires a means of searching, such as a WAIS service, and a download service, such as FTP.

→ Keep an archive of third-party shareware that adds to the functionality of your product. You need an FTP service to provide this benefit to customers. Maintenance costs are low, and because the shareware is coming from your server, it appears as though you are giving customers freeware—everyone likes something valuable for nothing!

→ Get valuable customer feedback or bug reports. Giving customers the means of providing customer feedback empowers them. It gives your company a means of immediately satisfying customer needs, and up-to-the-minute beta testing that allows your company to correct a problem before it becomes widespread.

→ Put your company on a mailing list server, such as Majordomo or listserv. These services often have sections for new product or service announcements. Using Majordomo relieves your company of the burden of creating and maintaining a mailing list.

→ Search lists of foundations to find sources of grant money. Presently, entire libraries of foundations are available. The job of finding foundations to which you can apply without using the Internet is about as difficult as writing the grant proposal. Computer-assisted searching takes the pain out of finding appropriate foundations to which to apply.

→ Allow customers to buy products and services over the Internet. This area is still a bit tricky. Before charging and shipping products to a client, it is important to confirm purchases with a phone call. Computer hackers love to take advantage of someone else's money. The authentication technology for the Internet is only partially in place. Allowing customers to buy over the Internet gives them an immediate way of fulfilling a buying decision. Your company's follow-up phone call is a way to make customer contact and determine if the customer might like additional products or services.

→ Communicate quickly with people outside your company using e-mail. A good solution to playing telephone tag is to switch to e-mail. E-mail is a hybrid of the telephone and the letter: its delivery is as fast as a telephone, and yet, like a letter, provides more permanent expression. E-mail has all the fun of "getting something in the mail," but none of the pressure of a telephone call. For these reasons, I know many people who are *e-mail junkies*: they pause mid-work to read their e-mail whenever new messages arrive.

→ Participate in research heaven. When your employees research topics, they often are limited to the local libraries, bookstores, and the lag between time of writing and time of publishing. On the Internet, your employees can browse through libraries in Egypt or Japan, and read documents on the same day they are written.

→ Post demonstration versions of your software, or show your product (or service) in action. You can see examples of this idea by ftping to `ftp.internet.net`.

For people both internal and external to your company, the Internet is a great means of increasing your company's visibility, customer service, and sales.

A New Principle in Customer Relations

The Internet can offer a new level of customer support, for example:

→ Telephone conversations are good, but inadequate when what the customer really needs is a document right away.

→ You can send software patches to customers to help "put out fires" when customers find problems in software.

→ You can offer customers all the advantages of online documentation, including hypertext links and timely updates.

→ The Internet offers customers visual aids.

Telecommuting

You can use the Internet to bring your company into the 21st century by enabling employees to telecommute. *Telecommuting* is most often thought of as "working out of your own home." It involves using communication tools, such as computers, fax machines, modems, and the Internet, to accomplish the same tasks you would if you were at your place of work.

Allowing employees to telecommute means they need passage through the company's firewall, e-mail, and FTP clients, at least, on their machine at home, and an Internet connection. In return, the company gets to reduce the amount of floor space it needs. The company saves the associated building, insurance, office equipment, and utility costs. Many employees work better at home, which you can measure by their productivity.

Laws in California actually require corporations to reduce auto pollution. Telecommuting satisfies state laws that require a corporation to prove efforts at auto emission reduction.

Instead of enlarging one facility to encompass your work force, your company can create satellite offices connected to the main office by the Internet. Satellite offices also offer reduced commute times for employees, which allows your company to draw its employees from a larger geographical area.

Keeping Up with the World

The Internet can keep your employees up-to-date on the latest developments in research. Magazines take a week to reach the newsstands; newspapers

do not report subjects in great depth. The Internet gives you access to research papers the same day they are loaded onto an Internet server.

Some of the brightest minds of our age are Internet users. They often offer expert advice for solving problems.

Reducing Costs

The Internet can play an important role in reducing your company's expenses. Consider the following examples:

→ Instead of paying for a long-distance phone call, you can e-mail the person and only pay for the local call to the Internet service provider.

→ Reduce mailing costs by switching over to using e-mail.

→ Replace the expensive costs of producing and mailing catalogs, technical manuals, press releases, white papers, and technical papers by offering the same materials on the Internet.

→ Reduce office space needs and utility costs by offering employees the opportunity to telecommute using the Internet.

→ Reduce the use of paper and associated materials by using e-mail and by making documents available using Internet tools.

What Businesses Are on the Internet

To get a feel for something new, being able to see what other people are currently doing is nice. This section suggests where you might look to see how businesses today are using the Internet.

Table 2.2 Companies Using Networks

Company	Number of Networks Registered with the Internet
Exxon	263
Transamerica	260
GTE	254
Unisys	216
Texas Instruments	188
Boeing	140
Motorola	140
Hewlett Packard	137
Commonwealth Edison	130
Sprint	102
Johnson Controls	85
Loral	85
Pacific Bell	74
Martin Marietta	69
SmithKline Beecham	67
Lockheed	66
Ford Motor	61
Bell Atlantic	58
General Electric	52
Intel	51

Table 2.2 shows you the kind of commitment many major companies have made to networking and the Internet. The statistics were compiled by Internet Info. To get updated statistics, e-mail them at info@internetinfo.com.

The list goes on. It is evidence of the commitment many of the country's major corporations have made to using the Internet. To get a listing of (almost) all the corporations that have a presence on the Internet, look at Netgenesis, a commercial Web site pointer at `http://www.netgen.com`; or look at *Interactive Age* magazine's list of the top 1,000 firms at `http://techweb.cmp.com/ia`.

The following list of companies should give you some idea of how businesses currently use the Internet.

Internet Shopping Network

The Internet Shopping Network is a hardware and software microcomputer store open around the clock for browsing and purchasing. They provide access to InfoWorld articles that review computer hardware so that you can make informed purchasing decisions.

Participation in the Internet Shopping Network is by membership, which is free. Credit card information is kept at the offices of the Internet Shopping Network so that credit card numbers are not continually broadcast across the Internet.

To reach the Internet Shopping Network (see fig. 2.1), use the following URL:

`http://www.internet.net`

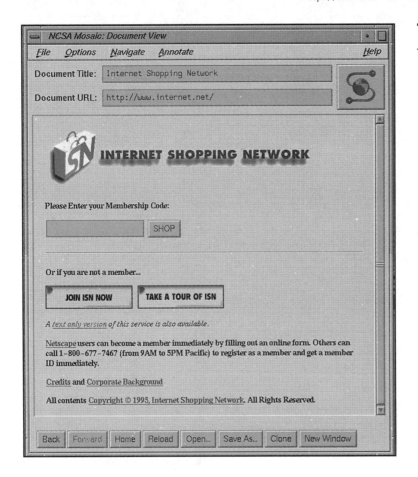

Figure 2.1

The Internet Shopping Network home page.

Figure 2.2

*The home page of
Federal Express.*

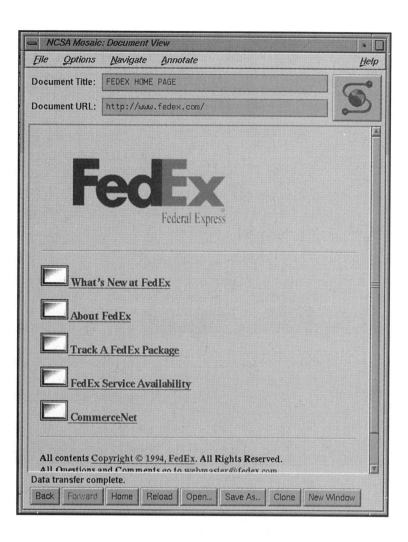

Federal Express

Federal Express ships packages all over the world.
You can access the service at the following URL
(see fig 2.2):

http://www.fedex.com/

Hewlett Packard

Hewlett Packard offers a service, called Access HP,
that tells users how to effectively use the Internet.
The company views this project as an extension of
their customer relations support services.

To reach the Hewlett Packard home page (see fig.
2.3), use the following URL:

http://www.hp.com/

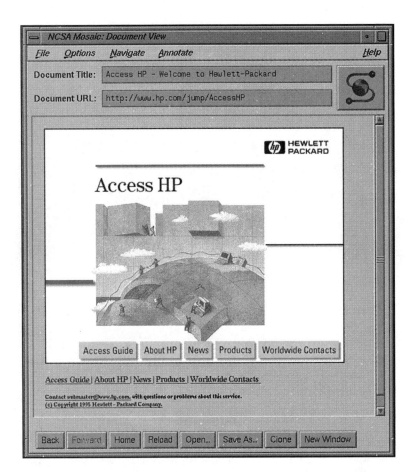

Figure 2.3

The Hewlett Packard home page.

CommerceNet

CommerceNet is a nonprofit consortium of high-tech companies, including Amdahl Corporation, Apple Computer, Inc., Bank of America, Citibank N.A., Digital Equipment Corporation, Intel Corporation, and others. The goal of CommerceNet is to create a working electronic marketplace.

To reach the home page of CommerceNet, use the following URL:

```
http://www.commerce.net
```

Paramount Pictures

You can see terrific previews of upcoming *Star Trek: Voyager* TV shows (in a video clip), listen to the captain and the holographic doctor talk to you, and examine previous episodes of *Star Trek: Voyager*. You should definitely visit this page; it is one of the best on the Web (see fig. 2.4).

To reach the home page of Paramount, use the following URL:

```
http://www.paramount.com
```

Figure 2.4

The home page of Paramount Pictures.

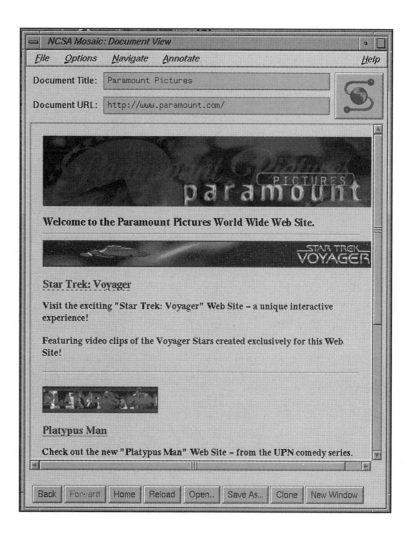

Canadian Airlines

Traveling somewhere? Perhaps Canadian Airlines can help arrange your travel plans.

To reach the home page of Canadian Airlines (see fig. 2.5), use the following URL:

```
http://www.CdnAir.CA
```

Other Business Examples

Table 2.3 provides the names and URLs of other businesses that have an ongoing presence on the Internet. Look at these examples to see parallels to your own company's use of the Internet.

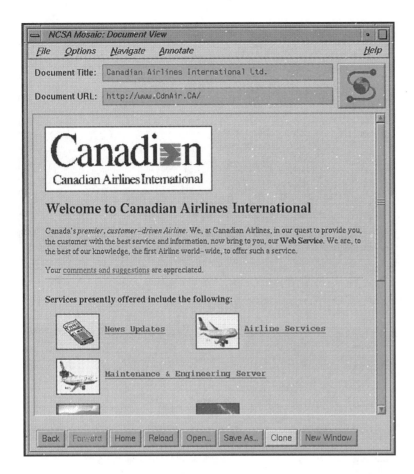

Figure 2.5

The Canadian Airlines home page.

Table 2.3   Interesting Business Home Pages

Organization URL	Description
Automobile Sellers	Automobile sales
http://www.clark.net/pub/networx /autopage/autopage.html	
Solar Panel Power	Information on and sales of solar panels
http://www.wilder.com/solar.html	
Arctic Adventours	Catalog of tours
http:/www.oslonett.no/data/adv/AA/AA.html	

Organization URL	Description
Lockheed `http://www.lmac.lockheed.com`	Press releases and public information
Bank of America `http://www.bankamerica.com`	Banking services
Digital Equipment `http://www.digital.com`	Computer information
Dun & Bradstreet `http://www.corp.dnb.com`	Stock market reports
Downtown Anywhere `http://www.awa.com`	Mall of stores
BizNet Technologies `http://128.173.241.138/shopping.html`	Mall of stores
NetMarket `http://www.netmarket.com`	Mall of stores
World Wide Web of Sports `http://www.tns.lcs.mit.edu/cgi-bin/sports`	Sports information
Branch Mall `http://florist.com`	Variety of stores
Grant's Florist `http://florist.com/flowers/flowers.html`	Flower store

The list of Internet users could fill an entire book. The examples listed above give you an idea of what is on the Internet now. You can imagine how much better the offerings will become.

Summary

In this chapter, you got to know Internet users a little better. You also got an idea of how businesses can use the Internet to their benefit. Finally, you took a look at some of the businesses that are already providing services on the Internet.

Preparations are well under way to provide a secure means of making purchases over the Internet. Recently, a joint venture between Netscape, IBM, three online services, and Terisa Systems, creators of secure-purchasing software called *Secure Hypertext Transfer Protocol* (HTTP), began to make secure purchasing a reality.

In the near future, perhaps as soon as the fourth quarter of 1995, it will be possible to perform secure financial transactions on the Internet. When that happens, commerce on the Internet will be at first a novelty, like slipping your credit card into the gas pump. But soon, Internet commerce will be as common as using your credit card at a department store.

New Internet tools become available every day. Just recently, Silicon Graphics announced breakthrough technology that enables users to navigate through a 3D, virtual reality (see `http://www.sgi.com/products/WebForce/WebSpace`). Imagine allowing people to wander through buildings you have created while they sit at home or work! As tools proliferate, businesses will have more and more ways to reach people effectively.

3

Advertising on the Internet

T he Internet, as we know it today, is an outgrowth

of NSFNET, the network of five supercomputers

founded by NSF (National Science Foundation). As

a government agency, NSF officers felt that it was

inappropriate for businesses to use the Internet for

profit. The Internet, in the beginning, was aimed

directly at educational institutions and government

research centers.

In response to NSFNET rules, several commercial networks were formed and linked to NSFNET. These commercial networks, such as UUNET, Performance Systems, and General Atomics, gave companies who wanted to do business on the Internet a welcome environment in which to operate.

Today, the complexion of the Internet is entirely different. Whereas businesses were once tolerated on the Internet, today they form the fastest growing segment of Internet service offerings. Virtually every branch of the business community is racing to the Internet to attract the attention of its 30 million users. From banks, to Hollywood, to special events, to home-grown businesses, business advertising is now embraced by the Internet community. To take advantage of advertising on the Internet, however, you have to understand its dynamics.

How Not to Advertise on the Internet

Some companies have found out the hard way that the Internet user community has an unwritten rule about advertisements: do not force them on anyone. If your concept of advertising on the Internet is represented by a cigar-smoking car salesman, wearing a wierd hat, screaming about the low price of his cars, you will have problems advertising on the Internet. The last thing you want to do is foist your message on users who do did not ask for your advertising message. You could do that, for example, by broadcasting e-mails to a large number of people, or by inserting advertisements into newsgroup discussions. Committing this kind of indiscretion, more often than not, will subject your company to flaming. Flaming is the equivalent of

hate mail. Flaming can range from nasty letters, to absurd service requests that jam and cripple your service.

How to Advertise on the Internet

The central theme to your marketing approach on the Internet should be to provide information and direct sales to interested parties. The information you provide can and should include information in addition to product and service literature—information that your customers will find interesting. If your business is selling computers, for example, you might offer information about the speed of the newest CPUs on the market. If your business is selling cars, you might offer information about the newest safety laws and tests.

One practice your company is unfamiliar with is direct user feedback about advertisements. Your company may have had phone calls and mail in response to advertisements. Internet feedback, however, is more plentiful, more immediate, and potentially (if your company gets flamed) more dangerous. These reasons make it important to obey Internet etiquette.

Three Advertising Principles

You can apply the following three principles to creating successful Internet marketing schemes:

→ Target a specific audience

→ Make your information valuable

→ Continually update the information

A company needs to know its audience. Advertising to the correct target audience returns the greatest sales per advertising dollar. Knowing your audience also enables you to structure the information on your service to the customer's greatest advantage. Gear the information on the service to the customer's needs, not the company's policy. The easier the information is to access, the more readily users will delve deeper into the information structure. An easy-to-use interface that offers information of value to your target audience should be the marketing goals for your Internet marketing plan.

Don't skimp on the information you offer. If you do not offer much information, your company might not attract attention. Rather, your company should strive to create a presence on the Internet; it should strive to be *the* resource for information in its field. You might publish, for example, technical manuals, research reports, installation guides, and service notes. Or you might make available information that seems only tangentially related to your service, but of great interest to Internet users.

The more often you update the information on your service, the more often people are interested in revisiting your service. Although such elements as your company logo remain the same, you should update a What's Hot list weekly, and other elements should look different and attract attention. Never let the service go stale.

The Internet offers businesses, from small to large, access to global markets, greater profitability due to reduced costs, and the opportunity to be the first acclaimed expert in its niche market.

Throwing Away Old Advertising Principles

Advertising in the standard mediums of television, radio, and printed matter is based on a central principle: a balance of cost and distribution—the more people an advertisement can reach, the more expensive the advertisement.

Advertising on the Internet dispenses with this central principle. The cost of connecting to the Internet is covered in Chapter 6. That cost is fixed, however, regardless of the number of people who can access the advertisement. Considering that over 30 million of people are connected to the Internet, the audience for an advertisement can be quite large. Like any advertising, however, if all you do is type a note, stick it in a bottle, and hope someone rescues it from the sea, your Internet investment return won't amount to much. The following sections look at some appropriate ways to effectively market your Internet service.

Multimedia Internet Interfaces Help Motivate Users

In the past twenty years, the Internet has been used by people who have wanted to do research, discuss ideas, and simply chat. The advent of true multimedia browsers, such as Mosaic, Netscape, and Chameleon, has lifted Internet communication off the page. Before these multimedia browsers, you could retrive only text-based information, such as the pages in this book, only instead of holding a research paper in your hands, it appeared on your computer (which you could later print). The new multimedia browsers include color pictures, clickable buttons, hypertext links, and audio/video (see fig 3.1).

 Hypertext links are highlighted words that you click on to open other documents.

Multimedia came along and made navigating a set of documents easy. If you want more information about a particular topic, you click on the hypertext word. If you want to go back to the previous document, for instance, you click on a "Back" button. If you want to see a product in action, you click on the button that initiates a mini-movie.

 To see movie previews, for example, Paramount Pictures now has an Internet service. When you connect, you can choose a movie and watch the same preview on your computer that you would otherwise watch in the movie theater.

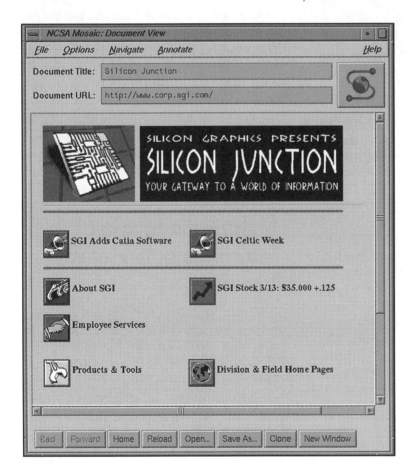

Figure 3.1

A multimedia document on the Internet.

Where Business Fits In

Making the user interface easier to operate does the following two things:

➜ Reduces the number of skills needed to operate in the Internet environment, thereby increasing the number of people who potentially can use the Internet effectively

➜ Provides the tools advertisers need to attract our attention

Marketing departments and agencies spend millions of dollars each year researching which colors attract us, how to lay out a page to attract our attention, how to lay out a page to hide information (such as a Surgeon General's warning), and how to motivate potential customers into acting.

All of those principles apply to WWW pages. Multimedia brings the Internet to a turning point. Now businesses have the tools they need to motivate users to act. Rather than reading about a product, users can see the products. Rather than reading about a service, users can hear about a service. Before multimedia browsers, advertising tools for the Internet were, at best, crude; with multimedia browsers, advertising can be as powerful as any on television, radio, or in magazines.

Appropriate Ways to Advertise on the Internet

You can use numerous appropriate ways of advertising on the Internet. This section lists some of the Internet sites that provide advertising mediums.

Before we discuss appropriate venues for advertising, let's discuss what not to do. One guiding principle is do not force your way into discussions in order to sell your products or services. This principle translates into the following guidelines:

➜ Do not send e-mail to great numbers of people.

➜ Do not advertise indiscriminately to newsgroups.

➜ Do not make false claims or promises. Vaporware is never appreciated.

The following is a list of Internet sites that provide appropriate advertising mediums for your business. You do not actually place advertisements for your services or products in most of these sites; rather, they are places that let others know that your company is an Internet site. In many cases, just letting the sponsors of the Internet sites know you want your company to be in their index accomplishes your need.

 note For more information on improving your business's exposure on the Internet, you should read the monthly newsletter, *The Internet Business Advantage*. You can inquire about subscriptions by e-mailing the following address:

`success@worth.com`

GNN

GNN runs a service called the What's New Page, which lists new services coming onto the Internet. To advertise on the What's New Page, you fill out a form provided by GNN, which you can receive by e-mailing the following address:

`wn-comments@gnn.com`

or by looking at the WWW page at the following URL:

`http//gnn.com/gnn/wn/whats-new.html`

On the form, you list your company's name, address, name of the resource, and a 50-word description of the service, which can contain hypertext links. The hypertext links enable you to beat the 50-word maximum and bring users directly to your company's home page. This listing is a must for companies offering a new Internet service.

Awards

As of 1994, there are prizes for Web sites. The best sites are advertised at the following address:

http://wings.buffalo.edu/contest/awards/index.html

You cannot exactly buy your way into this page, but you can make sure the awards sponsors consider your site.

CUI

CUI maintains a catalog of WWW services. You can use it when looking for specific topics.

http://cuiwww.unige.ch/w3catalog

EINet

EINet maintains a searchable index of WWW documents called Galaxy.

http://galaxy.einet.net/www/www.html

Special Interest Connections

Special Internet Connections (SIC) provides links to Internet services. The entries are indexed by category. Find a spot for your company.

http://www.uwm.edu/Mirror/inet.services.html

WWW Library

The World Wide Web Virtual Library maintains information about Web sites. The sites are indexed by category.

http://www.w3.org.hypertext/DataSources/bySubject
➡/Overview.html

WebCrawler

The WebCrawler maintains a list about document content and structure on the Web. WebCrawler lets you search by using keywords.

http://webcrawler.cs.washington.edu/WebCrawler
➡/WebQuery.html.

WWW Worm

Make sure to tell "the worm" about your Web site (the World Wide Web Worm, that is). The worm crawls through Web sites and catalogs service offerings.

http://www.cs.colorado.edu/home/mcbryan/wwww.html

Home Pages Broker

The WWW Home Pages Broker maintains an index of WWW pages indexed by content.

http://www.town.hall.org/brokers/Home.html

CommerceNet

CommerceNet maintains a list of company information, product descriptions of many companies. One of their goals is to provide a secure method to buy and sell merchandise on the Web.

http://www.commerce.net/

Shopping Network

If your company sells computer hardware or software, the Internet Shopping Network is for you. Users turn to the Shopping Network to see demonstration versions of software for a variety of platforms.

http://www.internet.net/

Commercial Services

For a list of commercial services available on the Web, Open Market provides a directory. Make sure that your company finds its way onto their list.

http://www.directory.net/

Internet Info

Internet Info collects valuable data and generates interesting statistics about business use of the Internet. They also publish a "New to the Net" service.

You can send announcements about your new service to the following address:

info@internetinfo.com

You can see their latest statistics by viewing the home page for the Internet Business Center at the following URL:

http://tig.com/IBC

Internet Business Center

The Internet Business Center (IBC) provides the link to Internet Info's statistics concerning business use of the Internet, called "New on the Net." You can view the business statistics by clicking on the "New on the Net" hyperlink at the following URL:

http://tig.com/IBC

The IBC is also a valuable resource for articles related to doing business on the Internet. You should browse through its offerings if you haven't already.

Interesting Business Sites

The Interesting Business Sites home page lists new and interesting services on the Internet. The home page is listed at the following URL:

http://www.rpi.edu/~okeefe/business.html

Become Active in the Internet

Rather than just waiting for Internet users to find your company, freely explore other Internet services and join discussions related to your company's products or services—without advertising your company. As conversations take place, relationships build, relationships build other relationships, and suddenly your company has an active presence in the Internet community. The point of each conversation should not be to tout your company. But when the opportunity arises naturally to point an Internet user to your company's home page, do so—gently.

Newsgroups with Which to Advertise

Newsgroups are forums for discussion centered on specific topics.

Advertisers obey an unofficial etiquette on the Internet; an etiquette that continues to change. The Internet is too anarchic to have an official mouthpiece. Etiquette, rather, develops in newsgroups. The penalty for disobeying such informal laws is the wrath of fellow Internet users, which can range from nasty e-mail to a flood of e-mail and download requests that tie up your server and render it useless.

> **n o t e** To subscribe to a newsgroup that discusses marketing on the Internet, send e-mail to `listproc@einet.net`. In the body of the e-mail use the following line:

```
SUBSCRIBE INET-MARKETING yourCompanyNameHere
```

Create Your Own Newsgroup

If you cannot find a newsgroup germane to your company, create one of your own. Call it `biz.CompanyName.general`. By creating a forum that invites user participation, your company can develop customer relationships, a niche market, and public trust.

Send Your Service Announcement to Catalog Maintainers

Some services maintain catalogs of all services offered on the Internet. Rather than wait for them to discover you, send them information about your service. You can submit your information to the following sources:

```
http://www.w3.org/hypertext/DataSources/bySubject
/Overview.html
```

or

```
http://web.nexor.co.uk/aliweb/doc/aliweb.html
```

Summary

In this chapter, you saw that the multimedia browsers have created an entirely new advertising environment on the Internet. These browsers employ all the power of color, interaction (for example, clickable buttons), audio, and video. These browsers allow businesses to use the Internet like it has never been used before.

The final section of the chapter gave a variety of appropriate venues for advertising the existence of your service. It is then the attractiveness of your home page and the quality of the information you are offering that determines how often your service is used.

Now that you have an idea how business can use and advertise on the Internet, it's important to understand the very basics of the technology involved so that you can make an informed decision as to what kind of connection to make to the Internet.

Getting Connected to the Internet

4

Understanding Basic Technology

I f you don necklaces of garlic whenever people start talking techno-jargon, relax. This chapter barely scratches the surface of the technical sophistication of the Internet. To offer an Internet service, you don't need to know the system architecture of the Internet in detail, but you do need to know the basics of TCP/IP to have some idea how different connections to the Internet work, and which type of connection your company should have to the Internet. So, before discussing TCP/IP, the next section talks about the technology of Internet connections in general.

Internet Connection Technology Primer

Chapter 6 discusses specific connections to the Internet in greater detail, including SLIP, PPP, ISDN, and other fancy acronyms about which you might not know much. But first let's get an overview of what it means to be connected to the Internet. Basically, there are three options, as follows:

→ A high-speed leased line from the telephone company using the TCP/IP protocol to an Internet service provider

→ Your computer does not speak TCP/IP, but does talk to a remote computer over telephone lines that does talk TCP/IP and is directly connected to the Internet

→ A combination of the first two, in which your computer talks TCP/IP over telephone lines rather than high-speed leased lines

The following sections look at each of the preceding options.

Using High-Speed Leased Lines

In this setup, the telephone company lays a dedicated line between your company and your Internet service provider, capable of data transmission rates between 14.4 Kbps and 45 Mbps. The higher the data transmission rate, the more users can access the Internet at the same time and the faster users' interactions are.

If your company wants to have a continuous presence on the Internet, you want this kind of setup. Such a setup requires some extra machinery: one or more servers, a router, a firewall host, and a CSU/DSU or a modem, as shown in figure 4.1.

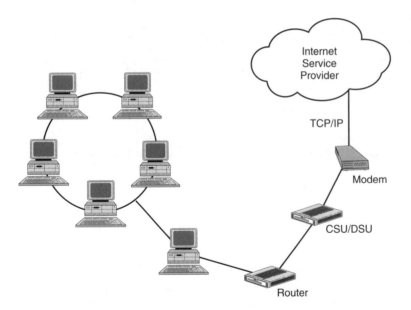

Figure 4.1

The environment for a leased-line connection.

The *server* is a dedicated computer that handles incoming Internet requests. You use it to store e-mail from the Internet, and to offer Internet services, such as Gopher, Archie, or the World Wide Web.

 If your company has continuous access to the Internet, you need to secure your LAN from would-be Internet intruders. One form of security is to put a firewall on the server. A firewall puts a barrier between your company's local network and people outside your organization. It protects against unauthorized snooping through your file system. Chapter 8, "Making Your LAN Secure," discusses security aspects in greater detail.

A *router* is a device that specializes in figuring out how to get Internet packets from one place to another. Routers contain tables of information about Internet servers all over the world and use that information to direct Internet messages to correct destinations across the intricate path of Internet connections. From start to finish, one Internet message packet might pass through 30 routers as it travels from the host to the target computer.

A *CSU/DSU* is a converter between analog and digital data. Instead of this converter, you can use a modem.

High-speed leased lines transmit data much faster than normal, voice-grade telephone lines. If you have a medium-to-large company, you probably need to use a leased line that has a transmission speed of 56 Kbps or greater. ISDN lines transmit data at this speed. T1 lines transmit data at this speed and higher.

For more information about ISDN and T1 lines, see Chapter 6, "Connecting to the Internet."

 Many individual users have dedicated Internet (telephone) lines running to their personal computers. The cost of this service, however, runs high: generally more than several hundred dollars a month. An individual can have a hard time justifying, or affording for that matter, such a cost. All the individual really needs besides a PC that can use the TCP/IP protocol is a high-speed modem. So, for those who have money burning in their pockets, this is a great connection to the Internet. Most individuals, however, access the Internet through work or a dial up service.

The advantage of using leased lines is the number of users who can use the Internet simultaneously—the higher the bandwidth, the more users can use Internet resources concurrently at an acceptable speed. Even the largest bandwidth network in the world can get bogged down by tons of users, for example.

Digital lines, such as ISDN and T1, provide greater bandwidth than analog dial up lines and, per given user load, faster performance.

Speed affects the following factors:

→ **Wait time for files and communication to reach you.** Faster is better—but unfortunately, more expensive.

→ **Choice of Internet browsers you can use.** High-speed connections give you the full range of Internet browsers, including the new, graphical, I've-got-it-all-in-my-multimedia-interface browsers, such as Netscape and Mosaic.

The extra equipment required by leased-line connections, and the high-speed leased line to the Internet, costs a great deal more than what Joe Schmoe pays for his shared, dial up account. If your company wants a permanent address on the Internet, you don't have much choice: you need either a leased or dedicated dial up line. As you read this book, you will see how the expense will be paid back many times over.

Dialing Up the Internet

At the other end of the spectrum from leased lines are dial up accounts. Equipment costs less, telephone rates cost less (usually), but the number of concurrent Internet users is necessarily less.

There are two kinds of dial up accounts: one that offers a shell service, and another that offers SLIP or PPP. The shell account provides a Unix interface: the command prompt. It is up to you to know the commands to accomplish your tasks. SLIP or PPP connections can offer, at a slightly higher cost, the opportunity to use graphical browsers and access WWW pages. They require your computer to run TCP/IP, however. We will discuss this situation in the next section. In this section, we assume that your computer does not know TCP/IP, and uses a shell interface.

The equipment configuration of a dial up, shell account includes a computer connected by a modem (over telephone lines) to a remote computer (that can talk TCP/IP) connected directly to the Internet, as shown in figure 4.2.

In this environment, your computer doesn't have a clue about TCP/IP. It lets the Internet service provider's remote computer do the speaking to the Internet. The user's computer simply becomes a *terminal emulator*—that is, it pretends to be the display and keyboard of the remote computer. This is because your computer does not talk TCP/IP, the protocol used on the Internet. All of the real Internet interaction takes place on the remote computer.

The advantage of this configuration is that you get Internet access when you want it by calling an Internet service provider, such as Netcom or Delphi, you get cheap rates, you spend less for equipment, and you get to use some Internet tools, such as e-mail. But cheaper is not necessarily better. When you use dial up, shell services, you cannot use data-intensive interfaces: those wonderful graphical interfaces currently so popular. Although you may be able to get text versions of documents on WWW services, they do not work well. When you use a WWW browser to click on a hyperlink, for example, the browser connects to another document. In shell accounts, however, hyperlinks are displayed as plain text. Unfortunately, there is no way for you to find out where the hypertext link leads. All the linking power of WWW documents becomes dead matter in shell accounts. When a Web document says, "Click here for more information," in a shell account you cannot click and you have no idea how to retrieve the more detailed information.

Dial up, shell accounts are for individuals who do not need continuous access to the Internet, who are happy just using e-mail, FTP, and Gopher, and who are happy not paying an arm and a leg for Internet access.

Running TCP/IP on Your Personal Computer

The third option provides a middle ground between the first two options. Here, your computer runs TCP/IP and speaks to an Internet provider through a modem and telephone lines, as shown in figure 4.3.

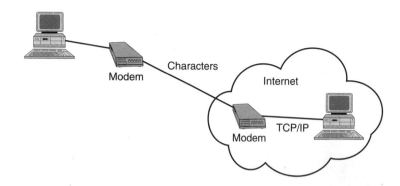

Figure 4.2

A dial up connection to the Internet.

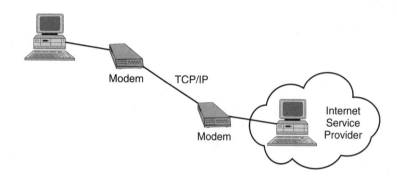

Figure 4.3

Running TCP/IP on your personal computer.

The element missing in figure 4.3 from figure 4.1 is the remote computer. Because your computer can run TCP/IP, it doesn't need a remote computer to do that. That helps because you eliminate the middleman and information can flow more quickly to your computer. Now you can use those graphical browsers you hear everyone talking about.

Now, where do you stand? This connection configuration is more expensive than a simple dial up, shell account because you have to run TCP/IP on your computer and your telephone connection to the Internet service provider (SLIP or PPP) costs more. But the setup is much cheaper than using a leased-line setup and its dedicated Internet server, router, firewall, and associated software. This intermediate setup enables you to use graphical browsers, which is good. What is bad, however, is

that you cannot connect the same number of users concurrently as you can with a leased line because network performance grinds to a halt.

This kind of hybrid connection environment is great for small companies and individuals who want to use graphical browsers. But companies that have many employees using the Internet, should use a leased line instead—probably a T1 or a fractional T1.

A Brief Introduction to TCP/IP

Now that you know how TCP/IP fits into the overall scheme of the Internet, you're ready to get up close and personal with TCP and IP. This discussion of TCP/IP barely scratches the surface of the topic. We don't talk in detail about the seven layers of network topology. To post a Gopher or WWW service on the Internet, you don't have to be a TCP/IP whiz. You do need to know the basics, though, if you want to understand what's going on.

Actually, TCP/IP is a *suite* of protocols, the most important of which are IP (Internet Protocol) and TCP (Transmission Control Protocol). The following sections talk about each of these and one more, UDP (User Datagram Protocol).

IP

IP chops up an Internet message (the data stream) into packages, called packets (usually around 200 bytes each), wraps each packet up to make it easy to carry (across the Internet), and then labels its contents and destination, as shown in figure 4.4.

Suppose, for example, that you want to look at a document that is on a remote server. After you request the letter be sent to you, IP chops the document it to pieces, wraps up each piece, and sends the pieces. Strangely enough, IP is not very reliable: it does not guarantee that all of the pieces of a message will reach their destination, nor does IP make sure that all of the packets get lined up in the correct sequential order.

Internet pathways lead from one router to another. The shortest route, however, is not always the fastest. Network load and network failures help determine the path that an Internet message takes as it routes from the server to the client. As the remote server transmits the document over the wire one packet at a time, the second packet might find a quicker path to reach your computer than the first packet. Consequently, the second packet arrives before the first packet.

 n o t e A *client* is an application that sends requests, such as performing a function. A *service* is an application that (sometimes) runs on a different computer that fulfills the request. If the client and service are on different machines, as they are in the case of the Internet, the connection between the two is carried out by stub files and the network.

The client address is one of the things IP puts on the packet. Computer addresses are 32-bit numbers. To make things simpler, these 32-bit addresses are split into four groups of eight binary numbers, separated by periods. The following is an example of a 32-bit address:

`10101010.10101010.10101010.10101010`

Each group translates into a decimal number between 0 and 256. A full address looks like the following:

`12.24.132.112`

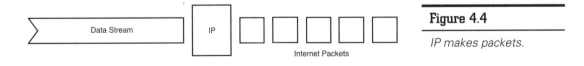

Internet Packets

Figure 4.4

IP makes packets.

The Internet address is called a *dotted octet*, because each decimal number represents an 8-bit binary number.

Each computer on the Internet has an address (one 32-bit binary number represents roughly 4.3 billion addresses). Your company, for example, might have an Internet address that begins with 12. If, for some reason, the Internet reserved 12 for only your company, any message sent by any computer in the world that had an address that began with 12 would be routed to your site.

Suppose you had two subnetworks on your local network. Each would be given a different subnet address (the middle two three-digit, decimal numbers), for example, 12.123.234 and 12.123.235. We've come from the entire Internet to your network with the first number, 12, and now to the specific subnet in your company's local network, either 12.123.234 or 12.123.235. Each computer on each subnet is identified by the last of the four decimal numbers. (If you have more computers on a subnet than numbers (256), you need to make a new subnet.) At last, the packets, which IP packages, find the intended recipient.

The addressing scheme is hierarchical, which makes it easy to use. Routers only have to have a table of all the networks on the Internet; that is, they only have to use the first of the four numbers to send a message. The local router has to figure out which computer on the local network should receive the Internet message. If routers had to keep track of every computer on the Internet, they'd have to use a pretty big table.

 note The route a packet takes from the server to the target computer can be updated dynamically. During its transmission, a packet might travel through 30 routers before finding its way to the target computer, and at each router the message can take one of many courses. This kind of network routing is called *connectionless routing.*

Some packet-switching networks, however, are connection-oriented (X.25 networks, for example). Before a transmission begins, a fixed route is defined between the server and target; the route is not dynamically updated.

A connection-oriented network taxes router memory and requires routing calculations. Connectionless networks do not tax router memory, however—routing calculations are performed by every router along the transmission path.

TCP

Because of network peculiarities, all of the Internet packets might come to the target computer totally out of sequence. That's where TCP comes in. TCP puts the packets in their correct order and determines whether or not all of the packets arrived. How can TCP do this?

Hidden in the address information of each packet is a sequence number. IP simply increments it as each packet is mailed out. TCP uses these sequence numbers to put the packets into sequence, and determines if any are missing. If one packet gets detoured to Timbuktu for some reason, TCP sends a message to the remote computer to resend the missing packet. TCP keeps asking for packets until they arrive. Once all of the packets arrive, they are merged back into the steady stream of data they began as on the remote server.

TCP adds one additional layer of organization to the incoming messages: it sorts messages by port numbers. IP numbers identify specific computers on the Internet; port numbers identify specific services running on the same computer. Port numbers are 16-bit, which range roughly from 0 to 65,000, with port numbers less than 1,024 reserved for services. Because you might have more than one service running on your computer, the port number makes sure the Internet message goes to the right one. On the same server, for example, you might have such multiple services running as Gopher, WAIS, WWW, Telnet, and so on.

There is a de facto standard for some port numbers. Port number 20 is used for FTP services, for example; port 70 is used for Gopher; and port 80 is used for HTTP (WWW) services.

UDP

The IP and TCP protocols facilitate Internet communications. There are times, however, when you can get away without using the TCP protocol (and putting up with its time-consuming reordering). If the Internet message to be sent can fit in a single packet (200 bytes), there is no need to reorder anything. In this case, you can dispense with TCP and use the UDP protocol.

The UDP protocol sorts things by port number so that messages can reach the correct service on the server. UDP port numbers, however, are not equal to TCP port numbers. TCP 50, for example, does not go to the same service, necessarily, as UDP 50, unless you set up a server to specifically do that.

UDP performs one other optional service: it checks to see if the data in the packet was somehow changed in transit. This checking is called *checksumming.* The problem is, however, that this service slows down performance—so people often turn it off.

Naming Addresses

Dotted octet numbers make 32-bit addresses a lot easier to handle. Still, remembering dotted octet numbers is not exactly easy. When you want to e-mail someone, it's really a problem if you have to remember that Bob's address is 12.123.234.111. Isn't it a lot easier just to use Bob's name as the address? Yes it is, and what enables you to do that is the Internet name service, called the *Domain Name Service* (DNS).

DNS maintains a table that maps Internet addresses, such as 12.123.234.111, to names, such as warp.engr.sgi.com. Such names can be longer or shorter, but the order of the parts of the name, separated by periods, follows a common logic. The name parts proceed from most specific to least specific, as you move from the first to last parts of the name. The first name is often the name of the computer. The next part is generally the subnet the computer is on. The second-to-last name part is often the company's name, and the last name part describes the kind of company it is, as shown in figure 4.5.

Figure 4.5

Parts of a name.

Extension	Description
.edu	Educational institutions
.com	Commercial Internet sites
.mil	Military installations
.net	Internet service providers

Occasionally, you will see a final two-letter code that identifies the country the server is in. Country codes are standardized in the International Standards Organization's document ISO 3166.

A server that can tell you an IP address if you give it a domain name is called a *Domain Name Server*. DNS clients ask these servers to return IP addresses for specified domain names. In completing its tasks, one DNS may ask another DNS for help, and so on, until an answer is found and a reply is sent to the DNS client.

You can also make an alias for a domain name. If, for example, you want to make a service on a server, serverName, available to FTP and WWW servers, you could create the aliases ftp.some.machine and www.some.machine, both of which point to the same server, serverName.some.machine.

Big Brother: inetd

It's great that you can put 65,000 (or even 10) services on the same server. Each service eats up a chunk of memory, however. What works best is to start a service only when it has a pending request, and to terminate it when a reply is sent to the client making the request. The problem is, how does a service know when to wake up?

That's inetd's job—it's the big brother of services that run on most Unix hosts. inetd is a daemon that

constantly monitors the host's port to see if other services should start up. But how does it do it? inetd monitors the port numbers of all service requests that come to a server. When a request comes in, inetd looks in /etc/services for the name of the service. After it has the name of the service to start, it looks in its configuration file, inetd.config, to get setup information. The configuration information in the file is similar in form to the following example:

```
gopher    stream tcp    nowait    guest /usr/sbin
➥/gopherd    -l
```

The first field, `gopher`, is the name of the service. This name much match exactly the name of the service as it is found in /etc/services. The second field, `stream tcp`, describes the kind of connection the service will make. In this case, `tcp` will handle the packet ordering so that the downloaded information appears to be a steady stream of data. The other option for second field, dgram udp, specifies that UDP, not TCP, will handle the packet ordering.

The third field, `nowait`, tells the service to spawn itself for each service request that comes to the server. The other option for the third field, `wait`, tells the service to handle the service requests sequentially, starting a new request only after finishing the current one.

The fourth field, `guest`, specifies the user ID used to run the service. The fifth field, `/usr/sbin /gopherd`, specifies the name and path of the service. The last field, `-l`, is the equivalent of a command-line option that influences the execution of the service—whether or not to enable logging, for example.

You can keep track of inetd's actions by looking in the log file, syslog (unless you turn off inet's logging).

Using Daemons

In cases in which services are started infrequently, inetd does a great job. A problem arises, however, when service requests come in every other second. In such cases, inetd starts and stops the Internet service unnecessarily. Each stop and start takes a finite amount of time and degrades system performance.

To correct this problem, you can run a service continuously. This option increases system performance because the service only reads configuration information once, but it also permanently consumes system resources. It is the job of the service, then, to monitor incoming requests. When multiple, concurrent requests of the same service are made, the service spawns itself, one for each request.

How Service Requests and Replies Happen

Now that you know that the Internet uses a client/service architecture, let's take a look at a complete communication sequence to get a feeling for how everything works.

Let's take a simple example of a WWW client requesting information from a WWW service. The sequence of events would transpire something like the following:

1. The user decides to look at a document offered in a company's home page. He requests the document by clicking on an icon.

2. The WWW client interprets the user's action and constructs an appropriate request IP packet.

3. The WWW client looks in /etc/services to find the correct port number for a WWW server. In this case, it finds the number 80.

4. The client finishes addressing the IP packet, or series of packets, with the TCP port number 80, and sends it to the WWW server across the Internet.

5. inetd sees a service request come in with a port number of 80. It looks in /etc/services to see what the name of the service is that it should wake up. It finds that 80 corresponds to WWW.

6. inetd uses the information in the configuration file, inetd.config, to start the WWW service with the correct options.

7. inetd backs out of the transaction to let the WWW client communicate directly to the WWW service.

8. The service processes the request by opening and reading the document file.

9. IP chops up the document and puts it in a series of packets and addresses each packet.

10. The document goes to the WWW client over the network.

 n o t e If the WWW document contains an image, a second TCP/IP connection is created between the WWW client and server to facilitate the download of the image.

11. The IP packets are cached on the WWW client machine. When they all arrive, TCP puts them in the correct sequence and presents them to the WWW client.

12. After the download is complete, the TCP connection is terminated and the WWW service terminates on the server.

13. The WWW client decides which of the series of packets to display. Some clients spawn external viewers in which the document is displayed.

Communication between Gopher clients and servers works in the same way as the WWW. Because Gopher documents cannot include graphic images, however, a second TCP/IP connection is never made.

FTP works in a different way altogether. Two TCP/IP connections are always created between FTP clients and servers. One handles the data download; the other manages the communication. The data TCP/IP connection comes and goes as needed. The managing TCP/IP connection, however, runs as long as the client is logged in to the service.

Summary

In this chapter, you took a look at how TCP/IP plays a role in different kinds of connections to the Internet. Then you dived into some basic concepts about TCP and IP. First, you learned about service requests and replies. You saw that when a service request reaches the server, inetd starts the appropriate service on the server, according to port number. You found out how Internet data flows through the maze of Internet connections between the server and target computer through routers. You saw that TCP puts back in order the Internet packets that IP chopped up and sent on their way to the target computer.

This chapter also discussed UDP, which is usually used only when the packet of data is very small.

Now that you understand the basic technology involved in the Internet, it's time to learn about and decide which kind of connection your company will have to the Internet.

5

Tools for Accessing Internet Information

Now that you have an idea of how you can use the Internet to enhance your business, and you know the basic mechanisms of how to retrieve data from the Internet, you might be interested in getting your business onto the Internet. Before you can do that, you need to decide the sort of service you want to provide. This section gives a brief description of the tools people can use to retrieve information on the Internet. Some tools are part of Unix, some are so common you might not think of them as Internet tools, and others require some explanation. The Internet services discussed in this chapter include the following:

→ finger

→ telnet

→ E-mail

→ FTP

→ WAIS

→ Archie

→ Gopher

→ World Wide Web (WWW)

Using finger

The finger command uses the fingerd service, which is a daemon inetd can start. fingerd comes with most versions of Unix. You use finger to find out who's on a particular host and some basic information about their usage. You can tell, for example, how long they've been logged in, where they're logged in, and their login name.

But that isn't all. You can add to the information printed out when someone fingers you by editing your .plan file. You can write whatever you want in the .plan file. If you make a .plan file for your business, you can point people toward other services your company might offer. The following is a simple .plan file:

```
When you have documentation needs,
use WriteIt! at URL: http://www.writeit.com
~
~
~
~
```

Now, when someone fingers me, they get the following:

```
warp 132% finger geckel
Login name: geckel In real life: George Eckel
Directory: /usr/people/geckel Shell: /bin/csh
Mail to geckel goes to geckel@warp.engr.sgi.com
On since Feb 23 11:40:16 on ttyq0 from :0.0
16 minutes Idle Time
On since Feb 16 05:01:48 on ttyq1 from :0.0
14 seconds Idle Time
On since Feb 16 05:01:51 on ttyq2 from :0.0
15 minutes Idle Time
On since Feb 16 05:01:56 on ttyq3 from :0.0
7 days 6 hours Idle Time
Plan:
When you have documentation needs,
use WriteIt! at URL: http://www.writeit.com
```

Okay, it's not exactly fancy, but your .plan file points potential customers in the right direction.

finger doesn't represent the level of Internet communication that the rest of this book is about. Because fingerd is probably already installed on your Unix host, learning how to operate it is relatively easy. We'll leave that task to you.

Although finger is a nifty, if simple, way of pointing people at a home page, it can also lead to security breaches. The information displayed by finger can help someone find a way into your system. For that reason, you might consider disabling finger (by eliminating it in inetd).

 For a more sophisticated use of finger, try using the GNU finger daemon, GNU fingerd. If **t i p** you set up a .fingerrc file in the business home directory, you can execute a script when someone fingers the business. You can FTP GNU fingerd from prep.ai.mit.edu in /pub/gnu/finger-1.37.tar.gz.

Using telnet

telnet is also included with most flavors of Unix. It's a service that allows you to call a computer over telephone lines and log in to it, just as though you were using rlogin to log in to a computer on a local network. After you telnet into a computer, you enter your user ID and password. The telnetd daemon looks for a login shell in /etc/passwd. If it finds one, it executes the shell script, which might be a menuing system.

Because telnet is part of standard Unix, you probably already know a lot about it. As an Internet service, it is somewhat limited, so it is not described in greater detail in this book. For the equivalent (and more popular) type of Internet service, look at the FTP chapters.

Getting and Sending E-mail

Having worked on a network, you are already familiar with e-mail. You can send and receive letters across network (and internetwork) lines. You can even broadcast messages to many people at once. The Internet has mailing lists that you can retrieve from or broadcast to. You might, for example, broadcast a message to an entire newsgroup or discussion group.

Of course, you want to broadcast messages sparingly. Flooding newsgroups with e-mail about your company every week is not proper Internet etiquette. Doing so likely would provoke the ire of Internet users.

The advantage of using e-mail as a way to communicate over the Internet is its immediacy. Most people on workstations have a mail client running. Rather than waiting for people to fire up their browsers and search across the Internet to find your company's home page, an e-mail arrives at their workstation and you reach them immediately. Again, it is not proper Internet etiquette to broadcast e-mail to a wide body of users in order to promote your company. Instead, you should use e-mail to foster your company's relationships with its clients.

E-mail is a great service, and its immediacy makes it stand out from all the other Internet services. Unless your company is going to set up a mail list service that uses organizing programs like listserv or Majordomo, you don't need to know any more about e-mail because you already have it set up and running. Because you should not send e-mail to advertise your business, we will not pursue this Internet service any further.

Offering an FTP Service

The majority of Internet traffic (36 percent) is FTP. E-mail comprises only 6 percent of Internet traffic, probably because it is most often used within local networks. But FTP, today, is the workhorse of Internet tools.

Connecting to a remote computer using FTP is similar to using telnet or rlogin, except that you do not have all the tools of a shell, and your access to files, called *archives*, is limited. You use FTP to transfer files. The files can be of any type; for example, they might be text files or binaries—FTP doesn't really care. Nor does it care about the platforms of the two computers. You might, for example, transfer files between a Silicon Graphics workstation and a PC (assuming they have FTP clients). Part of the reason FTP is the workhorse of the Internet is that FTP clients are so easy to get on every platform.

You can allow users access to your system either by logging into FTP using a user ID or the login anonymous. When you allow a user to FTP to a server using their user ID, you run the risk of someone on the Internet sniffing at what is going on, learning their login, and then gaining access to the FTP archive. This can be of little consequence to some companies, but a serious concern to others.

Using the anonymous login is the safest way to grant access to an FTP service because you can restrict anonymous users' access to your system's file system. By restricting their access, you restrict the harm they can do; and by assigning permissions correctly, you can limit the actions anonymous users can perform.

You might find that you can identify groups that should have greater (but still restricted) access than anonymous users get. To handle that situation, you define user groups and restrict their privileges in the FTP archives. Here, again, you run the risk of unauthorized people discovering user group IDs and climbing through your file system.

The following example FTP session with Microsoft gives you a flavor of the typical use of FTP.

```
SGI guest3% ftp ftp.microsoft.com
Connected to ftp.microsoft.com.
220 ftp Windows NT FTP Server (Version 3.5).
Name (ftp.microsoft.com:guest): anonymous
331 Anonymous access allowed, send identity (e-mail
name) as password.
Password:
230-¦
¦ Welcome to ftp.microsoft.com (a.k.a
➥gowinnt.microsoft.com)!
¦
```

```
¦ Please enter your full e-mail name as your
➥password.
¦ Report any problems to ftp@microsoft.com
¦
¦ Refer to the index.txt file for further
➥information
¦
230 Anonymous user logged in as anonymous.
Remote system type is Windows_NT.
ftp> pwd
257 d:/ is current directory.
ftp> ls
200 PORT command successful.
150 Opening ASCII mode data connection for /bin/ls.
dr-xr-xr-x 1 owner group 0 Oct 7 1994 bussys
dr-xr-xr-x 1 owner group 0 Oct 7 1994 deskapps
dr-xr-xr-x 1 owner group 0 Dec 21 1994 developr
-r-xr-xr-x 1 owner group 7445 Dec 14 1994
➥dirmap.htm
-r-xr-xr-x 1 owner group 4244 Dec 14 1994
➥dirmap.txt
-r-xr-xr-x 1 owner group 712 Aug 25 1994
➥disclaimer.txt
-r-xr-xr-x 1 owner group 860 Oct 5 1994 index.txt
-r-xr-xr-x 1 owner group 5628354 Feb 24 3:52 ls-
➥lR.txt
-r-xr-xr-x 1 owner group 546449 Feb 24 3:53 LS-
➥LR.ZIP
-r-xr-xr-x 1 owner group 28160 Nov 28 1994
➥MSNBRO.DOC
-r-xr-xr-x 1 owner group 22641 Feb 8 1994
➥MSNBRO.TXT
dr-xr-xr-x 1 owner group 0 Oct 7 1994 peropsys
dr-xr-xr-x 1 owner group 0 Nov 2 1994 Services
dr-xr-xr-x 1 owner group 0 Feb 7 14:31 Softlib
-r-xr-xr-x 1 owner group 5095 Oct 20 1993 support-
➥phones.txt
-r-xr-xr-x 1 owner group 802 Aug 25 1994
➥WhatHappened.txt
226 Transfer complete.
ftp> cd developr
250-Welcome to the Microsoft FTP Server. This
➥machine offers the
```

following materials and information for systems
➥and network products:

- Selected knowledge-base articles
- Selected product fixes
- Updated drivers
- Utilities
- Documentation

The developr directory is maintained by Microsoft
➥Developer Support.

Please report any problems with this area to
➥ftp@microsoft.com. Sorry, individual replies to
➥this alias may not be possible, but all mail will
➥be read. Please, this is not a product support
➥alias!

For further information refer to the readme.txt
➥file.

```
250 CWD command successful.
ftp> ls
200 PORT command successful.
150 Opening ASCII mode data connection for /bin/ls.
dr-xr-xr-x 1 owner group 0 Aug 24 1994 basic
dr-xr-xr-x 1 owner group 0 Nov 1 1994 DEVCAST
dr-xr-xr-x 1 owner group 0 Aug 24 1994 devutil
dr-xr-xr-x 1 owner group 0 Jan 18 10:56 drg
dr-xr-xr-x 1 owner group 0 Nov 21 1994 dstlib
dr-xr-xr-x 1 owner group 0 Aug 24 1994 fortran
dr-xr-xr-x 1 owner group 0 Aug 24 1994 fox
dr-xr-xr-x 1 owner group 0 Oct 7 1994 GEN_INFO
dr-xr-xr-x 1 owner group 0 Aug 24 1994 MAPI
dr-xr-xr-x 1 owner group 0 Aug 24 1994 masm
dr-xr-xr-x 1 owner group 0 Feb 17 10:38 MSDN
dr-xr-xr-x 1 owner group 0 Feb 7 16:52 MSJ
dr-xr-xr-x 1 owner group 0 Oct 12 1994 multimedia
dr-xr-xr-x 1 owner group 0 Aug 24 1994 ole
dr-xr-xr-x 1 owner group 0 Dec 21 1994 pc95
-r-xr-xr-x 1 owner group 1427 Aug 25 1994
➥readme.txt
dr-xr-xr-x 1 owner group 0 Feb 16 11:37 rfc
dr-xr-xr-x 1 owner group 0 Feb 14 16:22 TAPI
dr-xr-xr-x 1 owner group 0 Aug 24 1994 vb
dr-xr-xr-x 1 owner group 0 Aug 24 1994 visual_c
dr-xr-xr-x 1 owner group 0 Oct 7 1994 win32dk
dr-xr-xr-x 1 owner group 0 Aug 24
226 Transfer complete.
ftp> get readme.txt
local: readme.txt remote: readme.txt
200 PORT command successful.
150 Opening ASCII mode data connection for
➥readme.txt.
226 Transfer complete.
1427 bytes received in 0.39 seconds (3.61 Kbytes/s)
ftp>
```

Often, if a company has a firewall, employees cannot use FTP to connect directly to a remote machine; they must first log in to a company server and FTP from there. The company server can provide a gateway to the Internet. The following shows you such an example:

```
warp 165% rlogin guest@sgi.sgi.com
 For information about Silicon Graphics, please
call (415) 960-1980.


 For information concerning this machine, send mail
➥to postmaster@sgi.sgi.com
or call (415) 390-3410.
Last login: Thu Feb 23 13:59:25 by
➥dishong@155.11.199.11
IRIX Release 4.0.5 System V sgi
Copyright 1987-1992 Silicon Graphics, Inc.
All Rights Reserved.
Silicon Graphics ---- Mtn. View UUCP & Internet
➥Gateway
cwd=/usr/tmp/geckel
**** An instable version of mosaic is available
➥from
dist.wpd:/sgi/IS-services/xmosaic. Please install
➥it
 and run Xmosaic from your workstation.
Read news from your workstation. Avoid creating
```

```
➥temporary files in /tmp.
Big files in /tmp are deleted within minutes.
**** Put files for FTP access in ~ftp/private only,
➥not in ~ftp/pub. ****
 ~ftp/private is good for hiding files from snoopy
➥anonymous FTP users since they cannot run ls in
 ~ftp/private.
Use ftp.sgi.com instead of sgi.com in your
➥announcements of FTPable files.
SGI guest1%
```

FTP is great for transferring files, but terrible for browsing. If you have worked with a file structure of any size, you know how difficult it can be to navigate through it. Although files names can be descriptive, they're not descriptive enough. Some system administrators even put README files in every directory to give the browser some clue as to what is grouped in that directory. This is rather clunky navigation, however. If that was the only navigation tool available, you would learn to suffer with it. But why suffer? WWW browsers provide links to FTP for the purpose of downloading files. FTP archives, however, are easier to set up than WWW sources, since you do not need to transfer your documents into HTML (the language that makes graphical interfaces graphical—more on this in chapter 19). Although you might eventually like to offer a WWW service, you might start with an FTP service because your documents are already in the correct format.

Offering an Archie Service

Archie is a command-line search service that only looks in FTP archives. The following example offers a feel for how it works:

```
% archie cummerbund
Host  sgi.com
```

```
Location: /usr/tv
       FILE   xwr-r—r—FormalWear
```

In this example, we use archie to search for a document that contains the word *cummerbund*. archie discovers a reference to cummerbund on the host machine sgi.com, in the directory /usr/tv, in the file FormalWear.

Archie does not actually look through the FTP archives. It looks in *ls-lR files*, which are compressed, long-format, recursive listings of FTP archives.

The great thing about Archie is that it helps you find what you need in FTP archives. The downside of Archie is that it works only with ls-lR files and requires the client machine to have a decompression application, such as Unix's compress.

Archie is a great service, but it is not a service that you would use to promote your business. For that reason, this book will not discuss it further.

Offering a Gopher Service

Gopher is a text-based browser. If you think of information being stored in a hierarchical manner, Gopher is the tool that shows the hierarchy and enables you to easily navigate through it. Gopher shows you the hierarchy one level at a time by presenting menu choices that lead to documents or to other menus that allow you to refine your choice.

Figure 5.1 shows you an example of a Gopher menu.

You move to a menu item by selecting. In the text-based version, you move the arrow to the correct menu item and push Return. You can get further information about Gopher menu items by pushing the equals (=) sign. To select a Gopher menu item using a WWW browser, you just click on it.

Figure 5.1

A Gopher display.

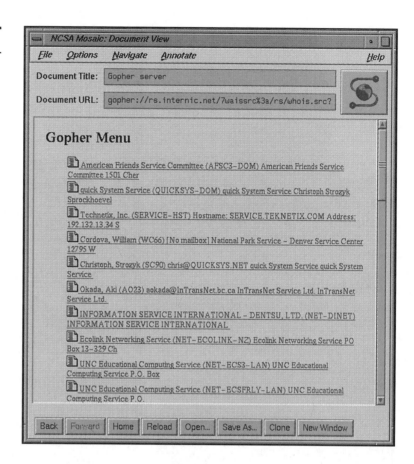

The menu options can lead to other documents or menus in the same remote host, or they can be links to other Gopher or FTP services.

System administration of Gopher is as easy as setting up logical and well-named directories. The names of the directories and files displayed in Gopher menus are actually located in files that are parallel to the source files. Naming the files and directories well helps users navigate the system.

The advantage of Gopher is its speed, which derives from its text-based nature. It allows users who have slow telephone-line access to browse the Internet easily. If your company wants to attract the attention of consumers who have only dial-up access to the Internet, you should provide a Gopher service.

The downsides of Gopher are that you have to set it up as a menuing system and that it can only handle text. Menu options can only be up to 80 characters long, which limits their ability to describe topics.

For more information about Gopher services, see Chapter 16, "Setting Up a Gopher Service."

 n o t e Although new Gopher clients—Gopher+—can handle some graphic elements, Gopher is essentially used to transmit text, or binaries.

Offering a WAIS Service

WAIS is the service you use if you want to find a document on the Internet. Most often it works by keywords. You supply several keywords and it searches for matches on Internet servers. It begins its search at the Directory of Servers—a server that maintains a list of all the other servers on the Internet. From that list, it determines which of the servers on the Internet are most likely to contain a match for the search data. WAIS then goes to those servers for a more detailed search. Figure 5.2 shows a WAIS display.

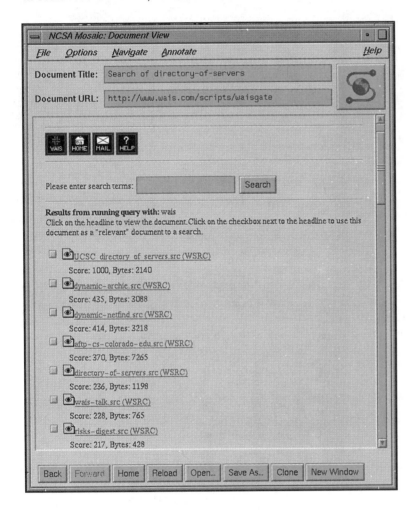

Figure 5.2

Searching with WAIS.

WAIS reports the number of times the keywords occur in the documents. You then can look at those documents.

Newer WAIS services provide even greater search options. After WAIS gives you the initial report of the number of times the keywords occur in each document, you can add additional keywords or wild cards to select the selected documents that better match the subject for which you are looking. Amazingly, you even can enter an entire document as selection criteria to find similar documents.

Although you can use text-based WAIS clients, graphical clients are far superior. WAIS can handle many different kinds of data, including GIF, TIFF, ASCII text, mail digests, NetNews archives from the Internet, and more. You also can work out support for other data types.

WAIS works best at finding word matches. That does not help much if you are trying to find a picture. You have to hope the title of the picture includes your keyword. Admittedly, system administrators can embellish the title to include many words, such as, mona_lisa_lady_half_smile.gif. But as of yet, you cannot scan in a picture to look for similar pictures.

The only other downside is the amount of disk space a WAIS service consumes. There are two parts to a WAIS service, the documents and the indexes of the documents. Rather than search entire documents for keywords, WAIS searches document indexes, which are built by indexing software. Unfortunately, these indexes can be huge, even larger than the data they represent. WAIS software developers know this situation must change.

Because WAIS helps you find documents you can then browse, offering WAIS in combination with a browser, such as WWW, is recommended.

For more information about WAIS services, see Chapter 13, "Setting Up a freeWAIS Service," and Chapter 14, "Managing a freeWAIS Service."

Offering a WWW Service

The biggest advantage of a graphical user interface (GUI) is that the tools within the GUI are visual and intuitive, and similar from one windowing system to another. Rather than having to learn a different set of commands for the PC world and the Unix world, Windows allows you to use what you learned in Microsoft Windows and apply it to the X Windows in Mosaic, a WWW, windows-based browser. By relying on a visual grammar that has been developed de facto by Microsoft Windows, Motif, and several other X Windows graphical interfaces, WWW clients flatten their learning curve.

Figure 5.3 shows a WWW client.

What is so powerful about WWW services is that they can send data to the WWW client in many media: text, colored text, pictures, video clips, audio clips, and hypertext. The protocol for WWW is Hypertext Transfer Protocol (HTTP). Hypertext Markup Language (HTML) is the language used to write WWW documents—it looks similar to normal text except for additional formatting information. Hypertext is the cornerstone of WWW navigation.

You are restricted in Gopher to selecting entire menu items. In WWW clients, you can click on hypertext words, which generally are underlined and have a distinct color (usually blue), on icons, and on pictures. These hypertext links can lead to documents on the same server, on a different server, or to a Gopher, FTP, or WAIS service. Before WWW services, only clients and services of the same types could transfer data; for example, a Gopher client could talk only to a Gopher service. A WAIS client, for example, could not receive data from an FTP service. WWW services tie together many of the other services. A WWW client, such as Mosaic or Netscape, can display a Gopher menu, as well as place hypertext icons before each menu choice that users can click on.

Mosaic and Netscape can play multimedia presentations. You can, for example, access the WWW service at Paramount Studios to see movie previews. (The download time for the two minute trailer isn't at all trivial, however. But to see on your computer the same movie trailer presented at movie theaters is a big accomplishment.)

WWW services, then, provide three important services for businesses:

→ They make the tools for browsing the Internet simple and easy to use.

→ They present powerful and colorful multimedia presentations.

→ They retrieve data from all kinds of services, such as Gopher and WAIS.

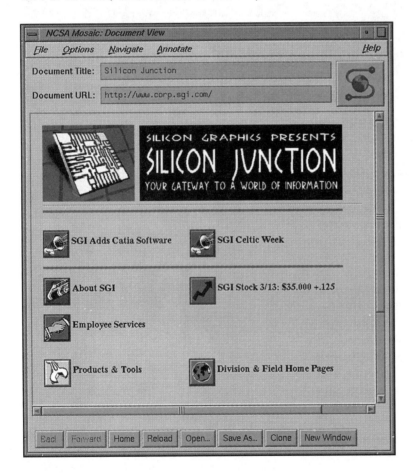

Figure 5.3

A WWW browser: Mosaic.

WWW services provide all the power your company needs to make exciting and motivating presentations. Accessing WWW services, however, used to be a problem because transferring the (sometimes huge) graphical files over slow connects was intolerable. Now, however, the newer modems (14.4 to 28.8 Kbps) and the cheaper rates for SLIP or PPP Internet connections make graphical interfaces available to all individuals. Netcom's SLIP connection, for example, is only a few dollars more per month ($20) than the text-based connection. Netcom's graphical client, Netcruiser, allows you to surf the net with nothing more than a modem. That means home users can access your company's WWW service—and that is good news for your business.

For more information about the World Wide Web, see Chapter 18, "Setting Up a WWW Service."

Deciding What Service to Offer

Now that you have had a taste of what the different services provide, you may be ready to make a decision about what your company wants to offer. The latest and greatest is the WWW service. There are few downsides to offering a WWW service. You probably want to do it. The only downsides are either the user does not have a WWW client, or you do not want to go through the process of converting your documents to true HTML (which is the tool you use to create hyperlinks and the graphical presentation). Some users cannot use WWW clients because their connection to the Internet or the speed of their modem is too slow. Because of the popularity of WWW, however, SLIP and PPP

connections will soon become more common than slower connections, and faster modems will become standard. All of this is good news to WWW service providers. In the meantime, users can use text-based WWW browsers, such as Lynx (without the power of audio, video, or graphics).

Providing a WWW service, however, requires a significant commitment to making the documents you offer graphical and full of hypertext links. This represents a significant investment of time and energy when creating a document. In the beginning, your company may simply not have the time, money, or motivation to change the format of stock company documents; your documents might not even warrant multimedia presentations. To provide these documents to the largest number of people, you might make these documents available through FTP; you might like to offer an FTP service. In the future, however, the more your documents incorporate multimedia, the more attractive they will be.

Summary

This chapter showed you the different Internet tools people use to access information over the Internet. By seeing the tools, you can decide what kinds of services your company wants to offer on the Internet.

Now that you have a sense about which Internet services you want to provide, it's time to learn how to get connected to the Internet.

Connecting to the Internet

The first obstacle you must overcome in using the Internet is getting connected to it. If only it were as easy as getting cable TV! There are many Internet providers, many categories of service, and many pricing structures. This chapter tries to demystify some of the concepts you must deal with, and thereby give you the confidence to select an Internet provider and a service category that is appropriate for your company.

This chapter looks at the categories of Internet service, examines your company's needs, and helps match your company's needs to the appropriate category of service.

 Some of you might wonder whether you can avoid the fees charged by Internet service providers by connecting directly to the Internet. Your company does not want to connect directly to the Internet 99.999 times out of 100. It's a business in itself. It's the business of Internet providers.

To connect to the Internet directly, you need a network of your own that spreads across the state (or country), contracts with similar networks for access to networks world-wide, high-speed ATM switches to deal with Internet data, and a crew of trained professionals to keep the operation running. If this is what your company wants to do, read no further; put down this book, because it does not describe how to become a part of the Internet's backbone.

Considering the overhead involved in becoming an Internet provider, you can see that paying Internet service providers is well worth it.

An Overview of Internet Service Categories

You can connect to the Internet in one of two ways:

→ Dial up account

→ Leased line

With a dial up account, you use your modem to call your Internet provider to connect to the Internet. When you are done working on the Internet, you hang up and terminate your connection to the Internet. The cost of your Internet service is either meted out on an hourly basis, a flat fee, or a combination of the two. You might, for example, get the

first 40 hours per month included in your monthly Internet bill, and then pay $2 per hour thereafter.

 Another cost is the price of the phone call. An individual has the advantage of not paying for local calls to the Internet provider. As a business, you are charged for all calls on a per minute basis.

There are two kinds of dial up accounts: dedicated and shared. On a dedicated line, only your Internet messages are transmitted. Dedicated lines are more costly, but because they do not share telephone lines with other telephone conversations, they are more accurate and achieve a higher average speed. In shared telephone lines, spurious noise can sometimes introduce errors in Internet messages.

When you connect to the Internet through a modem over ordinary telephone lines with a dial up account, the data-transmission rates vary between 2,400 bits per second (bps) to 28,800 bps. This transmission rate works very nicely for e-mail, running processes on remote machines, and even moderately well for WWW browsers. A dial up line can handle one call per telephone line. (You can use a network to spread this resource to more than one computer.) If your company only has a few people in it, and if these people do not want to use the Internet much (and when they do want to use it, e-mail or other text-based access is all they want to use), don't spend a dime more—use a dial up shell account to connect to the Internet.

A leased line is a dedicated telephone line that connects your company to the Internet provider. You do not need to dial up the provider; your company is always connected to the Interent through the provider. You pay for the leased line according to the volume of Internet traffic that crosses the wires. You also have to have a dedicated line laid to your company (which is expensive). Whereas individuals and small companies can choose to use dial up Internet accounts, medium to large companies almost have to use leased lines.

The break even point depends on the service your company chooses, but it is around four hours of Internet use per day. In other words, if you have a dial up account, you end up paying more than you would if you had a leased line for every minute you use the Internet over four hours per day. An individual can be quite happy using the Internet for less than four hours a day; a business with many users may find four hours too little.

Categories of Service

Your company can subscribe to three categories of Internet service. These categories differ in cost (both setup costs and monthly fees), speed, Internet browsers you can use, and number of Internet calls the service can handle. The three service categories are as follows:

➜ Shell

➜ SLIP and PPP

➜ Direct

Shell Account

A shell Internet account provides a Unix command line as a user interface when you connect to the Internet. On the command line you can use FTP, WAIS, and Gopher, for example, to connect to remote services and retrieve documents. For the longest time, this was the only type of Internet service available. The command line is not the sexiest of interfaces, but it is powerful. Those who mastered the commands have quick and easy access to many Internet providers.

Today, the shell account is still used because it is inexpensive, and because it offers much of what people want from the Internet: e-mail and downloading either documents or binaries. It also can work with the slowest (least expensive) modems. But just as we have seen command-line interfaces in software applications fall from favor, so too will the shell account. Now that the graphical browsers, such as Netscape, Netcruiser, Mosaic, and Chameleon, are becoming widely known, what at one time seemed like "enough" will no longer suffice. Because the shell account cannot use graphical broswers, it too shall fall from favor.

Although using the Internet for e-mail and FTP is important, as a company, there really is no reason to consider supporting only shell accounts; businesses need a more robust connection to the Internet. Much of the richness of the Internet is being created and offered through graphical services, namely, the World Wide Web (WWW). Full-screen programs that provide colorful, interactive, graphical interfaces to Internet resources (Mosaic and Netscape, for example), need to address the full screen of a computer. Shell access does not allow this. And though you can download text-only versions of WWW documents, you will not want to. The WWW offers too much to ignore it. To participate in the full range of offerings on the Internet, you need at least a SLIP or PPP connection.

SLIP and PPP

Two faster kinds of dial up connections that provide full Internet access are Serial Line Internet Protocol (SLIP) and Point-to-Point Protocol (PPP). With these connections, you can use graphical browsers, such as Mosaic and Netscape, along with all of the other Internet tools, such as WAIS, FTP, and Gopher, to explore the Internet.

Again, the Internet connection takes place through a modem over a dial up telephone line. This type of connection has suddenly become less expensive ($20 per month from Netcom). Because it offers access to graphical services, this type of connection is really the minimum your company should offer. Because this type of connection is not lightning fast, you would not want this type of connection for a large company because too many Internet requests would grind the network to a halt. This is a great connection type for individuals and small businesses.

For more information about SLIP and PPP, see "Using SLIP and PPP," later in this chapter.

Direct Connections

A direct connection provides full Internet access to the Internet using a dedicated phone line. ISDN (Integrated Services Digital Network), described later, is such an example. Because a direct connection is made through a dedicated telephone line, you can attain much greater transmission rates, and thereby service a greater number of employees.

A leased connection provides the greatest transmission rates: between 9,600 bps to 45 Mbps! Companies that use a leased line from a local telephone company can have a permanent Internet address. This kind of connection is appropriate for medium to large sized companies.

Which connection type your company should use depends on your company's needs.

Defining Your Company's Needs

When making a choice between the different connection types, you have to look in the crystal ball to see how your employees will use the Internet, how often they will use it, and whether the number of employees in your company will grow within the next several years.

If yours is a company of only a few people, or if only a few people in your company will use the Internet, your solution probably is to buy the fastest modem available and purchase a dial up PPP connection. Start-up costs, including the cost of the modem and the connection fees, are low (at the time of this writing, around $275 for the modem, $25 for the connection fees). You are faced with a monthly connection fee, perhaps $20 per month, plus usage fees per hour. Your monthly fee, for example, might entitle you to connect to the Internet 40 hours per month; any time beyond that might cost $2 per hour. If you are using a "business" telephone line, you also pay the phone company for the phone call for the duration of time you connect to the Internet.

In addition to low start-up and maintenance costs, you get the benefit of being able to choose (or switch to) most service providers. If you have dedicated lines, you tie your company into the Internet service provider through which your company is connecting to the Internet.

The downside of a dial up PPP connection, of course, is bandwidth. The more people your company has accessing the Internet at the same time, the slower the performance. That is a general rule, of course, but more apparent with smaller bandwidth connections.

In addition to the number of people accessing the network, the kinds of Internet clients users use can also reduce network speed. As Internet tools become more user-friendly and exciting (such as Mosaic, Cello, and Netscape), they become hogs for more and more system resources. When Mosaic downloads audio/video/graphics, the files may be so large that they crush network performance. It's probably an unwritten rule that the nicer the interface, the heavier weight it is.

Number of users is one criterion you need to define for your company. Here are several other points you should consider:

→ Will the number of Internet users grow significantly over the next two years?

→ How often will the Internet users use the Internet?

→ What kinds of Internet services do you need— just e-mail, or multimedia browsers such as Netscape?

→ Do you plan to set up a company advertisement on the Internet?

→ How much can you afford?

Understanding Bandwidth Terminology

The more bits per second that a connection can provide, the higher the bandwidth. Standard bandwidths for Internet services follow:

→ 9,600 bps

→ 14.4 Kbps

→ 28.8 Kbps

→ 56 Kbps

→ 128 Kbps

→ 384 Kbps

→ T1 (1.5 Mbps)

→ T3 (which ranges up to 45 Mbps)

T3 connections are usually only used by Internet service providers to connect, for example, the networks at one end of a state to another with their backbone networks. T3 is very expensive. Only the very largest companies can justify the expense of a T3 connection.

Using a Dedicated or Shared Telephone Line

Your company can use two kinds of telephone line connections to take care of your Internet needs: shared or dedicated phone lines.

Dedicated phone lines are great because they eliminate, to a great extent, spurious noise that is common in telephone lines. When noise is encountered, network packets need to be retransmitted, and the general performance of the network slows. If there is a great deal of noise, the carrier signal can be lost and the connection can be broken.

Setting up a dedicated phone line is expensive, however, because you have to pay the phone company to run a line between your company and your Internet service provider. The cost of that service is computed on a per mile basis.

The start-up costs for a dedicated line are enormous in comparison to the shared telephone line options. Usage costs from dedicated lines are lower than for using regular telephone lines, however. The breakpoint is at about three hours of Internet usage per day. If people in your company use the

Internet for more than three hours each day, the local telephone bill will be greater than the corresponding usage fee for the dedicated phone line. Given that consideration, you might amortize the cost of setting up a dedicated line over a number of years by virtue of saving local phone charges.

Considering Connection Costs

The following figures are general, but they give you a benchmark by which to compare connection costs. First, examine the costs involved in setting up the phone connections for your company.

If you use a modem with a normal telephone line, the phone company already took the trouble to bring a telephone line into your company. There is no setup charge. If you need the higher capacity that a dedicated line offers, however, you can run a new line to your company (called a *dedicated line*) or continue to use a shared line but with a higher bandwidth capacity (called *Frame Relay*). For these services, you can expect to pay the phone company the following:

Unfortunately, the charges do not stop there. There are additional costs for hardware and software, as well as their upkeep. To set up an Internet service, for example, you need a router, a dedicated workstation (the server), and a CSU/DSU (which digitizes the signal), plus associated server software. This assumes that your company already has a LAN in place.

No one wants to spend money if they don't have to. But put these costs in perspective. If your company made a single direct mailing of a 200-page catalog to 250,000 people at a cost of $1.75 for printing and mailing, your total expenditure would be about $437,500. That cost far exceeds the cost of setting up a T1 line and a World Wide Web service. (A WWW service can provide audio/visual presentations.) In addition, the T1 service does not have the potential of reaching 250,000 people; it has the potential of reaching close to 30 million people!

Now consider changing the printed catalog for the next edition; that adds another $50,000 plus the cost of the printing and mailing again! With an

Service	T1 FR	128 Kbps FR	56 Kbps FR	Dedicated TI	Dedicated 56 Kpbs
Installation	$1,700	$1,700	$1,000	$1,500	$1,500
Monthly Charge	$650	$320	$125	varies by distance	varies by distance

The following charges are associated with each connection type:

Service	T1 FR or dedicated	384 Kbps FR	128 Kbps FR	56 Kbps FR dedicated
Installation	$4,000	$4,000	$4,000	$700
Monthly Charge	$1,500	$1,000	$900	$900

Internet service, there are no start-up fees for the second edition of the catalog, so there are no fees comparable to reprinting and remailing the catalog. The only expenses involved with revising the catalog are the cost of the phone service, the fees charged by the Internet service provider, and the cost of updating the service on the server. Altogether, these costs are far less than the cost of printing a second edition of a catalog.

Given this perspective, you can see that setting up a service on the Internet can be a bargain!

System and Personnel Requirements

Now that you know what kinds of services are available and what they can do for your company and customers, you need to know how much it is going to cost in terms of hardware and labor hours. The previous sections discussed the cost of accessing the Internet using the telephone company. This section describes other cost factors: hardware requirements per Internet service and personnel.

Determining Hardware Requirements

Chapter 4, "Understanding Basic Technology," discussed the hardware requirements based on the type of Internet connection you have through the telephone company. Leased lines, for example, require the most hardware and incur the greatest start-up costs, but they offer the greatest benefits.

This section looks at other hardware requirements on a per-service basis, including the following:

➔ Network bandwidth

➔ Computational load

➔ Disk space requirements

Determining Network Load

Now that you have an idea of the possible types of Internet connections, how do you choose the one that is right for your company? Part of the answer depends on the services you want your company to offer and receive; the other part of the answer is based on the popularity of your service.

As mentioned earlier, if your company wants an ongoing presence on the Internet, it needs to be connected by a dedicated dial up line or a leased line to the Internet. These lines also give your employees the opportunity to use graphical browsers, such as Mosaic. Not only can employees use graphical browsers to obtain information from outside services, they can use graphical browsers on company services as well.

If you determine that a leased line is the way to go, you still need to determine how much bandwidth your company needs. Does it need 56 Kbps (probably the minimum) or 1.5 Mbps? Look at the bandwidth requirements associated with each service type.

There are two basic parts to Internet communications: a service request and a service reply.

In terms of network load, service requests by any type of client—FTP, Gopher, WAIS, WWW, or Mail archive—are relatively light, with several exceptions. Uploading files using FTP can generate a considerable amount of network traffic. WAIS requests can be small, unless you use an entire document as a search criterion. Then, WAIS can generate significant network traffic. And if you use e-mail to broadcast a message to many user IDs, you can burden the network.

Service replies to client requests, however, often can generate a great deal of network traffic. The question is, how can you anticipate the amount of network traffic and purchase the appropriate fraction of T1 service?

Determining Computational Load

Chances are, you can't get away with using a pocket calculator to perform your service's computations. But you won't need a supercomputer either. How fast is fast enough? The following guidelines might give you a clue.

By far, the most CPU-intensive service is WAIS. Its job of searching indexes by keywords or by entire documents easily can bog down a CPU. In addition, WAIS is responsible for opening index files and determining just how closely index files match the keyword search. And WAIS does not help you much. It does not offer any tools to limit access to the service during high system loads, so everything just slows down. To accommodate a WAIS service, you need a fast processor.

The least CPU-demanding service is a mailing list service. They refer to alias files, but they do not tax the CPU. When e-mail is broadcast to large mailing lists, however, the CPU is taxed according to the size of the mailing list. The Unix program sendmail, designed to deliver mail on many flavors of Unix, was not really designed for high-volume mailings.

All the other services—Gopher, FTP, and WWW— tax the CPU in proportion to their popularity and the size of the files they process. WWW services, for example, often can be CPU-intensive because

they use images in their documents, and images make file sizes very large.

Because it is FTP's job to transfer entire files, FTP often can bog down CPUs while performing its tasks.

Regardless of the CPU you choose to run your service, you will need to monitor its usage. As your services gain in popularity, you will need to run faster and faster machines. Maybe some day your service will be so popular you will need a supercomputer. (But don't start off with one!)

Determining Disk Space

With the price of disk drives plummeting, getting extra large disk space is less of an issue, economically, these days. Still, you might wonder how much disk space you should allot for your service. Again, the type of service helps determine the amount of disk space your service will consume.

Most services only require the amount of disk space that is consumed by the files your service is offering. FTP archives, for example, take up a finite amount of space. You need to allow a little additional space to accommodate such things as README files, configuration files, and index files. Gopher, for example, uses index files to display menu choices. FTP uses small programs to list available files for anonymous users. A megabyte or two is usually sufficient to handle this extra overhead. So, if you can compute the number of megabytes your files will consume, you can make an educated guesstimate about the size of the disk drive to use with your services.

Exceptions to this rule are WAIS and Mail services. WAIS index files can swell to the size of the data files they represent. So, if you are offering a WAIS service, consider using a disk drive equal to twice the size of the data.

Mail services can use additional disk space because when the messages are queued, the headers and the message bodies sit on the disk under the queue directory.

Unfortunately, there is a *caveat* you should consider. Security can be an issue in Internet offerings. Some security schemes require that a copy be made of the data your service will offer. That requirement at least doubles the disk space you might otherwise estimate.

Manning the Post

After you have all your hardware in place and are connected to the Internet, you have to get someone who can make it all work. The ideal candidate for this job should have a unique blend of talents. He or she must have some system-administration experience in the Unix world, as well as an artistic eye so that he or she can design an attractive and effective graphical interface.

Here are some additional tasks that an Internet system administrator must perform:

➜ Keep current the information on the service.

➜ Continue to surf the Internet to find additional links to documents maintained by your company.

➜ Check the links to other services to make sure that your documents are not leading users on a wild-goose chase. (After about three or four messages saying that the document is not ready or the service is not willing to give it to you, smoke starts pouring from many people's ears.)

➜ Respond to user inquiries.

Obviously, the data that you are making available to others on the Internet is very important. The more helpful and relevant the documents and programs to Internet users, the more your documents and programs will be used. Sometimes, however, administrators forget that what users first see is not the documents and programs your service is offering; instead, it is the interface designed by the Internet system administrator. The interface might be a menuing system for Gopher or a home page for WWW. If the directories are not arranged well in your FTP service, if the README files are incorrect or poor in an FTP service, if the WWW links are bogus, if the WWW interface is not intuitive, or if the person fires off angry e-mails at users who have questions, it doesn't really matter how good the data is in your service; no one is going to use it. The Internet system administrator position is crucial for the success of your service. Think twice before setting the salary level of the position.

Making the Decision

After you have looked at the makeup of your company, guessed about the number of people you will employ in the near future, and made an intelligent guesstimate about the amount of Internet usage, you can apply these rules of thumb:

➜ 56 Kbps is the minimum transmission speed for companies employing 10 or more people who regularly use interactive applications over the Internet.

➜ T1 is the recommended connection type for moderate to large companies in which employees regularly use interactive applications over the Internet.

→ If your employees will use interactive Internet applications, such as WWW browsers, you need a greater bandwidth.

→ Buy as big a transmission rate as your company can justify—you probably will need to double it in three to five years.

Your company probably will need to increase the size of its service, because the Internet applications in the future will continue to demand higher transmission rates to run at a reasonable speed. Remember when your 286 ran applications just fine until you tried to run Microsoft Windows on it? All of a sudden, you found out that applications had outpaced your hardware. With the growth of multimedia browsers, tomorrow's Internet applications likewise will outstrip today's transmission requirements.

The following sections describe the connection types in more detail.

Determining Hardware Requirements for Dial Up and Proxy Connections

For a dial up or proxy connection, you need a modem connected to a telephone line. You can use a regular phone line or a dedicated 14.4-Kbps line.

Over the past several years, a variety of modem protocols have hit the marketplace. The latest is V.34, which runs at 28,800 bps and effectively doubles the speed of the previous front-runner, the V.32bis protocol. With data compression, a V.34 modem can transfer data at a rate of up to 115,200 bps.

There is, of course, an upper limit as to the maximum transmission rate that a voice-grade telephone line can handle. To get much past the transmission rate touted by the V.34 protocol, you have to stop using standard telephone lines.

The V.34 modem is significant for companies because it makes services available to them, such as World Wide Web services, that are unavailable when you have to use slower modems.

When purchasing such modems, be careful that its features are not proprietary.

To configure a modem, set the speed and settings of the port to the same numbers. If your modem uses V.34, for example, set the modem and the serial port to 115,200 bps, 8 data bits, no parity, and 1 stop bit (8,N,1).

Using the Dial Up Connection

To use a dial up connection, you must use one of the many service providers. There are two types of service providers: those that offer limited Internet access but provide many ancillary services (such as stock quotes, movie reviews, and so on) and those that offer full Internet access only. Examples of the first type of service follow:

→ CompuServe (800-848-8990)

→ America Online (800-227-6364)

→ Prodigy (800-776-3449)

→ GEnie (800-638-9636)

→ MCI Mail (800-444-6245)

None of these services gives you access to the full Internet. You can get e-mail through all of these services, although you might have to pay for each e-mail you receive and send!

In part, these online services make their money by offering to subscribers specialized software that accomplishes specific tasks, such as monitoring the stock market. Most of this software is available, in some form, as shareware on the Internet, however. It therefore is in the interest of these companies to limit their customer's access to the Internet.

Although many of these companies provide many useful services, such as stock quotes and access to the Internet, they generally charge for these services. So be careful that you know what your costs are before subscribing to one of these online services.

Looking at Internet Providers for Dial Up Connections

There are other companies set up just to give people access to the Internet. They might not offer people the same high-end services that you might get on CompuServe, for example. However, there are no hidden charges either.

There are many local Internet providers and several national providers. These companies generally provide you with an account on a server running Unix that handles e-mail for you. Some services provide menu systems or graphical-user interfaces to help guide your interaction on the Internet; others simply provide the equivalent of a shell. If you are unfamiliar with Unix, make sure the Internet provider supplies a menu system or a GUI to make life in the fast lane of the information superhighway easy. Otherwise, you might putt putt around, spinning in circles until you get your Unix commands down.

What comes with such unrestricted access to the Internet, often, is... freedom (!) and no one to hold your hand. If what you want access to is a stock-quoting service, you will have to find such a service yourself, with the aid of the multitude of Internet books now on the market. If you are daunted by not having someone to guide you around the Internet, however, see what kind of technical support the Internet provider offers, if any. (But it shouldn't take much Internet surfing to find a wealth of information.)

The following are three national Internet providers:

→ Delphi (800-695-4005)

→ Netcom (800-501-8649)

→ Performance Systems International (800-82-PSI-82)

The trick with these services is that you need to live near one of their local dial-in numbers (because you are footing the bill for the local call).

Delphi is located in Boston. If you do not live near Boston, you log in to Delphi using SprintLink or Tymnet. Delphi uses menus as its navigation system, which, unfortunately, can be tedious.

Netcom has many Sun workstations around the country, so it has many more local dial-in numbers than Delphi. Netcom also offers a graphical-user interface called Netcruiser to help you find the information you want on the Internet.

Performance Systems International originally serviced the defense industry. Consequently, it is a reliable system. It too offers a graphical user interface. You must pay for the third-party software interface, however.

Using SLIP and PPP

Two protocols operate in the environment of a proxy connection: SLIP and PPP. Both work through a modem over shared (or dedicated) telephone lines.

SLIP (serial lines on Internet protocol) was created as shareware and is available widely on the Internet. SLIP transmits Internet packets over serial lines.

SLIP is simple and reliable. More important, SLIP gives users access to the full suite of Internet tools—including Mosaic, Gopher, FTP, and telnet. All these tools run as though your machine were connected directly to a network. For all these reasons, the various shareware versions of SLIP became very popular.

SLIP can be frustrating, however. The virtue of its simplicity is also its problem: it can handle only IP; it cannot handle such protocols as Appletalk, Novell Netware, OSI, and so on. Although it is interesting that there are many versions of SLIP shareware, the problem is that there is not a common protocol. Although the protocol is described in RFC 1055, there is no standard SLIP—only varieties that partially conform to RFC 1055. Finally, SLIP is not a secure protocol. There is no way to authenticate a SLIP connection.

 n o t e A *secure protocol* means that your Internet messages cannot be read or changed by others.

Authenticating a connection means that you can identify the participants in the connection.

A task force called Internet Engineering Task Force (IETF) worked for several years to improve SLIP. The result of its work is a standard called PPP, Point-to-Point Protocol, RFC 1548. It shares with SLIP the capability to provide users access to a full suite of Internet tools, such as Mosaic, Gopher, FTP, and telnet, on a serial line, but it also provides many more features than SLIP.

The following list of features gives you some indication of how much better the PPP protocol is than SLIP:

→ PPP can negotiate compression techniques and maximum frame sizes.

→ PPP can provide low-level authentication.

→ PPP can use control characters that can pass through to the application.

→ PPP provides loopback detection.

→ PPP offers sophisticated monitoring.

Most of this functionality is hidden from the user: these attributes are negotiated at connection time. Therefore, it is not harder to make a connection with PPP than it is with SLIP.

PPP supports dynamic IP address handling. When a connection between two computers is made, PPP allows the target computer to use an IP address from a list of shared addresses. That IP address remains constant during the connection. When the connection is terminated, the assigned IP address returns to the shared list for use by other computers. The capability of the PPP protocol to use shared IP addresses is called *dynamic IP address handling*. This feature enables PPP to connect with any target computer, regardless of its network addressing. And, as the popularity of the Internet continues to grow, IP addresses will grow scarce. Using a set of shared IP addresses is a way of stretching the number of IP addresses available.

Some Internet service providers offer a discount on service prices if you accept an IP address that is tied to the Internet service provider. This type of registration stays with your company while you are with the Internet service provider, but is revoked if you switch Internet service providers. This is one way that the Internet is dealing with the exploding need for IP addresses.

You can hunt around the Internet for a shareware version of SLIP or PPP, or you can purchase a copy. The price, between $100 and $700, depends on the platform. For the Unix platform, a company called Morning Star Technologies, Inc., among others, sells PPP software called MST-PPP. On smaller platforms, such as the PC and the Mac, there is Chameleon and MacSLIP, respectively.

 Some companies, such as Telebit and Rockwell International, package together a modem, SLIP, PPP, and router. Putting SLIP and PPP on a router reduces the processing burden from other servers.

There are SLIP-only configurations that PPP cannot access. However, some versions of PPP, such as MST-PPP from Morning Star, also support SLIP and can allow connections to systems that only support SLIP.

For new dialup networks, you should use PPP instead of SLIP.

Using ISDN

If your company's goal is to use the Internet to do such things as video conferencing, you need a bandwidth broader than 28.8 Kbps. ISDN was conceived in 1968 when 64 Kbps seemed like a great deal of bandwidth. Today, telephone companies offer single- and double-line ISDN service. Throughput of a single line is actually 56 Kbps; double-line throughput is 128 Kbps. This bandwidth is acceptable for video conferencing. The MPEG images often have a slight stop-action look to them, but establishing a connection is as simple as making a phone call.

ISDN works over dedicated telephone lines. The machinery used to rout ISDN calls is normal telephone machinery. For that reason, ISDN is the choice of telephone companies to bring larger bandwidth services into businesses and the home.

Although it is fine for a business to have an ISDN connection to the Internet for faster access, in order to do video conferencing, all video conferencing sites need ISDN connections.

On the downside, telephone companies charge for ISDN calls just as they charge for regular business calls—they charge per minute for the length of the connection. Because there is a similar rate structure for ISDN and normal phone calls (calls are more expensive during business hours), ISDN connections can get expensive. The expense is holding back a wider appeal of ISDN. If the telephone companies instituted a flat-fee structure, ISDN's popularity would rise.

Using Switched 56k

A service that is very similar to ISDN and that already exists in many areas is Switched 56k. You can use it to connect to ISDN (and Switched 56k) sites. Switched 56k requires special cabling by the telephone company.

ISDN and Switched 56k have a similar downside: both are metered calls. The time of day affects the cost of the calls. Whether the call is local or long distance also affects the cost of the call.

The variation on Switched 56k that offers a fixed rate is a dedicated 56k (DDS) line. Dedicated lines cost more to install, but that extra cost can be amortized over the length of the service.

Using a Leased Line

To really get a higher bandwidth than that offered by ISDN, you need to use a leased line. For medium to large companies, leased lines are the only practical alternative. Transmission speeds vary between 9,600 bps and 45 Mbps. Not surprisingly, the cost of the equipment and service varies accordingly.

The lower end transmission speeds use an analog signal. In such cases, you can get away with using a simple modem to connect to the leased line. But if you need higher throughput, and you probably do, you will use a digital signal that requires additional machinery, including the following:

→ A router (used as a gateway)

→ A CSU/DSU (which converts the digital signal)

→ A host computer

→ Associated software

A router decides which IP messages are bound for the local network and which are bound for the Internet. Although you can use a process on a Unix machine as a router, it is much faster to use a dedicated router, such as those built by Cisco, Wellfleet, and others. It would be silly to pay for a higher transmission rate and then create a bottleneck in the system by not purchasing a dedicated router. If you insist, however, on using a Unix machine as a router,

strip it of its other jobs so that additional processes do not slow down its routing performance.

The host computer can store Internet mail messages which machines on the local network can access at their convenience.

Extra machinery is never cheap, but the cost of routers, CSU/DSUs, and host computers has fallen dramatically to a point that small- to medium-size companies can afford.

There are other cost factors involved after you get into an environment with routers and servers. To isolate a local network from the Internet, for example, you need a firewall. *Firewalls* provide a barrier to people outside of your company who try to access your local network. This prevents people outside of your company from using the Internet to probe your company's sensitive files. There are many ways of implementing firewalls. They can be server applications, part of the router, or part of an operating system. Each firewall has its own price tag and provides a different level of security.

Also, in terms of additional costs, there's the small matter of maintaining the system with highly trained professionals. But cost is only one factor in the entire equation that makes Internet access very attractive.

At the high end of the transmission speed is the T3 line, capable of transmitting data at 45 Mbps. This is a great service, but it's far too expensive to be practical to most businesses except Internet service providers. Most commonly, Internet service providers use T3 connections as the backbone links between major networks. These providers also use T3 lines to connect the areas at each end of their service area, such as northern and southern California.

A more reasonably priced leased line is the T1. Its maximum transmission rate is 1.544 Mbps. This speed is more than enough for just about every major corporation. You even can get partial service (and pay less). You can get a T1 line as low as 64 Kbps, for example, or you can purchase fractional T1 service in 64-Kbps increments. You could have a T1 service at the following transmission rates: 64 Kbps, 128 Kbps, 192 Kbps, and so on, up to 1.544 Mbps.

Using Service Providers

Regardless of how you get connected to the Internet, your company will need the service of an Internet service provider. There are many, and many offer immediate fax-back information services.

Getting an Internet Address

One attractive feature of getting a leased T1 line is that your Internet service provider generally gives your company a permanent Internet address and a domain name. If your company wants a permanent presence on the Internet (for example, your company wants to offer a WWW service), a permanent Internet address is a requirement.

 Whether or not your company gets a permanent Internet address is up to the Internet service provider. Before you choose one, make sure you know if they will provide your company with a permanent presence on the Internet.

SLIP and PPP connections also require Internet addresses and domain names; dial up shell accounts do not.

Your Internet service provider can provide you with all the information you need to get a permanent Internet address. If you want to prepare yourself for the questions your provider will ask in order to perform that service for you, you can look at the Internet registration template from the agency that assigns Internet addresses and domain names, InterNIC, by gophering to rs.internic.net. Once there, select

```
/InterNIC Registration Services (NSI)/Internet
Registration Archives/templates/Internet-number-
template.txt
```

One question on the form that requires some forethought and planning is the class of Internet address that your company needs.

There are three classes of Internet addresses: A, B, and C. A Class C address can handle up to 255 nodes on a single segment, whereas a Class B address can handle up to 65,535 nodes per segment. If your company has less than 255 addressable computers on a local network, use a Class C. If your company has more, you must use a Class B address.

 Because Internet addresses are running short, it is unlikely for any company to get a Class B address.

You cannot base your decision of an Internet address class simply on what your company has today. You must guesstimate how many computers will be on your network in the next five years. You have to consider how many subnets you have.

Domain names should be similar to your company's name. Silicon Graphic's domain name is sgi.com, for example, and Hewlett-Packard's domain name is hp.com. If you want to see whether the domain name you are considering is claimed already by another company, you can gopher to rs.internic.net.

Once there, select the InterNIC Registration Services (NSI) menu item, and then select "Whois Searches." Enter your prospective domain name to check for duplication.

Give your service provider all the required information so that he or she can register your Internet address and domain name on behalf of your company. Once assigned, the address and domain belong to your company, not to the Internet service provider.

Summary

In this chapter, you looked at many ways of connecting to the Internet. You also briefly looked at some of the machinery required by such connections.

After looking at your company's Internet needs, you should use the following rules of thumb:

→ If yours is a small company in which the employees intend to use the Internet infrequently, you should use PPP over a high-speed modem with a dial up account.

→ If your company wants a permanent presence on the Internet, generally, you want to get a dedicated dial up or leased line connection.

→ If your company wants to set up a satellite location of five or more people who run data-intensive applications, 28.8 Kbps dial up accounts will not suffice. Instead, use ISDN or a fractional T1.

→ If your only network application is teleconferencing between two specified sites, use ISDN.

→ If yours is a company with 10 or more people who use the Internet regularly, use a dedicated dial up or a fractional T1 connection.

→ If you want your company to advertise on the Internet, use a fractional T1 or a dedicated dial-up connection.

All but the very largest companies find T1 adequate for their needs.

Remember that your Internet needs are sure to grow. With that in mind, do not choose ISDN if your transmission rates already are near the maximum throughput rates of ISDN (128 Kbps). ISDN does not offer faster service. It often is better to start with a fractional T1 link than ISDN, because you can increase the amount of T1 you use as your company grows. This flexibility avoids the nightmare of throwing away good machinery that simply is inadequate for the job.

Legal Considerations

I t is not within the scope of this book to provide a

full discussion of the legal issues connected with

Internet use and commerce. Even if there were

room, I could not write in rich detail about the

intricacies of Internet law because the courts have

not yet made many judicial decisions about what is

legal on the Internet. You may have read about

judgments against hackers and people posting illicit

materials on company servers, or more recently

about the congressional ban on smut, but Internet

law is still in its infancy.

This chapter might, however, be one of the most important in the book, not because it unveils and clarifies mysterious ideas, but because court costs are monstrous. Making even an innocent mistake can cost you more than you care to think about. You need to add legal concerns to your checklist of important items to consider as you create your service, and as you maintain it. If ever you are in doubt about whether you need permission to use something on the Internet, get permission. If ever you get the feeling that you are on uncertain legal grounds, get a lawyer to spend a couple of hours with you. Although legal advice costs ridiculous sums of money, costs of legal actions will truly stun you.

This chapter covers the basics of Internet law. Currently, most of the applicable laws are carry-overs from the publishing world. As the Internet matures, Internet law will become defined. So do not treat this chapter as the definitive source for Internet law, but rather as a starting place.

Protecting Your Materials

As an Internet service provider, your service offers some combination of documents and programs. Some of these items you might want people to copy and distribute freely. You might, for example, want sales brochures distributed as widely as possible. You might, however, want to maintain control over other items, either to receive credit or remuneration for the work. If, for example, you have written the next, greatest WWW browser, you might like to get paid for your talent and time. Or you might have documents that reflect significant research, or have creative work that you want to keep under your name for future remuneration opportunities.

The following are the four kinds of intellectual property that you can protect:

- → Trademarks
- → Patented designs
- → Trade secrets
- → Copyrighted material

Trademarks

Trademarks are logos, company names, and product names that are owned by individuals or companies. Trademarks prevent others from capitalizing off the good name of existing companies and products. You would not, for example, want to call your next computer the Coca-Cola™ Machine. It is to your company's advantage to leverage off of successful company and product names, but it is a right for which you must pay.

Patented Designs

If you design a new piece of hardware, you can patent the design and the hardware with the U.S. Patent Office. Because the patent is made public by the government, it is fine to publish a document about the design. What you cannot do, however, is freely use a product that requires a license; for example, encryption technology found on the Internet is free to non-profit users, but requires a license for use by for-profit businesses.

 note Encryption technology poses another problem. It is illegal to encrypt documents and programs that are exported. The government likes the opportunity to see what is leaving the country to determine if the contents violate national law. The government does not, for example, want the recipe for making atomic weapons going to North Korea.

Trade Secrets

Trade secrets are products or ideas created and owned by individuals and companies. If you are a software developer, no doubt you signed a form for your company, as a condition of employment, that said anything you created was the property of the company, not you. These creations are part of a company's assets. Companies pay many people's salaries to develop such assets; they do not want this information freely distributed.

It is imperative that your company maintain the secrecy of these ideas or mark them clearly as property of your company so that your company can prosecute people who steal such things.

Conversely, make sure that your service does not reveal the secrets of other companies. Even if the vice president of a company turns over to you some great ideas, like the formula for Coca-Cola, their corporate policy might not allow them such latitude, and your company will soon hear from their legal department. Always get written permission from responsible corporate officials before using trade secrets.

Copyrighted Materials

The intellectual property that you probably will make the most use of is copyrighted materials. If you are making documents available to Internet users, you need to copyright the documents you want to control.

Getting a copyright is easy. You submit two copies of a document to the U.S. Copyright Office no later than three months after its initial publication, and display copyright information prominently in the document. Copyright declarations look similar to the following:

Copyright © 1995 DreamsAlive, Inc. All rights reserved.

Even if you forget to include that information, the copyright office gives you five years to correct the oversight.

The address of the U.S. Copyright Office is as follows:

Copyright Office
Information and Publications Section
Library of Congress
Washington, DC 20559

Copyrights are actually automatic. As soon as you create a document, it is yours (unless you have agreed to something else with, for example, an employer). Registering your document with the copyright office helps prove that you are the author of it. Make sure you register your documents before you make them available to others on the Internet so they do not register the document before you!

Copyrights remain in force until 50 years after the death of the author (or, if jointly created, the death of the last surviving author). For companies, copyrights remain in force for 100 years after the creation of the document, or 75 years after its publication, whichever is shorter.

Avoiding Legal Problems

The following list by no means exhausts the topic of what you should not do on the Internet. It does, however, provide a quick review of some "gotchas" that merit your attention.

Seek Permission

Everything on the Internet looks free. Everyone can access just about everything. You might wonder why anyone would care that you make the same content available again in your document.

In fact, many Internet authors relish the idea of someone promoting their materials (as long as they receive some credit). It is crucial, however, that you get permission to use materials that are not yours.

Avoid Libel

People writing Internet documents are protected under the First Amendment of the U.S. Constitution, which establishes the right of free speech. Such freedom does not, however, extend into the area of defamation of character. You do not, for example, want to publish your story about a real person taking illegal drugs or worse, unless you are willing to weather the storm of a court case. Nor do you want to publish information that you know is false. Finally, you do not want to publish a document on the basis of hearsay. If the information source is wrong, you could be libel for gross negligence. As you would expect, the more severe the error, the more severe the consequence.

You also cannot cut and paste together paragraphs from someone else's work and change a couple of words here and there. This violation is termed "fair use."

What you can do, however, is use someone else's ideas if you put those ideas into your own words. No one can claim ownership of ideas. You may, however, choose to include some reference to the other document in a bibliography.

Export Problems

Do not export encrypted files. The government takes a dim view of people selling national secrets, so it is a national policy not to export encrypted materials.

You also may not export encryption technology under any circumstances. Again, the government does not like to be the odd man out when it comes to encryption technology. If, for some reason, you want to make this technology available to U.S. Internet users, you should require user registration and authentication of identification.

Avoid Pornography

Pornography is not illegal in all states and countries, but it is in many. Just because your porn server is located in a state that allows pornography, you are not exempt from the laws of other states where Internet users might access your service. If porn is your business, you had better require—at least—user registration and authentication of the user's location and age.

Pirated Software

Even if software is freely available on the Internet, it is not okay for you to offer the same software as though it were yours.

Checking Uploaded Material

Here's the catch: You may adhere stringently to all of the above guidelines, but if someone commits any of the illegal actions described above on your server, you get part of the blame. Criminals are not dumb. They do not want to make pirated software or pornography available on their servers; they want to make pirated software and pornography available on others' servers, perhaps yours.

If you allow people to upload files to your server, it is doubly important that you check and recheck what is on your server. Even if you do not allow uploads, you should still be vigilant about checking for the following:

→ Unusually high numbers of FTP sessions

→ Any fsp (File Sharing Protocol) sessions or log files

→ Unusually large amounts of disk space consumed by a single user

→ Any mention of your service in any of the security and hacking related Usenet news groups

If you find anything out of the ordinary, it is very important to document it before taking any action of your own. Also before giving them an account, make users sign an agreement that details what they can and cannot do. Include a list of penalties if they violate the policy. This is especially important if you are a commercial provider.

Summary

This chapter gave only a brief description of some of the legal topics that you should concern yourself with. It described ways to protect your materials and avoid legal problems.

The brevity of the chapter does not reflect its importance in the creation of your service and its role in routine administrative maintenance. If you build one of the services incorrectly, you get the chance to reconfigure it without much consequence. If, on the other hand, you handle one of the above-mentioned legal issues incorrectly, your company might suffer huge consequences.

Making Your LAN Secure

Opening the door to the Internet community is exciting, it's good for business, and it helps your employees. The door, unfortunately, swings both ways, and you never know what's going to come in. You can use the 99 percent rule to describe the necessity of local area network (LAN) security—99.999 percent of the people who access your service do so with good intentions. The 0.001 percent, however, who intend otherwise, require that you spend time and money protecting your LAN from piracy and sabotage.

Although you can protect your LAN in a number of different ways, the use of a firewall offers the most common and effective approach by far. A *firewall* is application software that sits on a computer between your LAN and the Internet. All Internet messages must pass through the firewall. To reach the LAN from the Internet, you must have a firewall account that defines your user ID, password, group ID, and system-administrator-given permissions. Permissions include any combination of reading, writing, or execution of files in the LAN. You might give read-only permissions to a user, for example, so he or she can only read files, not change them.

The discussion of security issues deserves a book of its own. This chapter defines firewalls, discusses the strategies you can employ to make your LAN secure, and informs you of the free firewall software on the Internet. For a thorough discussion of firewalls and LAN security, refer to *Internet Firewalls and Network Security*, published by New Riders Publishing.

Guarding the Gateway

First and foremost, the job of the gateway computer is to monitor the connection between the Internet and your LAN. The gateway computer accomplishes this task by examining the IP address and port number of each IP packet coming and going.

A firewall implements the security policies defined by your company. A firewall should prevent any actions your company deems unacceptable from taking place, should log suspicious events, and should alert personnel when suspicious events occur.

Kinds of Firewalls

This chapter discusses just two of the two most popular kinds of firewall setups:

→ Inline host

→ Monitoring host

Inline Host

The inline host places the gateway computer directly in the path between the Internet and the LAN, as shown in figure 8.1.

This setup prevents a direct connection between the Internet and your company's LAN. Both the Internet service and the LAN client talk to the inline host.

The inline host uses programs called *proxies* that hand data from the LAN to the Internet, and vice versa. Proxies generally run on the inline host and are invisible to users. You can configure proxy software to prevent direct Internet/LAN communication based on the following:

→ Source addresses or ports

→ Destination addresses or ports

→ Passwords

To gain access to a LAN through the firewall, proxy software often requires users to enter a gateway ID and a password. Without these entries, an Internet user cannot gain access to the company's LAN.

Monitoring Host

A monitoring host does not sit directly between the Internet and your company's LAN. As figure 8.2

Figure 8.1

The inline host.

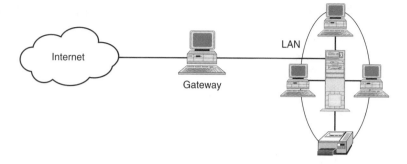

shows, a router sits between the Internet and the LAN; the monitoring host monitors all communication between the Internet and the LAN.

The router is often configured to allow all IP packets from the LAN to pass unimpeded to the Internet. IP packets traveling in the other direction can be restricted according to the address of the Internet server or destination port.

When LAN Internet clients communicate with Internet services, any virus on an Internet service can pass through the firewall. Make sure the services accessed by LAN Internet clients are secure. Newer services are favorite targets for Internet demons. Even old services, however, are susceptible to infection. Stayed tuned to newsgroups for information about virulent services.

Getting Firewall Software

Now that you know what a firewall is, you need to decide where to get firewall software and decide where in your system to place it. This section talks about three of the most popular firewall applications. You might also use FTP to retrieve /pub /firewalls/firewalls.ps/Z from ftp.tis.com.

Using the Firewall Toolkit

The Firewall Toolkit runs on the gateway computer. It contains a variety of useful tools and proxy services that help connect LAN users to the Internet, and restrict access to your services.

The netacl file in the Firewall Toolkit contains access tables. It works with inetd to determine whether or not to start all inetd-controlled services, such as ftpd and httpd, in response to service

Figure 8.2

The monitoring host.

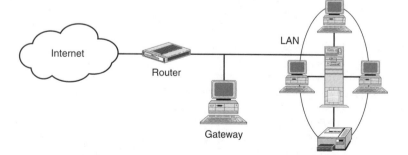

requests. Other tools provide important functionality; they include the following:

→ **smap** and **smapd.** Provides basic mail-handling functions—they accept mail and place it in a chroot()'d directory

→ **FTP daemon.** Enables you to run anonymous FTP on the gateway computer, and enables LAN to access Internet FTP services

The Firewall Toolkit also contains a variety of proxy services that connect LAN users to the Internet. These services include the following:

→ **ftp-gw.** An FTP proxy

→ **plug-gw.** A socket-to-socket service

→ **tn-gw.** A telnet proxy

The advantage of these proxies is that you do not have to modify LAN Internet clients in order to access Internet services through the proxy on the gateway computer. On the other hand, instead of taking the time to change the configuration of the client once, with the Firewall Toolkit, you have to use a two-step process every time you want to read an Internet service. First you connect to the gateway computer where the proxy software runs; then you connect to an Internet service by typing the following at the proxy prompt:

```
> connect InternetHostName
```

With this in mind, you have to decide if not modifying Internet clients on your LAN is worth everyone's trouble when accessing Internet services.

To get the Firewall Toolkit, use FTP to get it from ftp.tis.com in /pub/firewalls/toolkit/fwtk.tar.Z.

Using the CERN WWW Service in Proxy Mode

When in proxy mode, the CERN WWW service works in much the same way as the Firewall Toolkit—LAN Internet requests go to the service, which in turn automatically makes requests of Internet services. Like the Firewall Toolkit, LAN Internet clients are not directly connected to Internet services. Unlike the Toolkit, the separate connection between the gateway computer and the Internet service is transparent to the LAN client. To the client, it appears as if he is connected directly to the Internet service.

To allow the CERN service to automatically connect to Internet services and hand the information to LAN Internet clients transparently, you have to change environment variables for the Internet client. For an NCSA's X Mosaic client, for example, you have to set the following variables:

```
setenv http_proxy *http://www.company.com:80/*
setenv ftp_proxy *http://www.company.com:80/*
setenv gopher_proxy *http://www.company.com:80/*
setenv wais_proxy *http://www.company.com:80/*
setenv file_proxy *http://www.company.com:80/*
```

Another advantage of the CERN WWW service is that it can cache Internet service documents. Because it makes all connections to Internet services, it can use the cached version of a document rather than requesting that document over the Internet. This feature reduces response times and network load.

To get the source code for the CERN WWW service, refer to Chapter 18, "Setting Up a WWW Service."

Using SOCKS

The SOCKS software package includes a SOCKS library that has standard socket calls, such as connect(), bind(), listen(), and accept(). These library functions enable the SOCKS service to communicate with external services.

The SOCKS service runs on the gateway computer. It runs as an intermediary, passing LAN Internet requests to remote services, and service answers to LAN Internet clients. The proxy service comes with versions of FTP, telnet, finger, and whois. The service is available to get from ftp.nec.com in /pub/security/socks.cstc/socks.cstc.4.2.tar.gz. From the same source—ftp.nec.com—you can get freeware that allows SOCKS to provide a proxy service for ping, Archie, Gopher, and WWW service requests.

Placing the Gateway Computer

The gateway computer that runs the firewall software can be located in three places:

→ It can be between the Internet server and the company's LAN.

→ It can run as the Internet server.

→ It can be outside both the Internet server and the company LAN.

Placing the gateway computer between the Internet and the service introduces significant security risks to your LAN. Although it is possible, it is not a practical solution, and so is not discussed.

Some people call the connection between your machines and the Internet the *demilitarized zone*—the border between friendly and unfriendly forces. If you place your service in the demilitarized zone, and place the gateway computer between that zone and your LAN, your service does not benefit from firewall protection; only your LAN does. Because access to your service does not require access to your gateway computers, this configuration provides your LAN the greatest protection. Your gateway computer, however, must provide proxy software so that LAN users can access the Internet, including your service.

If your service resides on the gateway computer, both internal and external users have easy access to the service. The service, however, is vulnerable to attack, making the gateway server untrustworthy.

If your gateway computer sits outside your LAN and Internet server, your service receives the maximum protection, and LAN users can easily access your service. The gateway computer still needs proxy software, however, to enable Internet users to access your service.

In part, you need to decide how you want to use the firewall software—do you want to protect your service, or do you want to protect your LAN? If you want to protect your service, you must locate the service on the gateway computer or inside it. Locating the service inside of the gateway computer, however, presents communication problems with Internet clients. With every solution, a balance between ease of communications and security ensues—the easier it is to communicate with the Internet community, the more vulnerable the service; the more secure the service, the more difficult it is for the Internet community to communicate with that service.

If you want to protect your LAN, do not locate your service on the gateway computer; locate the service outside the gateway computer. Any virus that compromises your service might also infect the machine on which it is running. This is especially bad news if your firewall runs on the same machine—thus compromising your firewall security.

Locating a service outside of the gateway computer to prevent the gateway from becoming compromised, however, leaves the service much too vulnerable in the inline configuration. In this configuration, the Internet connection plugs right into the server running your Internet service. You need a router outside of the Internet server to protect it, as is prescribed in the monitored configuration.

An even safer configuration is to add a second router to the monitored configuration inside the gateway computer but outside of the LAN. The second router adds an extra layer of security to protect the LAN from invasion should the gateway computer become infected.

As you can see, providing an Internet service opens your service and LAN to some risk. You can minimize that risk by using the procedures suggested in this book.

The following sections discuss the considerations you must take into account when deciding where to locate your gateway computer relative to your service. Briefly, you should locate anonymous FTP services on the gateway computer in an inline configuration; a WWW service is best located in a monitored configuration inside the router but outside the gateway computer.

Inline Configuration

In terms of security, the last thing you want is a wayward application (infecting the machine carrying your service) to make connections with other machines on your LAN. Remember, however, that an FTP transaction uses two connections—one in which the FTP client navigates the service, and a second, set up by the service to the client, that allows the uploading or downloading of data. The tricky aspect of FTP, then, is its inherent use of a mechanism—connecting the service to client machines—that endangers the client machines receiving FTP requests. One result of the dual connection is the difficulty of locating the gateway computer inside the service.

With the inline configuration, it is hard to imagine a time when you would want any services to run outside of the gateway computer. This configuration makes your service too vulnerable. The configuration also makes it difficult for LAN users to access your own service.

The best location for an FTP service in the inline configuration is to run the service on the gateway computer. FTP provides its own security features, such as running ftpd in a limited directory space using chroot(), and running it as a nonprivileged user. Both LAN and Internet users have easy access to your service.

You can locate your WWW service on the gateway computer. This configuration makes your service equally accessible to Internet and LAN users. CERN's version of httpd provides the proxying mechanism that enables LAN users to safely access Internet services. Unfortunately, a virus that affects the WWW service on the gateway computer can very easily infect all the LAN users. For this reason, this configuration is not considered secure.

Monitored Configuration

Because the router in the monitored configuration provides security, it is possible to locate the FTP service outside the gateway computer, but inside the router. To provide even more security, you can add a second router between the gateway computer and the LAN. The second router protects the LAN from viruses that have infected the gateway computer. The addition of a second router, however, makes access to the service from the LAN more complicated.

One solution is to put the FTP service on the gateway computer. The problem here, as mentioned previously, is that if the service is compromised, the gateway computer might also become compromised, disabling firewall protection. The addition of a second router minimizes this risk but does not eliminate it. Running FTP on the gateway computer, however, is a reasonable solution.

 n o t e With all FTP services, remember you can use inetd, netacl, and xinetd to restrict user access to FTP services.

You can also use the proxy mode of FTP, called PASV. This mode requires the FTP client to open both FTP connections, enabling the inner router to block other FTP connection attempts between the (possibly infected) gateway computer and the LAN. The drawback to this method is that both service and client need to be configured to use PASV.

You can configure the outside router to only permit access to Internet requests for the WWW service on port 80. On the inside router, you can choose to only permit access to messages initiated by WWW clients on the LAN. Given these conditions, it is safest for you to set up your WWW service outside of the gateway computer so that it is less likely to be compromised if the service is compromised.

Putting the WWW service on the gateway computer is also an acceptable solution but slightly less secure than the previous configuration.

You might also want to position the service between the gateway computer and the inner router. This configuration makes it more difficult for Internet users to access the service. Also, if the service becomes infected, no firewall protection exists between the service and your LAN.

A Grab Bag of Security Addenda

Security experts daily propose and revise a plethora of security ideas offering varying degrees of protection. To join in these discussions, e-mail to majordomo@greatcircle.com. You will be instructed how to join the mailing list. In the meantime, look at the groups' FAQs (Frequently Asked Questions), which you can use FTP to get from ftp.greatcircle.com in /pub/firewalls/FAQ.

The following list offers some additional security issues to keep in mind:

→ Routers almost always interface directly with the Internet, and as such, offer security measures. It is beyond the scope of this book to discuss what various router makers have to offer, but you should take advantage of router security.

→ Try to find ways to break into your own service. Because this task is so open ended, it often does not get done. You understand, though, how much better it is for you rather than someone else to find an Achilles' heal in your service configuration.

→ Regularly scan all files for viruses. Get new virus software as quickly as it becomes available.

→ Formalize one or more plans that you can execute when you detect intrusion. Do not try to sharpen your skills at intruder detecting in the heat of the moment. Decide whether, for example, you want to shut down the service, the server, or the Internet connection.

→ Enable logging on your service and scan it automatically for questionable actions. Do not place the log files on the gateway or service servers.

→ Create and enforce user access restrictions. Routers, in addition to services, can facilitate these restrictions.

→ Keep backups of everything important.

→ Where to place the gateway computer relative to the service

→ The security implications of the services you are offering

→ What kind of machinery adds security to your system

→ The advantages and disadvantages of different configurations of that machinery

It seems unfair that all the time and money spent securing your system is aimed at only 0.001 percent of the people using the Internet. Unfortunately, the effects of viruses can be disastrous. The "Good Time" virus, for example, erases your hard disk and damages your CPU. These viruses necessitate that security be one of the highest concerns of the Internet system administrator.

Summary

Considering the consequences of crime is a way of life when you offer services to the Internet community. Due to motivating factors too numerous to consider, some people enjoy invading and wrecking entire LANs. This chapter presented some ideas that can help you protect your service and LAN. Important issues to consider include the following:

p a r t

Setting Up and Managing Internet Services

Understanding Linux

As the most sought after and widely used public implementation of Unix, Linux is a complete and ever-growing entity with a worldwide following all its own.

This chapter introduces Linux, provides a brief history of Linux, and explains how to install the Slackware version of Linux provided on the CD-ROM accompanying this book.

A Brief History of Linux

Linux traditionally has been associated with the Unix geniuses who sit in front of their computers night and day. Linux has gained increasingly widespread use, however, in business, academia, and personal productivity.

Linux (pronounced with a short i, as in LIH-nucks) is a clone of the Unix operating system, and it runs on Intel 80386 and 80486 computers. It supports a wide range of software, from TeX to X Windows to the GNU C/C++ compiler to TCP/IP. It's a versatile, bona fide implementation of Unix, freely distributed according to the terms of the Free Software Foundation's General Public License.

Linux can turn any 386 or 486 PC into a workstation. It gives you the full power of Unix at your fingertips. More businesses implement Linux every day, particularly in the realm of financial services, hospital administration, and distributed computing.

What makes Linux so different—and so appealing to everyone—is that it's a free implementation of Unix. It was, and continues to be, developed by a group of volunteers, primarily on the Internet, exchanging code, reporting bugs, and fixing problems in an open-ended environment. Given this type of environment, why do people bet their businesses on it? Because they have access to the internal operating system. Patches and updates for any number of different things ranging from additional hardware support to security are available daily, whereas a company might have to wait weeks, months, or even years for the same patches from a commercial vendor.

Unix is one of the most popular operating systems in the world because of its large support base and distribution. Originally developed as a multitasking system for minicomputers and mainframes in the mid-70s, it has since grown to become one of the most widely used operating systems anywhere, despite its sometimes confusing interface and lack of central standardization.

Versions of Unix exist for many systems, ranging from personal computers to supercomputers such as the Cray Y-MP. Most versions of Unix for personal computers are quite expensive and cumbersome. Commercial implementations range from $500 to thousands of dollars.

Linux is a freely distributed version of Unix developed primarily by Linus Torvalds at the University of Helsinki in Finland. The first official Linux release was in October 1991. Although relatively young compared to "real Unix," probably as much, if not more, development effort exists for Linux than for most implementations of Unix.

Today, Linux is a complete Unix implementation that offers X Windows, TCP/IP, and most of the freely available software packages. Many Internet service providers use it as a low cost way to provide their users with facilities, and you commonly see INN, C-News, and UUCP also running on it.

One of the most startling facts about Linux is that many people have executed benchmarks on 80486 Linux systems and found them comparable with mid-range workstations from Sun Microsystems and Digital Equipment Corporation.

Supporting Hardware

Before installing the software, you need to be aware of Linux's hardware requirements. If you already have hardware, chances are it's supported, because Linux supports more hardware and peripherals than some of the commercial implementations do.

Processor

Linux currently supports systems that have an Intel 80386 or 80486 CPU, including all variations of this CPU type, such as 386SX, 486SX, 486DX, and 486DX2. As the Intel Pentium chip supports the 386/486 instructions set, Linux should install and run with little or no extra difficulty. Linux works with non-Intel "clones," such as AMD and Cyrix processors, as well.

If you have a 80386 or 80486SX, you also might want to use a math coprocessor, although you don't have to have one (the Linux kernel can do FPU emulation if you don't). Linux supports all standard FPU couplings, such as IIT, Cyrix FasMath, and Intel coprocessors.

The system motherboard must use ISA or EISA bus architecture. These terms define how the system interfaces with peripherals and other components on the main bus. Most systems sold today use ISA or EISA bus. Linux doesn't currently support IBM's MicroChannel (MCA) bus, found on machines such as the IBM PS/2. Linux also supports systems that use a local bus architecture for faster video and disk access. You should have a standard local bus architecture, such as the VESA Local Bus ("VLB").

Memory Requirements

Compared to other implementations of Unix, Linux requires very little memory. You need at the very least 2 MB of RAM, although 4 MB would be better and is recommended. The more memory you

install on your system, the faster Linux runs. In addition, Linux utilizes all the RAM installed in your system. Linux runs happily with only 4 MB of RAM, including all the bells and whistles such as X Windows, Emacs, and so on. However, more memory is almost as important as a faster processor. Although 8 MB is more than enough for personal use, you might need 16 MB or more if you expect a heavy user load on the system.

Most Linux users allocate a portion of their hard drive as swap space, which acts as virtual RAM. Even if you have a great deal of physical RAM in your machine, you might want to use swap space. Although swap space certainly doesn't replace for actual physical RAM, it can let your system run larger applications by swapping out inactive portions of code to disk.

Hard Disk Requirements

You can run Linux from a floppy disk, if the words slow and cumbersome don't bother you. Considering the almost daily dip in hard disk storage cost, your system probably has some kind of hard disk.

The amount of disk space you need before you can install Linux depends very much on the distribution you install. Some distributions are larger than others. Some are minimal implementations, whereas others are full-blown releases.

You must have an AT-standard (16-bit) controller. The kernel contains support for XT-standard (8-bit) controllers; however, most controllers today are AT-standard. Linux should support all MFM, RLL, ESDI, and IDE controllers. The general rule for non-SCSI hard drive and floppy controllers is that if you can access the drive from MS-DOS or another operating system, you should be able to access it from Linux.

Linux also supports a number of popular SCSI drive controllers, although support for SCSI is more limited because of the wide range of controller interface standards. Supported SCSI controllers include the following:

Adaptec AHA1542B

AHA1742A

AHA1522

AHA1740

AHA1740

Future Domain 1680

TMC-850

TMC-950

Seagate ST-02

UltraStor SCSI

Western Digital WD7000FASST.

To install Linux, you must have some free space available on your disk. You can install Linux across multiple disks. Linux can share the disk space with MS-DOS and OS/2 with the Linux Loader. The amount of hard drive space you need depends greatly on your specific needs and the amount of software you want to install.

Compared to other commercial and publicly available Unix implementations that require hundreds of megabytes of disk space, Linux can run in as little as 10 to 20 MB. However, the amount of software and applications you can use is limited by this amount. The documentation that comes with the given distribution should provide the information you need for decision making. If you want to install all of the software from the CD-ROM, you need approximately 700 MB of disk space. If you want

to run a small WWW site, for example, you need a disk partition of approximately 100 MB to install Linux, the HTTPD server, and some HTML files.

Remember to figure in your disk space and some additional space for a swap area. Should Linux not have enough physical memory in which to load all your running applications, some of the contents of RAM are written to the swap space.

The swap space is used as virtual RAM, or memory. As each program loads, memory is consumed. When Linux runs out of memory, it writes some of this memory to the swap area so it can be used by other programs. For example, if you have 16 MB of RAM and a 16 MB swap space, Linux thinks you have 32 MB of RAM. This enables you to execute programs that need a lot of memory.

Video Requirements

As do most operating systems available today, Linux supports all standard Hercules, CGA, EGA, VGA, and Super VGA video cards and monitors for the default text-based interface. In general, if the video card and monitor coupling works under another operating system such as MS-DOS, it should work fine with Linux.

Graphical environments, such as X Window, have their own video hardware requirements. You should refer to the Xfree86 server information included with your distribution for these requirements. Once you have Linux installed, you can also check the online documentation for the requirements of each server.

Mice and Pointing Devices

Generally you use a mouse only in graphical environments. You can associate several Linux applications, however, with a mouse. Linux supports all standard serial mice, including Logitech, MM series, Mouseman, Microsoft (2-button), and Mouse Systems (3-button). Linux also supports Microsoft, Logitech, and ATIXL busmice, as well as the PS/2 mouse interface. In addition, Linux supports trackball pointing devices that use these interfaces.

CD-ROM Drives

CD-ROM drivers have several different interface types, which has compounded the problem of making them available for Linux. If you have a SCSI host adapter and a SCSI CD-ROM, you shouldn't have any problems with Linux. The same is true for IDE interface drives. Linux also provides support for some proprietary interfaces, including the NEC CDR-74, Sony CDU-541, and Texel DM-3024. Linux supports the Sony internal CDU-31a and the Mistsumi CD-ROM drives as well.

Tape Drives

Like the CD-ROM drive, several versions of tape drive are available. Any SCSI-based tape should operate properly with Linux. Some have been explicitly verified, such as the Sanyo CP150SE; Tandberg 3600, Wangtek 5525ES, 5150ES, and 5099EN with the PC36 adapter. You also could add a Floppy tape module to the system to support the Colorado and other QIC-40 and QIC-80 tape drives that work off the floppy disk controller.

Printer Support

Linux supports the complete range of parallel printers. If you can access your printer under MS-DOS, you most likely could under Linux as well. If your printer requires special software under DOS to work, then it will not work under Linux. The Linux printing software consists of the Unix standard lp and lpr software. This enables you to print remotely to printers elsewhere on the network.

Network Interface Cards

Linux supports many popular Ethernet and LAN adapter cards, including 3Com's 3c503, 3c503/16, and 3C509; Novell's NE1000 and NE2000; Western Digital's WD8003 and WD8013; and Hewlett Packard's HP27245, HP27247, and HP27250. Other network interface cards reportedly also work, and Linux developers regularly add support for additional hardware.

Sound Devices

For audiophiles, Linux supports various sound cards and related software, such as CDplayer (a program that can control a CD-ROM drive as a conventional CD player, surprisingly enough), MIDI sequencers and editors (which enable you to compose music for playback through a synthesizer or other MIDI-controlled instrument), and various sound editors for digitized sounds.

Online Documentation

Several forms of documentation are available for Linux, depending on what you have available. On the CD-ROM are three directories: /guide, /howto, and /viewer. If you have MS-DOS and Windows running with a CD-ROM, you should install the Multimedia viewer, in which all the files in the /howto directory are prepared as hypertext in a Windows help file format. The Multimedia viewer makes finding information regarding specific questions you might have about Linux very easy. Figure 9.1 illustrates one page in the Multimedia browser.

```
┌─────────────────────────────────────────────────────────┐
│ ■                    Linux HowTo                    ▼ ▲  │
├─────────────────────────────────────────────────────────┤
│ File   Edit   Bookmark   Help                           │
├─────────────────────────────────────────────────────────┤
│ Contents │Go Back│ History │ Search │  <<  │   >>  │     │
├─────────────────────────────────────────────────────────┤
│How To Index                                              │
│                                                        ▲ │
│ 3.   HOWTO Index                                         │
│                                                          │
│The following Linux HOWTOs are currently available. The list is small, because this is a relatively new project.│
│                                                          │
│  BogoMips HOWTO, Explanation and anecdotal reporting of BogoMips ratings for various machines.│
│  Busmouse HOWTO, by Mike Battersby (mike@starbug.apana.org.au).│
│      Information on using busmice with Linux and XFree86.│
│  Linux CDROM HOWTO, by tranter@software.mitel.com (Jeff Tranter).│
│      Information on CD-ROM drive compatibility for Linux│
│  Linux Distribution HOWTO, by Matt Welsh (mdw@sunsite.unc.edu).│
│      A list of many of the major Linux distributions available via anonymous FTP and via mail order on│
│      diskette, tape, or CD-ROM. Also includes other Linux-related goodies that you can only get via mail│
│      order.                                              │
│  Ethernet HOWTO, by Paul Gortmaker (gpg109@rsphysse.anu.edu.au).│
│      A HOWTO about the various Ethernet device drivers which are available for Linux. Should be read along│
│      with the NET-2 HOWTO by anyone using Ethernet for TCP/IP on Linux.│
│  Ftape HOWTO, by Kai Harrekilde-Petersen (ftape@mic.dth.dk).│
│      A HOWTO describing the setup and use of various QIC ftape drivers for Linux.  ▼│
└─────────────────────────────────────────────────────────┘
```

Figure 9.1

The Multimedia HOWTO Browser.

Alternatively, if you don't have MS-Windows, you can find the same information in a text-based configuration in the /howto directory. The /guide directory also contains a wonderful document entitled install.txt, a generic reference manual that covers installing Linux and discusses the different utilities and programs, its history, future direction, development work, and how to operate it.

After you install the system, you have full access to the standard online manual pages using the traditional Unix man command.

Installing Linux

This discussion of how to install Linux focuses on the Linux distribution included with this book. Although it doesn't pretend to be the definitive reference, it does introduce readers to the process of installing Linux on their computers.

Because Linux can easily exist with DOS, and even share DOS partitions, installing Linux from a DOS environment is easy. If you don't have DOS installed on the computer on which you want to install Linux, you need access to a DOS-based system that has a CD-ROM driver you can access from DOS.

Creating a Boot and Root Disk

This discussion assumes that you have access to a machine that runs MS-DOS and that you can access a CD-ROM drive on this system. The Linux CD-ROM that comes with this book has a directory called /slakinst (see fig. 9.2). The /slakinst directory contains a number of other directories, including /boot12, /boot144, /root12, and /root144. The /bootXX directories include the kernel and boot code for both 5.25- and 3.5-inch floppies.

Figure 9.2

The Linux CD-ROM directory structure.

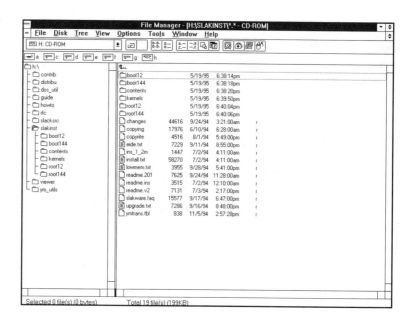

```
File Manager - [H:\SLAKINST\*.* - CD-ROM]
=  File  Disk  Tree  View  Options  Tools  Window  Help
H: CD-ROM

a    c    d    e    f    g    h

h:\                        ...
├ contrib                  boot12           5/19/95   6:38:14pm
├ distribu                 boot144          5/19/95   6:38:18pm
├ dos_util                 contents         5/19/95   6:38:20pm
├ guide                    kernels          5/19/95   6:39:50pm
├ howto                    root12           5/19/95   6:40:04pm
├ rfc                      root144          5/19/95   6:40:06pm
├ slacksrc                 changes    44616  9/24/94   3:21:00am    r
├ slakinst                 copying    17976  6/10/94   6:28:00am    r
│ ├ boot12                 copyrite    4516  8/1/94    5:49:00pm    r
│ ├ boot144                eide.txt    7229  9/11/94   8:55:00pm    r
│ ├ contents               ins_1_2m    1447  7/2/94    4:11:00am    r
│ ├ kernels                install.txt 58270 7/2/94    4:11:00am    r
│ ├ root12                 lowmem.txt  3955  9/28/94   5:41:00pm    r
│ └ root144                readme.201  7625  9/24/94  11:28:00am    r
├ viewer                   readme.ins  3515  7/2/94   12:10:00am    r
└ ym_utils                 readme.v2   7131  7/3/94    2:17:00pm    r
                           slakware.faq 15577 9/17/94  6:47:00pm    r
                           upgrade.txt  7286  9/16/94  8:48:00pm    r
                           ymtrans.tbl   838  11/5/94  2:57:28pm    r

Selected 0 file(s) (0 bytes)        Total 19 file(s) (199KB)
```

You should try to use the modern kernel because it contains most of the device drivers. If you cannot boot or install using that kernel, you need to be more specific about the kernel you use. If you have a SCSI device such as your CD-ROM and a network card, then you should try the scsinet kernel. If the selected kernel does not match your system, it may not boot. If that happens, then you should select another kernel and try the boot process again.

To create a boot disk, you must run the DOS utility program rawrite.exe, which you can find in the CD-ROM's /dos_util directory. This program copies the disk image from the CD-ROM to the floppy disk. Figure 9.3 illustrates the execution of the RAWRITE program.

When you use the rawrite command, it accepts no command line arguments, but prompts for the names of the source file and the destination disk drive.

You use the same procedure to create the root file system disk. To create the two disks using the modern kernel and a scsinet root file system, for example, you would use the following command sequence. This command sequence assumes that the CD-ROM is drive H:, and the target disk drive is drive A:.

```
c:\> H:\dos_utils\rawrite
RaWrite 1.2 Write disk file to raw floppy diskette

Enter source file name: h:\slakinst\boot144\modern
Enter destination drive: a:
Please insert a formatted diskette into drive A:
➛and press -ENTER-
Number of sectors per track for this disk is 18
Verifying image to drive A:. Press ^C to abort.
Track: 01 \Head: 0 Sector: 13
c:\> H:\dos_utils\rawrite
RaWrite 1.2 Write disk file to raw floppy diskette
```

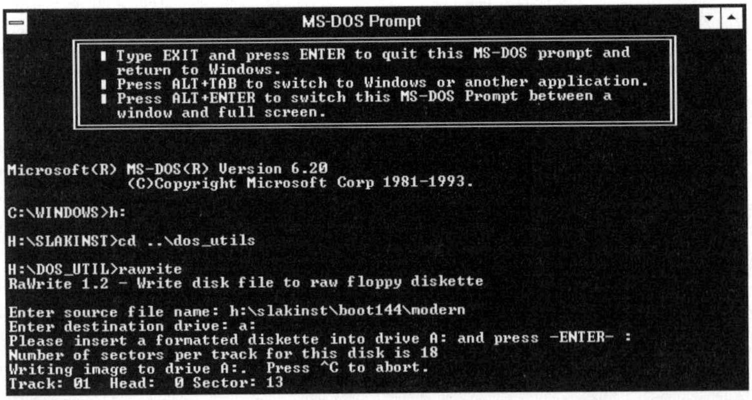

Figure 9.3

Creating a boot disk
with rawrite.exe.

```
Enter source file name: h:\slakinst\root144\scsinet
Enter destination drive: a:
Please insert a formatted diskette into drive A:
➥and press -ENTER-
Number of sectors per track for this disk is 18
Verifying image to drive A:. Press ^C to abort.
Track: 01 \Head: 0 Sector: 13
c:\>
```

Make sure that you clearly label the disks so you don't have problems later during the install. After you create the two disks you need here, you can proceed to boot the Linux system and begin installing.

When you boot from the Linux boot disk, you see a Boot: prompt. Read the screen carefully. If you have no arguments to pass to the boot program, simply press Enter. *Do not change the floppy diskettes yet.*

Pressing Enter at this point loads and prepares the kernel. The modern kernel distribution tries to recognize the different pieces of hardware configured in the system. When the system is ready for you to insert the root file system disk, it prints a message saying so on-screen and waits.

After you insert the root file system floppy, press Enter to load Linux. After Linux loads, a login prompt appears. Log in as root; you don't have or need a password yet.

Creating Hard Disk Partitions

At this point, you have a floppy disk-based system. But you want to install Linux and its application environment on the hard disk, so you need to create some partitions—like MS-DOS and other PC-based operating systems, you must create disk partitions on which to install Linux. The following illustrates running fdisk to create several disk partitions for Linux.

```
# fdisk
Using /dev/hda as default device!

Command (m for help): p

Disk /dev/hda: 16 heads, 63 sectors, 827 cylinders
Units = cylinders of 1008 * 512 bytes

Command (m for help):
```

If you want to create Linux partitions on more than one hard disk, remember to run fdisk on each hard disk, because you must set up each partition separately.

A variety of options are available for fdisk, the most commonly used one being to specify the name of the hard disk you want to set up. If you have only one disk, fdisk uses that device.

Table 9.1 lists a number of commands that fdisk offers to enable you to manipulate the partition table. You can obtain a listing of these same commands and descriptions by typing **m** (the m command) at the `Command (m for help):` prompt.

You use the n command to create a new partition. You probably don't need to worry about most of the other options. You use the q command to quit fdisk without saving any changes, but to quit fdisk and write the changes to the partition table to disk, you use the w command.

The first thing you should do now is display your current partition table and write the information down for later reference. Use the p command to do this, as shown on the next page:

Table 9.3 fdisk Commands

Command	Action
a	Toggles a bootable flag
d	Deletes a partition
l	Lists known partition types
m	Generates a list of these commands and descriptions
n	Adds a new partition
p	Prints the partition table
q	Quits without saving changes
t	Changes a partition's system id
u	Changes display/entry units
v	Verifies the partition table
w	Writes table to disk and exit
x	Extra functionality (experts only)

```
Command (m for help): p

Disk /dev/hda: 16 heads, 63 sectors, 827 cylinders
Units = cylinders of 1008 * 512 bytes
Command (m for help): p

Disk /dev/hda: 16 heads, 63 sectors, 827 cylinders
Units = cylinders of 1008 * 512 bytes

 Device Boot Begin Start End Blocks Id System
/dev/hda1 1 1 300 151168+ 83 DOS-32 bit

Command (m for help):
```

In the preceding example, a single MS-DOS partition starts at cylinder 1 and ends at cylinder 300, leaving 527 of the total 827 cylinders available for disk partitions.

You need to create two partitions in this disk space: one partition for the root file system, to contain all the Linux utilities (you don't need to have more than one file system for data, but it does give you better control over where files install on your system), and the other partition for the swap space. The following illustrates creating the swap space as the second partition.

```
Command (m for help): n
Command action
e extended
p primary partition (1-4)
p
Partition number (1-4): 2
First cylinder (301-827): 301
Last cylinder or +size or +sizeM or +sizeK (204-
➥683): 351
Command (m for help):
```

Now you've created your swap partition. The fdisk program asked you to enter the number for the partition you wanted to create. Because partition 1 al ready existed, you created a partition

numbered 2. The first cylinder corresponds to the partition's starting point. Leaving a gap between the partitions is pointless.

When fdisk prompts for the last cylinder value, you have several options. You can provide an explicit last cylinder value, or you can respond with several other answers. If you don't know how many cylinders to make the partition but you know you want an 80 MB partition, for example, respond to the prompt with +80M. From this value, fdisk will calculate the number of cylinders.

For your swap space, though, you don't need such a large partition. Even with the values given in the following example, you have a 25 MB swap partition! You can calculate this easily using fdisk's p command's output, as shown in the following:

```
Command (m for help): p

Disk /dev/hda: 16 heads, 63 sectors, 827 cylinders
Units = cylinders of 1008 * 512 bytes

 Device Boot Begin Start End Blocks Id System
/dev/hda1 1 1 300 151168+ 83 DOS-32 bit
```

The preceding shows that the units for this disk are cylinders of 1008×512 bytes (which is 516,096 bytes), and that times 51 cylinders (351–300) gives a size of 26,320,896 bytes (26 MB).

Because this is your swap partition, many distributions of Linux require that you specially identify it for the installation program, for which you use fdisk's t command to set the label on the partition. You must use the distribution that accompanies this book, shown in the following:

```
Command (m for help): t
Partition number (1-4): 2
Hex code (type L to list codes): L
```

```
 0 Empty 8 AIX 75 PC/IX b7 BSDI fs
 1 DOS 12-bit FAT 9 AIX bootable 80 Old MINIX b8
➥BSDI swap
 2 XENIX root a OS/2 Boot Manag 81 Linux/MINIX c7
➥Syrinx
 3 XENIX usr 40 Venix 80286 82 Linux swap db CP/M
 4 DOS 16-bit <32M 51 Novell? 83 Linux native e1
➥DOS access
 5 Extended 52 Microport 93 Amoeba e3 DOS R/O
 6 DOS 16-bit >=32 63 GNU HURD 94 Amoeba BBT f2 DOS
➥secondary
 7 OS/2 HPFS 64 Novell a5 BSD/386 ff BBT
Hex code (type L to list codes):82
Command (m for help): t
```

You use the same procedure to create the root file system. The following illustrates the entire procedure.

```
Command (m for help): p

Disk /dev/hda: 16 heads, 63 sectors, 827 cylinders
Units = cylinders of 1008 * 512 bytes

 Device Boot Begin Start End Blocks Id System
/dev/hda1 1 1 300 151168+ 83 DOS-32 bit
/dev/hda2 301 301 351 25704 82 Linux swap

Command (m for help): n
Command action
e extended
p primary partition (1-4)
p
Partition number (1-4): 3
First cylinder (301-827): 352
Last cylinder or +size or +sizeM or +sizeK (204-
➥683): 827
Command (m for help): a
Partition number (1-4): 3

Command (m for help): p
```

```
Disk /dev/hda: 16 heads, 63 sectors, 827 cylinders
Units = cylinders of 1008 * 512 bytes

 Device Boot Begin Start End Blocks Id System
/dev/hda1 1 1 300 151168+ 83 Linux native
/dev/hda2 301 301 351 25704 82 Linux swap
/dev/hda3 * 352 352 827 239904 83 Linux native

Command (m for help):w
#
```

This example shows you the fdisk commands a and w in action for the first time. You use the a command to toggle the Boot flag. You want Linux to be bootable, so select it as the boot partition. You use w to write the partition table back out to the disk and exit fdisk.

 note Before you continue to the next installation step, write down the information from the partition table. You need it later to complete the installation, and it's essential should you ever need to resolve a problem in the future.

Before you can continue, you should prepare the swap space. Although you can do this during the installation, you really should do so before you begin the installation, especially if you have less than 4 MB of RAM.

Preparing swap partitions consists of two tasks: establishing a file system for the swap, and turning swapping on. To perform the first task, use the mkswap command as follows:

```
# mkswap -c /dev/hda2 25704
```

You use the mkswap command to set up disk partitions or disk files to use as swap space. The -c option instructs mkswap to check the space for bad blocks first. The device name /dev/hda2 is the name you gave your swap partition. The final argument, 25704, is the size of the partition you created earlier.

Swap space isn't limited to a separate disk partition, although doing it that way is the most common practice. You also can place swap in a file, much like the MS-Windows and OS/2 approach to swapping. To do so, use the commands shown in the following:

```
# dd if=/dev/zero of=swapfile bs=1024 count=8192
# mkswap swapfile 8192
# sync
```

The commands in the preceding example create a file of 8,192 bytes in length, called swapfile, in the current directory. The count= argument for the dd command controls the size of the swap file. If you want more space, increase this value. As when you create the partition, you need to use the mkswap command to create the structure for the swap file. The final sync command causes the information to be written to the disk and clears the disk buffers of any information pending for disk writes.

The second command you use with swapping—the swapon command—turns swapping on for that device or swap file and accepts on the name of the device for which you want to enable swapping. You also can use the swapon command if you want Linux to use additional swap partitions or swap files once it's up and running. The following illustrates use of the swapon command.

```
# swapon swapfile
# swapon /dev/hda2
```

You now have completed the initial work to install the Slackware distribution of Linux on your system.

Installing the Software

Installing the Slackware version of Linux is quite simple, actually much less difficult than setting up the disk partitions. You do need to follow some specific instructions here, however, to install successfully from the CD-ROM.

To begin installing, run the setup command, which results in a screen filled with the information shown in the following.

```
+---Slackware Linux Setup (version HD-2.0.1) --+
¦ ¦
¦ Welcome to Slackware Linux Setup. ¦
¦ ¦
¦ Hint: If you have trouble using the arrow keys
➡on your keyboard, ¦
¦ you can use '+', '-', and TAB instead. Which
➡option would you like? ¦
¦ +-------------------------------------------+ ¦
¦ ¦ HELP Read the Slackware Setup HELP file ¦ ¦
¦ ¦ KEYMAP Remap your keyboard ¦ ¦
¦ ¦ QUICK Choose QUICK or VERBOSE install mode
➡[now: VERBOSE] ¦ ¦
¦ ¦ MAKE TAGS Tagfile customization program ¦ ¦
¦ ¦ TARGET Select target directory [now: /] ¦ ¦
¦ ¦ SOURCE Select source media ¦ ¦
¦ ¦ DISK SETS Decide which disk sets you wish to
➡install ¦ ¦
¦ ¦ INSTALL Install selected disk sets ¦ ¦
¦ ¦ CONFIGURE Reconfigure your Linux system ¦ ¦
¦ ¦ PKGTOOL Install or remove packages with
➡Pkgtool ¦ ¦
¦ ¦ EXIT Exit Slackware Linux Setup ¦ ¦
¦ +-------------------------------------------+ ¦
+----------------- --------------------+
¦ < OK > <Cancel> ¦
+----------------------------------------------+
```

You really should read all the HELP files you can regarding installation, but the setup program is configured so that if you start at the top of the list and work through all the steps, establishing a functional Linux system should pose little or no difficulty.

The HELP option provides information on how to move around the options in the setup program, and what each of the sections do. After you read the Help section, you don't need to change anything for KEYMAP (unless you aren't using a US-English based keyboard), QUICK, MAKE TAGS, or TARGET. The current target is the root file system of your Linux partition, which typically is where you install the distribution.

Selecting the Source Media

The first option you must configure is the SOURCE media, which establishes where you will install from. The following shows the SOURCE menu.

```
+----------------- SOURCE MEDIA SELECTION -------+
¦ ¦
¦ Where do you plan to install Slackware Linux
➥from? ¦
¦ ¦
¦ +-------------------------------------------+ ¦
¦ ¦ 1 Install from a hard drive partition ¦ ¦
¦ ¦ 2 Install from floppy disks ¦ ¦
¦ ¦ 3 Install via NFS ¦ ¦
¦ ¦ 4 Install from a pre-mounted directory ¦ ¦
¦ ¦ 5 Install from CD-ROM ¦ ¦
¦ +-------------------------------------------+ ¦
+-----------------------------------------------+
¦ < OK > <Cancel> ¦
+-----------------------------------------------+
```

If you have installed Linux on a different partition, such as under an MS-DOS partition, you can use the first option to install it from that location. Should you want to install this distribution from floppy disk, be prepared: it takes about 75 1.44 floppy disks to install all the components from the Slackware distribution, and that doesn't include any of the

additional utilities and programs included on the CD-ROM.

When you first install, you can't install through NFS (the Network File System) because you won't have networking configured or available yet. You can install from a premounted directory if the Linux distribution files are installed on another Linux disk or the CD-ROM currently is mounted.

You select the last option from the source media selection screen to install from the included CD-ROM. The following shows the CD-ROM selection menu.

```
+------------- INSTALLING FROM CD-ROM ----------+
¦ ¦
¦ In order to install Slackware Linux from a CD-
➥ROM, it must ¦
¦ contain the distribution arranged beneath a
➥source directory ¦
¦ in the same way as if you were to install it
➥from a hard ¦
¦ drive or NFS. The source directory must contain
➥subdirectories ¦
¦ for each floppy disk. Your CD-ROM should be
➥compatible with ¦
¦ this format if it contains a mirror of the
➥Slackware FTP site. ¦
¦ ¦
¦ What type of CD-ROM drive do you have? ¦
¦ +-------------------------------------------+ ¦
¦ ¦ 1 SCSI [ /dev/scd0 or /dev/scd1 ] ¦ ¦
¦ ¦ 2 Sony CDU31A [ /dev/sonycd ] ¦ ¦
¦ ¦ 3 Sony 535 [ /dev/cdu535 ] ¦ ¦
¦ ¦ 4 Mitsumi [ /dev/mcd ] ¦ ¦
¦ ¦ 5 Sound Blaster Pro (Panasonic) [ /dev/sbpcd ]
➥¦ ¦
¦ +-------------------------------------------+ ¦
+-----------------------------------------------+
¦ < OK > <Cancel> ¦
+-----------------------------------------------+
```

Remember that Linux doesn't support every CD-ROM drive on the market. If you don't have one that it does support, you might be out of luck. You're best bet aside from buying a new CD-ROM drive is to find someone who can loan you one or make you install floppy disks. Here, you install from a SCSI CD-ROM.

If you choose SCSI CD-ROM, you must select the CD-ROM device from which you will install, as shown in the following:

```
+------------- SELECT SCSI DEVICE -------------+
| Which SCSI CD-ROM are you using? (If you're not
➡sure, |
| select /dev/sr0) |
| +--------------------------------------------+ |
| | /dev/scd0 SCSI cd 0 | |
| | /dev/scd1 SCSI cd 1 | |
| +--------------------------------------------+ |
+----------------------------------------------+
| < OK > <Cancel> |
+----------------------------------------------+
```

If you aren't sure which one to use, try /dev/scd0, not /dev/sr0 as suggested. The informational prompt in the setup program in the preceding example is incorrect.

Selecting the Linux Distribution

After you select the CD-ROM from which you want to load the distribution, you must indicate which Linux distribution you are loading (use the next selection screen, shown for all CD-ROM install types and illustrated in the following).

```
+----------- SELECT SOURCE DIRECTORY-----------+
| Now we need to know which directory on the CD
➡contains the Slackware |
| sources. This location may vary depending on the
➡cd you have. There |
```

```
| are default selections for the Slackware
➡Professional CD (including |
| an option to run mostly from the CD), InfoMagic
➡CD, TransAmeritech |
| CD, and the Linux Quarterly CD-ROM. There may be
➡other directories |
| containing other versions - enter a custom
➡directory name if you |
| like. Which option would you like? |
| +--------------------------------------------+ |
| | slakware Slackware Pro: install to HD | |
| | slackpro Slackware Pro: run from CD | |
| | slackware.111 TransAmeritech CD | |
| | packages/slackware Linux Quarterly CD-ROM | |
| | distributions/slackware InfoMagic CD-ROM | |
| | Custom Enter your own directory name | |
| +--------------------------------------------+ |
+----------------------------------------------+
| < OK > <Cancel> |
+----------------------------------------------+
```

The distribution included with this book is the Slackware 2.0.1 release, provided by InfoMagic. So here, the logical choice is the InfoMagic CD-ROM selection. However, the CD-ROM has been prepared with DOS style short file names to be DOS-readable as well. Names like "distribution" are saved as "distribu" on the CD-ROM. Some CD-ROMS won't be able to find this distribution, and will print a message like the one shown in the following:

```
+---------- ERROR: DIRECTORY NOT FOUND ----------+
| The Slackware source directory could not be
➡found. |
| You'll have to reconfigure your source media
➡before |
| you can install. |
| |
+------------------------------------------------+
| < OK > |
+------------------------------------------------+
```

If you're up against such a situation, work through these screens again and from the selection menu and choose "Custom" from the SOURCE menu, then enter the following path:

/distribu/slackwar

Using this path causes the installation program to look in the directory /distribu/slackwar, which it can find, and then to start the installation.

Selecting the Disk Sets

The next phase is to select the different disk sets you want to install. You shouldn't just install them all, because the CD-ROM easily contains more than 500 MB of uncompressed utilities and programs. The following shows the disk set windows.

```
+-------------- SERIES SELECTION --------------+
¦ ¦
¦ Use the spacebar to select the disk sets you
➥wish to install. ¦
¦ You can use the UP/DOWN arrows to see all the
➥possible choices. ¦
¦ Press the ENTER key when you are finished. If
➥you need to ¦
¦ install a disk set that is not listed here,
➥check the box for ¦
¦ custom additional disk sets. ¦
¦ ¦
¦ +------------------------------------------+ ¦
¦ ¦ [ ] CUS Also prompt for CUSTOM disk sets ¦ ¦
¦ ¦ [X] A Base Linux system ¦ ¦
¦ ¦ [ ] AP Various Applications that don't need X
¦ ¦
¦ ¦ [ ] D Program Development (C, C++, Lisp, Perl,
etc.) ¦ ¦
¦ ¦ [ ] E GNU Emacs ¦ ¦
¦ ¦ [ ] F FAQ lists, HOWTO documentation ¦ ¦
¦ ¦ [ ] I Info files readable with info, JED, or
➥Emacs ¦ ¦
```

```
¦ +--------v(+)-----------------------------+ ¦
+----------------------------------------------+
¦ < OK > <Cancel> ¦
+----------------------------------------------+
```

The CD-ROM contains 17 disk sets, not including any customs sets. To select the one you want to install, highlight the option you want to select and press the spacebar.

Installing the Disk Sets

After you choose the disk sets you want to install, select INSTALL from the setup menu to start the installation. The program installs all disk sets and applications marked as required by Linux without user intervention. The installation program prompts you for each optional package as to whether you want to select the option. Choosing yes installs the package; choosing otherwise doesn't.

Configuring your Linux System

With the disk sets installed, you must configure the system and some components to ensure that it reboots after you finish. The steps in this configuration include the following:

→ Creating a Linux Boot disk

→ Modem configuration

→ Mouse configuration

→ Network configuration (if installed)

→ Linux Loader configuration

You definitely should go through the configuration options. Configuring the Linux Loader (LILO) and making a boot disk are musts. If you don't have a modem or a mouse, however, you don't need to install those components.

At this point, you can exit the setup command, because installation is now complete.

Restarting

Now that the installation is complete, you must reboot your system so that you can boot off your hard disk (see the following for the necessary commands).

```
# sync
# reboot
```

These commands flush the disk buffers, and reboot the system. Any currently running processes stop and the system restarts. As the system restarts, you see messages that resemble those in the following, depending upon your system configuration:

```
Kernel logging (proc) started.
Console: colour EGA+ 80x25, 8 virtual consoles
Serial driver version 4.00 with no serial options
➡ena
tty00 at 0x03f8 (irq = 4) is a 16450
tty01 at 0x02f8 (irq = 3) is a 16450
lp_init: lp1 exists, using polling driver
ftape: allocated 3 buffers alligned at: 001F8000
Calibrating delay loop.. ok - 33.22 BogoMips
aha152x: BIOS test: passed, porttest: ok, auto
➡config
aha152x: vital data: PORTBASE=0x340, IRQ=11, SCSI
➡ID=
scsi0 : Adaptec 152x SCSI driver; $Revision: 1.0 $
scsi : 1 hosts.
  Vendor: SONY Model: CD-ROM CDU-55S Rev: 1.0
  Type:   CD-ROM ANSI SCS
Detected scsi CD-ROM sr0 at scsi0, id 3, lun 0
scsi : detected 0 SCSI disks 0 tapes 1 CD-ROM drive
➡t
Scd sectorsize = 2048 bytes
```

```
Memory: 14508k/16384k available (780k kernel code,
➡38
This processor honours the WP bit even when in
➡superv
Floppy drive(s): fd0 is 1.44M
Swansea University Computer Society NET3.014
IP Protocols: ICMP, UDP, TCP
PPP: version 0.2.7 (4 channels) NEW_TTY_DRIVERS
➡OPTIM
TCP compression code copyright 1989 Regents of the
➡Un
PPP line discipline registered.
SLIP: version 0.7.5-NET3.014-NEWTTY (4 channels)
CSLIP: code copyright 1989 Regents of the Univer-
➡sity
eth0: 3c509 at 0x300 tag 1, 10baseT port, address
➡00
3c509.c:pl15k 3/5/94 becker@super.org
Checking 386/387 coupling... Ok, fpu using
excep➡tion
Linux version 1.1.18 (root@fuzzy) #4 Tue Sep 13
18:35
Partition check:
 hda: hda1 hda2 hda3
VFS: Mounted root (ext2 filesystem) readonly.
Adding Swap: 25700k swap-space
```

```
Welcome to Linux 1.1.18
login:
```

The installation of your system is complete. You can now log in as root to perform any other necessary configuration tasks. You should create a user for yourself rather than use root all the time. To add a user, use the adduser command. You can obtain instructions on adduser by typing the following command:

man adduser

The process of adding a user is important because you should not log in and work regularly as the root user. The adduser command prompts for you for the information that it requires. The process of adding a user is demonstrated in the following:

```
pc login: root
Last login: Sun Aug 13 23:59:44 on tty1
Linux 1.0.9. (POSIX).
You have mail.
pc:~# adduser

Adding a new user. The username should be not
➥exceed 8 characters
in length, or you many run into problems later.

Enter login name for new account (^C to quit):
chrish

Editing information for new user [chrish]

Full Name: Chris Hare
GID [100]:

Checking for an available UID after 500

First unused uid is 501

UID [501]:

Home Directory [/home/chrish]:

Shell [/bin/bash]:

Password [chrish]: aaaaa

Information for new user [chrish]:
Home directory: [/home/chrish] Shell: [/bin/bash]
Password: [aaaaa] uid: [501] gid: [100]

Is this correct? [y/N]: y

Adding login [chrish] and making directory [/home/
chrish]
```

```
Adding the files from the /etc/skel directory:
./.kermrc -> /home/chrish/./.kermrc
./.less -> /home/chrish/./.less
./.lessrc -> /home/chrish/./.lessrc
./.term -> /home/chrish/./.term
./.term/termrc -> /home/chrish/./.term/termrc
./.emacs -> /home/chrish/./.emacs
```

```
pc:~#
```

Because your user is now created, you can perform any other system administrator tasks, or you can log out and log back in using your new user name.

Summary

This chapter presented Linux, its general hardware requirements, and how to install the Slackware distribution included with this book. Anyone who has been around Unix for any period of time will be impressed by Linux. New users to the Unix environment will wish they had some of this functionality at their office.

If you experience difficulties or have questions regarding the installation, your best source of reference is the HOWTO documentation in the Multimedia Help viewer for Windows, which is included on the CD-ROM.

10

Setting Up an FTP Service

F inally, you're at a point where you can actually

make a service work. Congratulations! If you're

reading this chapter, you believe your company can

benefit from an FTP (File Transfer Protocol) service.

FTP is, in fact, one of the most widely used ser-

vices on the Internet. Nearly every host has an FTP

client or service—not too surprising when you

consider that the FTP service, ftpd (or in.ftpd),

comes with most standard flavors of Unix. You can

usually find ftpd in the /usr/etc (or /etc) directory.

n o t e If you do not want to offer an FTP service on your server, skip to the chapters that discuss the services your company wants to offer.

ftpd is great for services that do not require strict security and do not handle large archives. If either issue matters for you, however, you probably would benefit from implementing the WU version of ftpd. (WU stands for Washington University in St. Louis, MO.) The next chapter discusses this service. Read on, however, because many things in the standard implementation of ftpd are also true for the WU ftpd daemon.

You can offer two kinds of FTP service: *user oriented* and *anonymous*. In the first case, users use their user IDs to log in to an FTP service; in the second case, they use the generic user ID, anonymous.

You really don't want to implement a user-oriented service because of the danger of security breaches. User IDs are broadcast over the Internet in plain text, which makes them vulnerable to mischievous hackers. If they can find a user's ID and password, they can use the system with the permissions of the user whose ID was detected.

You can restrict the permissions of specific users. There is, however, a significant administration task of establishing permissions for multiple user IDs. You might very well establish such permissions for people within your company, or even for people in a company working on a joint project with your company, but certainly not for people in the Internet community.

With anonymous FTP, you can restrict the kinds of actions users can take by defining the permissions of the anonymous user ID accordingly, and you can restrict users' access to your file system. Although you might give some of your employees user-oriented access to your FTP service, we will not even consider offering anything but an anonymous FTP service to the Internet community.

Naming Your Service

There is a de facto standard for naming FTP services. By no means is it required, but it is the name users will try first and find easiest to remember. The format is

`ftp.domain.type`

in which *domain* and *type* are variables. *Domain* represents the alias domain name of your FTP server (often your company's name). *Type* represents the type of organization yours is; for example, edu is used for educational institutions, com is used for businesses. The following FTP service (of the company supporting the WAIS service) is a good example of an FTP name:

`ftp.wais.com`

Naming your FTP service www.domain.type, or abc.domain.type, or zzz.domain.type is not illegal, but it is not a good idea. You also do not want to use the real name of your host server in the name of your FTP service. If you change your FTP service from one server to another, you do not want to have to tell everyone accustomed to the old name to switch to the name of the new FTP server (which might change again in the future). You could easily lose your standard user base. Instead, you should use an alias for your server. To set up an alias for a server, edit the domain name services (DNS) database files by adding a line similar to the following:

```
ftp IN ftp.domain.type  real.domain.type.
```

Substitute your company's domain name for *domain*. Make sure that *real.domain.name* is the real domain name of the FTP server. Note the period that ends the line.

If you change your server, there is a lag time on the Internet determined by the time-to-live defined by your domain name service. The time-to-live variable is an expiration date for Internet servers. When it expires, other name servers must release data about your zone from their cache. If you plan to switch servers, reduce the time-to-live variable accordingly.

Configuring an FTP Service

inetd, the big brother of services, invokes ftpd. It watches port 21 for TCP packets. For every service request—TCP packet—that arrives at port 21, inetd creates a new copy of ftpd to service the request.

n o t e For more information about inetd, refer to Chapter 4, "Understanding Basic Technology."

Many implementations of Unix already have an FTP service, ftpd, set up in inetd's configuration file, inetd.config. You often find inetd.config in the /etc directory. Some Unix implementations have a sample line in inetd.config (commented out) that sets up ftpd. If your configuration file has such a sample line, uncomment it. If you do not have any configuration information for ftpd in your inetd.config file, add a line in the file similar to the following:

```
ftp  stream tcp  nowait  root /usr/etc/ftpd ftpd -l
```

Chapter 4 includes a thorough explanation of the syntax of this line. (And soon we will look at the command-line options for ftpd.) Suffice it to say that this entry prescribes that TCP is responsible for reordering the FTP packets when they arrive at the client, that inetd should spawn a new service for each FTP request, that /usr/etc is the directory where ftpd lives, and that you want to start ftpd with the −l (logging) option. The entry in your inetd.config file might have a different location for ftpd, and might use different command line options.

Depending on the computer platform, ftpd has several other options, as explained in the following table:

ftpd Option	Description
−l	Turns on logging.
−d	Writes verbose debugging information in syslog.
−t *seconds*	Sets the timeout period in seconds. The default is 15 minutes. In other words, if the FTP session is inactive for 15 minutes, ftpd terminates it.
−T *seconds*	Sets the maximum timeout period, in seconds, that a FTP client can request. By default, the maximum timeout period an FTP client can request is 2 hours. If that is too long, use this option to shorten it.

ftpd Option	Description
–u permission	Sets the umask value, on some flavors of Unix, for files uploaded to a server using an FTP service. The default permission is 022: group- and world-readable. Clients can request a different mask.

The most common option is the logging option, –l. Having this option on is nice because it enables you to monitor FTP connections and check for foul play. This option logs to syslog every failed and successful FTP session. If you specify the option twice, the get, put, append, delete, make directory, remove directory, and rename operations and their file-name arguments are also logged. If you specify this option three times, log entries for get and put include the number of bytes transferred.

The –d option option logs all the commands and arguments sent by the client, except for arguments from the PASS command.

After you set the configuration file, the system must reread the file before it can take effect. The best way to do that is to use the kill command to pass a hang-up signal (SIGHUP):

```
% killall -HUP pid
```

in which pid is the process ID of inetd. But how do you get the pid? If you are using Unix System V, you use

```
% ps -ef ¦ grep inetd
```

The equivalent for the BSD distribution of Unix is

```
% ps ax ¦ grep inetd
```

The following example shows you the output of the ps command:

```
furnace 5% ps -ef ¦ grep inetd
    root   246    1  0   Apr 25 ?          0:45
➥/usr/etc/inetd
    geckel  6099 5796  2 10:19:19 pts/11   0:00
➥grep inetd
```

The second field in each line is the process ID.

Setting Up the Anonymous User

Now that you've configured the service, you must create a user that has the appropriate set of permissions and access to the file system. You set up the anonymous user in the server's /etc/passwd file. Before doing anything else, ftpd checks this file for whether a user exists. If you fail to create the anonymous user, ftpd prevents a user who logs in as anonymous from accessing any FTP archives.

You do not want to match any user or group IDs for the anonymous user to any system-level IDs. Hackers can use those IDs to access the entire file system through telnet or rlogin. You can prevent such a security breach by putting an asterisk (*) in the password field for all user IDs except anonymous. The asterisk prevents any entry from working in the password field. If there are utilities on your system that do not require a password to log in, you should set the login shell to /bin/false so that the asterisk safeguard is not overridden.

 note Many man pages might suggest that ftpd ignores the login shell. Don't believe it; many versions of ftpd use it.

You might, for example, construct the anonymous user in the following way:

```
ftp:*:500:25:anonymous FTP  user:/usr/ftp:/bin
➥/false
```

In this example, `/usr/ftp` is the user login directory, which is what you use as the root directory
for anonymous FTP clients. If the login directory is
the client's root, that user does not have access to
anything higher in the file system than /usr/ftp; he
or she has access only to directories and files lower
in the file system. These provisions give your system the level of security it needs by restricting the
users' access to file system.

The root of the anonymous user file system does
not have to be under /usr. If you are offering a lot of
data in your FTP service, you might allocate a separate disk, file system, or both for anonymous FTP
use.

You restrict file access by using the change root
command, chroot(). If ftpd calls this function and
uses the anonymous user login directory as its argument, all absolute references begin at the login
directory. For example, if a user were to change
directory to root (cd /), he or she would only get to
/usr/ftp. Or, for example, changing to /bin really
moves the user to /usr/ftp/bin.

ftpd calls chroot() only if the FTP user is anonymous.
Therefore, users who use user IDs to log in are not
restricted to the file system specified by their login
directory. So, not allowing user ID access to FTP
archives confines FTP users to the restricted file
system, thereby protecting files outside that file
system.

Reorganizing Your Files

One ramification of using chroot() to restrict users'
access to your system is that you need to move all

the files that ftpd needs into the restricted login
directory. To do that, you need to set up a new directory structure that places several standard directories under the login directory. The following
table shows the directories you need to copy.

Directory	Description
bin	Contains the program ls, which supports the list commands.
dev	Use mknod to copy /dev/zero into ~ftp/dev with the same major and minor device numbers. Rld uses this file.
etc	Contains passwd and group. These files enable the ls command to display owner names instead of numbers. The password field in passwd is unused; it should not contain real passwords.
lib	Copy the files /lib/rld and /lib /libc.so.1 into lib. ls needs them in order to run.
pub	Contains the archive files available to FTP clients.

The important executable you want to copy to /usr
/ftp/bin is ls.

 Do not copy the /etc/passwd or /etc/group
files into /usr/ftp/etc, because it would allow
anonymous FTP users to copy the files with
encrypted passwords to their machines for their own devilish
purposes. With this information, third parties might be able
to crack the encryption. You should put a minimal amount of
information into the passwd and group files. For example, if
the FTP archive contains files created by ftp and bin, your
password file should look similar to the following:

```
ftp:*:500:1:anonymous user:/users/ftp:/bin/false
bin:*:2:2:/:/bin/false
```

If FTP archives are given group access to *user* and *other*, your group file might look like the following:

```
user:*:1:
other:*:3:
```

Login Directory Permissions

So you don't want hackers to upload computer vermin into your service? Using the set of permissions listed in table 10.1 for the subdirectories under the login directory can help.

Table 10.1   Permissions for Subdirectories

Directory	Owner	Permission	Comments
/	root	555	Make the home directory unwritable.
bin	root	555	Make this directory owned by the super-user and unwritable by anyone.
dev	root	555	Make this directory owned by the super-user and unwritable.
etc	root	555	Make this directory owned by the super-user and unwritable.
lib	root	555	Make this directory owned by the super-user and unwritable.
pub	root FTP administrator	555	Users can read and execute the archive files.
upload	root other	777 733	Users can upload files, delete and replace existing files.

Directory	Owner	Permission	Comments
dist	root FTP administrator	555	Users can read and execute the special archive files.

All directories can be accessed by group *other*.

All users must to be able to read and execute (that is, search through) files in the login directory, or you don't have much of a service.

You make the /bin directory executable, because it contains only the ls binary, so users can use it, but unwritable so that nefarious users cannot replace your ls binary with one of their Trojan Horses that suddenly brings your system to its knees.

The /etc directory contains valuable information about user permissions and group membership. The last thing you want is users resetting their system permissions and group memberships. Consequently, you need to make the directory unwritable.

The /pub directory contains your FTP archive files. These files must be readable and executable so that users can search through and download interesting files. On the other hand, you do not want to give users write permission to the directory, because then users could replace or delete archive files that you strenuously maintain. Users cannot upload files in this directory.

Creating the /upload directory is optional. It gives users a place to upload files to the server running the FTP service. Separating these files into their own directory is a form of *damage control*. If someone wheels in a Trojan Horse, hopefully its damage is confined to the /upload directory. If you see no

reason to permit uploads, don't include the /upload directory.

The permission set for the /upload directory permits users to write and execute in the directory, but not read from it. This permission set is somewhat inconvenient because it prevents users from looking at files others upload to the server. On the other hand, it prevents users from perverting or deleting those same files.

 note A byproduct of allowing users to read one another's uploaded files is that they can post files on your server completely unrelated to your service. These uploaded files can be bland or blasphemous. For the sake of your company's image, you don't want to inadvertently support the greatest porn or WaReZ (pirated software) archive in the country.

If you feel that protecting /upload files from in-house users of your system (not FTP users) who have access to this file is necessary, you can set the sticky bit on the permissions set by changing the permission to 1733.

The /dist directory also is optional; it's really nothing more than a regular FTP archive that you might find in /pub except that the files in /dist are documents or binaries that your company supports. They should not be programs that your company sells. They might be patches to programs, utility add-ons, driver updates, or tools that give added value to your products. Because these binaries are not

Table 10.2 Permissions for Programs and Files

File	Owner	Permissions	Comments
/bin/ls	root	111	Users can execute ls to search the FTP archive files.
/etc/passwd	root	444	Users can only read file ownership.
/etc/group	root	444	Users can only read about group member-ship.

generic programs, you need not fear people copying, renaming, and publishing these programs under their names.

Again, you run into the same danger of someone uploading something into /dist somehow. You can combat such raiders by making the media that contains this directory read-only (by putting the files on a CD-ROM drive, for example). You might put as many of your files as you can on such media if the files and directories are not likely to change much.

Inside the /bin and /etc directories, you also must use chmod to set the permissions for the standard programs and files, as shown in table 10.2.

Naming the System Administrator

Everyone likes a helping hand. Part of the job of the Internet system administrator is to provide that service to the Internet community. You should set up two mailboxes for yourself, one that handles your normal e-mail, and another that handles Internet system administration requests. To make it easier for users to reach you, you should use a common alias rather than your e-mail address; for example, you might use ftp-system-admin.

You can point the ftp-system-admin alias at your user ID. This directs all FTP system administration concerns directly to your mailbox. Your aliases file is probably under /etc . To set up the alias, use the following syntax:

```
ftp-system-admin   real-user-ID@domain
```

Then again, you may choose not to make the ftp-system-admin user ID an alias for your ID because you might like to keep separate your Internet FTP mail and your other mail.

If you set up an alias, it doesn't take effect until the system rereads the dbm-format database, which you can do by executing new aliases.

Trying Out Your FTP Archive

Before you announce to the world that you have a great FTP service, you really should test it. If you can, let as many people as possible bang on the service to see if you can catch any bugs, inconsistencies, or anything that would frustrate real users to the point of not using the service. Also, you should try to break into restricted areas of the file system and compromise files that should not allow such nonsense. Write the hackers guide to your service—then fix it before anyone else does.

If you have problems, you can look at the entries in the syslog file—assuming you turn on logging (–l) for ftpd in the inetd.config file. If you did not start ftpd with logging enabled, change the inetd.config file by adding the –l option at the end of the FTP configuration line, then make inetd reread the configuration file by executing the following command, where *pid* is the process ID of the inetd service:

```
% killall -HUP pid
```

The /etc/syslog.conf file should specify the location of the log files, usually /var/log. Keep a window open with the syslog file in it. To watch the syslog file, use the tail command (tail –f) while you use an FTP client to interact with your FTP service. Change directories, list the files in the directories, and download a several files to make sure all is working as planned.

Do a long listing of all the files and directories to make sure the permissions, owners, and groups are correct. Use the tables earlier in this chapter for guidance.

What Your Session Should Look Like

If everything is working okay, when you use your FTP client to ftp to your service, you should get a set of responses similar to the following (user input is in italics):

```
% ftp ftp.company.com

Connected to ftp.company.com
220 sizzle.asd.sgi.com FTP server (Version
➥4.2.321.2 Wed Feb 15 03:24:32 GMT 1995) ready.
Name (ftp.company.com:clinton): anonymous
331 Guest login ok. Use email address as password
Password: clinton@washington.com
230 Guest login ok, access restrictions apply.
ftp> cd /hot_topics
250 CWD successful
ftp> binary      --- specify binary to download
➥binary or non-ASCIIfiles
200 Type set to I.
ftp> get one_great_program.tar.Z
200 PORT command successful.
150 Opening BINARY mode data connection for
➥one_great_program.tar.Z
226 Transfer complete.
ftp> quit
221 Goodbye.

%
```

To actually use the program, you would do the following:

```
% uncompress one_great_program.tar.Z
% tar xvf one_great_program.tar
```

The beginning of the syslog file should look similar to the following:

```
Feb 15 03:24:32 sizzle inetd[121]: ftp/tcp:
➥Connection from sizzle (12.3.2.4) at Wed Feb 15
➥03:24:32 1995

Feb 15 03:24:32 sizzle ftpd[121]: Connection from
➥sizzle at Wed Feb 15 03:24:32 1995
```

What Might Go Wrong

If the path to the service in the inetd.config file is wrong, you might get a message in syslog similar to the following:

```
Feb 15 03:24:32 sizzle inetd[121]: ftp/tccp:
➥Unknown service
```

If a directory should be executable but isn't, you get a message similar to the following:

```
ftp> ls
200 PORT command successful.
150 Opening ASCII mode data connection for /bin/ls.
. not found
226 Transfer complete.
ftp>
```

If ftpd is not on the host machine, you might get an error similar to the following:

```
ftp: connect: Connection refused
```

If you try to log in as anonymous, but have not set up the anonymous user correctly, you get a message similar to the following:

```
520 Guest login not permitted.
Login failed.
Remote system type is UNIX.
Using binary mode to transfer files.
ftp>
```

What files? It did not really transfer any files. You're not even logged in, which you can confirm by trying to ls.

When you try to download an archive file, it should be readable. If not, you get an error message similar to the following:

```
ftp> get download_file /tmp/mine
200 PORT command successful.
550 download_file: Permission denied.
ftp>
```

If you made a mistake with the permission set for a directory, and a directory that should be readable is not, you get a message similar to the following:

```
ftp> ls
200 PORT command successful.
150 Opening ASCII mode data connection for /bin/ls.
. unreadable
total 2
226 Transfer complete.
ftp>
```

If you cannot upload a file, make sure the /upload directory is writable.

If you cannot change to one of the directories under the login directory, check to see that they are executable.

This is hardly a complete list of what can go wrong. But it at least gives you a flavor of problems you might see and what you need to do about them. After banging away on your service for a good while, open it to the people in your company. If they cannot break the service, pop the champagne corks and open the service to the eyes of the Internet world.

Summary

In this chapter you learned how to set up the configuration file for inetd, inetd.config. You added, populated, and set appropriate permissions for all of the directories under the login directory. You also set appropriate permissions for some of the files in those directories. All along you've tried not to create a hacker's paradise by being lax about file access and directory and file permissions.

You created a user, named anonymous, to give FTP clients access to your service, and, at the same time, to chroot() them to a restricted set of directories in your file structure. You also learned that you could set up additional users and passwords to give users access to additional directories under the login directory.

After you got everything set up, you had the chance to bang on your service long and hard to make sure that it was bullet-proof. You watched the syslog file using tail to debug errors that you found. And then you gave the Internet community a valuable new resource by giving your blessing to your company's new FTP service.

Now that your service is up and running, you might wonder if any upkeep is required. Are you kidding? Whenever did files and directories take care of themselves? Chapter 12 discusses how to properly manage your service.

11

Setting Up a More Secure FTP Service

The preceding chapter explains FTP in detail. One of FTP's drawbacks is its lack of security features. It relies on firewall software (see Chapter 8, "Making Your LAN Secure") to grant or deny access to users. What if there were a more secure version of FTP?

Actually, one does exist—the Washington University (WU) (in St. Louis) version of FTP. In addition to the FTP features Chapter 10 describes, the WU version includes the following:

→ Control over user access based on group ID and class. A class is the combination of a user type and domain name (or IP address).

→ Automatic compression (or decompression) and tar of files on the server just before they are downloaded.

→ Sophisticated tracking of uploads and downloads in log files.

→ Automated service shutdown.

The added security measures alone warrant consideration of the WU version of FTP. The other additions make this version even more attractive.

Getting the Source Code

With Linux Slackware distribution, it is not necessary for you to get the source code for this service, as it is included (and already compiled) with the distribution. This makes getting the FTP service operational much easier because you do not need to compile the source code. Furthermore, the version on the CD-ROM included with this book is the currently available Slackware release.

Consequently, if you are interested in knowing where to get the source code, read on. Otherwise, you can skip ahead to the next chapter, where you focus on how to configure the wu-ftpd server and place it into operation.

You can get the source code for WU FTP from `wuarchive.wustl.edu` in the file `/packages/wuarchive-ftpd/wu-ftpd-2.4.tar.Z`, as follows:

```
ftp> ls
200 PORT command successful.
150 Opening ASCII mode data connection for /bin/ls.
total 201
-r—r—r— 1 root archive 318 Apr 14 1994 CHECKSUMS
-r—r—r— 1 root archive 7761 Apr 14 1994
➥patch_2.3-2.4.Z
-r—r—r— 1 root archive 184907 Apr 14 1994
➥wu-ftpd-2.4.tar.Z
cd226 Transfer complete.
ftp> get wu-ftpd-2.4.tar.Z
local: wu-ftpd-2.4.tar.Z remote: wu-ftpd-2.4.tar.Z
200 PORT command successful.
150 Opening BINARY mode data connection for
➥wu-ftpd-2.4.tar.Z (184907 bytes).
226 Transfer complete.
184907 bytes received in 56.97 seconds (3.17
➥Kbytes/s)
```

 n o t e This chapter discusses version 2.4 of the software. If you find a later version, you might want to build that instead. If you do, check the NOTES file for differences between what is discussed in this chapter and the installation notes for the new version.

The archive server at Washington University supports a maximum of 250 anonymous FTP users. There are other archive sites that have the wu-ftp source code, and these might be more available than the Washington University site.

To uncompress and untar the source code, execute the following command:

```
% zcat wu-ftpd-2.4.tar.Z | tar -xvf -
tar: blocksize = 16
x wu-ftpd-2.4/doc/examples/ftpaccess, 422 bytes,
➥1 block
x wu-ftpd-2.4/doc/examples/ftpconversions,
➥455 bytes, 1 block
```

```
x wu-ftpd-2.4/doc/examples/ftpgroups, 37 bytes,
➥1 block
x wu-ftpd-2.4/doc/examples/ftpusers, 83 bytes,
➥1 block
x wu-ftpd-2.4/doc/examples/ftphosts, 190 bytes,
➥1 block
```

After uncompressing and untaring, notice the new directory, wu-ftpd-2.4:

```
%ls
wu-ftpd-2.4
wu-ftpd-2.4.tar.Z
```

The new directory, wu-ftpd-2.4 contains the following directories and files:

```
warp 295% cd wu-ftpd-2.4
warp 296% ls
```

```
FIXES-2.4 Makefile    build      doc     support
INSTALL   README    config.h   src     util
```

Table 11.1 describes the contents of the directories.

Installing the Service

Building the service is a multistep process. This section explains each step in detail.

1. Edit src/pathnames.h to accurately reflect the path names in your system. The table on the following page describes the path names in pathnames.h file.

Table 11.1   Description of Subdirectories in wu-ftpd-2.4

Subdirectory	Description
FIXES-2.4	Describes bug fixes and revisions from the previous software version
INSTALL	Describes how to install the service software
Makefile	Provides the Makefile instructions to run the make program
README	Describes the contents of the directories
build	Contains information necessary for the build
config.h	Contains the configuration variables
doc	Contains documentation on a variety of topics
src	Contains the source code for the service
support	Contains syslog and user authentication programs
util	Contains compression software and a log analysis package

Path Name	Description
_PATH_BSHELL	The absolute path name of the file on the server that contains the executable for the Bourne shell; default is /bin/sh
_PATH_CVT	The absolute path name of the file—ftpconversions—that contains the commands ftpd uses to compress, uncompress, and tar files; the default is /usr/local/etc/ftpconversions
_PATH_DEVNULL	The absolute path name of the file, on the server, that contains device information; default is /dev/null
_PATH_EXECPATH	The path name, relative to the chroot()'ed directory, of the directory of the executables users can use; default is /bin/ftp-exec
_PATH_FTPACCESS	The absolute path name of the file—ftpaccess—that contains user-access information; default is /usr/local/etc/ftpaccess
_PATH_FTPUSERS	The absolute path name of the file—ftpusers—that contains a list of users who may not access the service; default is /etc/ftpusers
_PATH_LASTLOG	The absolute path name of the file on the server that contains the last logins of users and terminals; accessed by the list command on your server
_PATH_PIDNAMES	The absolute path name of the PID files that store the PIDs of running ftpd's; the default is /usr/local/daemon/ftpd/ftp.pids-*%s*, where *%s* is replaced by the name of the class using the ftpd
_PATH_PRIVATE	The absolute path name of the file that contains group membership and group password information; default is /etc/ftpgroups
_PATH_UTMP	The absolute path name of the file—utmp—residing on your server, that contains user and accounting information for such commands as who, last, write, and login
_PATH_WTMP	The absolute path name of the file—wtmp—residing on your server, that contains user and accounting information for such commands as who, last, write, and login
_PATH_XFERLOG	The absolute path name of the file that logs file uploads and downloads; default is /usr/adm/xferlog

2. Edit the conf.h file.

Most likely, you do not have to modify the file at all. All the options in it are enabled by default. To disable any of the options, comment them out.

The following table offers a brief description of each variable:

Variable	*Description*
UPLOAD	Allows users to upload files to the server
OVERWRITE	Allows users to overwrite files as they upload them
HOST_ACCESS	Enables system administrator to allow or deny users access to the service based on their host name
LOG_FAILED	Logs failed attempts to log in to the service
NO_PRIVATE	Allows the use of private files
DNS_TRYAGAIN	Specifies that the service should try one more time if a DNS lookup fails

3. Build the service.

The build is different depending on the platform on which the service runs. The source code contains build scripts for the following platforms:

aix : IBM AIX

bsd : BSDI bsd/386

dgx : Data General Unix

dyn : Dynix

hpx : HP-UX

isc : ISC

lnx : Linux (tested on 0.99p8)

nx2 : NeXTstep 2.*x*

nx3 : NeXTstep 3.x

osf : OSF/1

sgi : SGI Irix 4.0.5a

sny : Sony NewsOS

sol : SunOS 5.x / Solaris 2.x

s41 : SunOS 4.1.x (requires acc or gcc 2.3.3 or better)

(If you must use gcc 1.4.2, mail me for a patch)

ult : Ultrix 4.x

If you are installing ftpd on a different platform, you have to create your own configuration file by copying and editing each of the following files:

```
% cp src/config/config.gen  src/config/config.Name
% cp src/makefiles/Makefile.gen  src/makefiles/
➥Makefile.Name
% cp support/makefiles/Makefile.gen  support/
➥makefiles/Makefile.Name
```

Name is the name of your computer platform.

note There is no preconfigured file for the Linux platform. Consequently, any patches or new versions that you want to install will require that you retrieve the entire version and build a configuration file for Linux.

Correcting the configuration information is specific to your platform, so it is not within the scope of this book. In general, the config.*Name* file contains information about system and library calls that the service needs to use. The Makefiles are general enough to support most platforms, but you should check the defines.

When you have set the Makefile and configuration files, build the service by executing the following command:

```
% build Name
```

Name is a three-letter abbreviation that describes your computer platform, such as aix or bsd.

 n o t e Building ftpd requires an ANSI C compiler. You can FTP one from prep.ai.mit.edu in the file /pub/gnu.

If the compiler complains that strunames, typenames, modenames, or other variables are undefined, install support/ftp.h as /usr/include/arpa/ftp.h and do the build again. Replacing the old ftp.h is not a problem because the new ftp.h is a superset of the old file.

If the compiler complains that pid_t is undefined, add the following line to src/config.h:

```
typedef int pid_t;
```

4. Install the service by executing the following command:

```
% build install
```

5. Edit the configuration file for inetd, inetd.conf, to start ftpd when receiving a FTP request.

6. Restart the system by sending the hang-up signal so that the new configuration specifications can take effect.

On BSD-ish systems, use the following command:

```
%kill -1 'ps -acx ¦ grep inetd ¦ cut -c-5'.
```

On SGI systems, use the following command:

```
% /etc/killall -HUP inetd
```

7. Install GNU tar and put a copy in the anonymous ftp hierarchy.

This software enables users to create .tar.Z files on the service host before receiving them over the Internet. You can download a copy of GNU tar from wuarchive.wustl.edu (IP address: 128.252.135.4) in the /gnu subdirectory.

8. Place a copy of compress in ~ftp/bin. This enables users to compress files before receiving them over the Internet.

9. From the doc/ directory, copy the ftpconversions, ftpusers, and ftpgroups files to the directories defined in pathnames.h.

10. Create at least one class in ftpaccess. For an example, look in doc/examples/ftpaccess.

11. Place any executables anonymous users can run in the directory specified by pathnames.h for _PATH_EXECPATH. The default is /bin/ftp-exec. Consider carefully what you put in this file.

12. Make sure the configuration files are set up correctly by running bin/ckconfig.

13. Hold your breath. Everything should be working now!

Installation Notes

Place into /etc/shells a list of all the valid shells in your system. If users do not have all the shells listed in this file, they cannot log in to the service.

Make sure the following files are in the chroot()'d FTP subdirectory:

→ All messages (deny, welcome, and so on)

→ Shutdown

→ The executables contained in the file defined by _PATH_EXECPATH

Read the INSTALL file for platform-specific build problems and corrections.

For additional help, you should subscribe to two mailing lists: wu-ftpd and wu-ftpd-announce. You can subscribe to both by sending e-mail to listserv@wunet.wustl.edu.

New Directories

Several new, important files have been added to the WU ftpd service; they include the following:

→ ftpaccess

→ ftphosts

→ ftpconversions

These three files, not present in the standard ftpd service, reflect the added functionality of WU ftpd.

The ftpaccess file contains information that permits or denies user access to the service. Chapter 12, "Managing an FTP Service," discusses this file in greater detail.

The ftphost file contains information that permits or denies users from specified hosts access to the service. This file, too, is discussed in greater detail in the following chapter.

The ftpconversions file defines what programs should run as a filter, depending on the prefix/suffix of the file to be uploaded/downloaded. For example, a .Z indicates that uncompress is automatically run on a server file before sending it. The executables that perform these tasks reside in the directory specified by the _PATH EXEC PATH variable in the pathnames.h file:

ftpd uncompresses the file before downloading it. Conversely, if a file on the service is named *fileName*, you can make the following FTP request:

```
ftp> get fileName.Z
```

ftpd compresses the file before downloading it. You exercise these options depending on whether or not you have the uncompression software on your workstation. Always download the compressed version of the file if you have the uncompression software.

The ftpconversions file matches file extensions and executables. All files that have the extension .Z, for example, get compressed, if they are not compressed already.

The formal syntax of the entries in the ftpconversions files is as follows:

```
prefix:suffix:prefAdd:SuffAdd:command %s:  \
objType:option:errorText
```

Table 11.2 describes each of the fields.

Table 11.2   Formal Syntax of ftpconversions File Entries

Field	Description
prefix	The prefix to the retrieved file name that triggers the conversion
suffix	The suffix to the retrieved file name that triggers the conversion
prefAdd	The prefix added to the converted file
suffAdd	The suffix added to the converted file
command	The command to be executed (along with any options) according to the prefix or suffix added to (or subtracted from) the requested file name by the user; %s is replaced by the name of the requested file
objType	The kind of object specified by the file name, including T_ASCII for a text (ASCii) file, T_DIR for a directory, and T_REG for a non-text file
option	Works with the ftpaccess directory to define the kind of executed command, and to determine whether or not the user has permission to execute such a command; some users might not, for example, be able to untar files; or another example, a user who cannot uncompress a file (using Unix compress) might also be prevented from uncompressing a file with the extension .zip if the ftpaccess directory defines .zip and .Z as part of the same group
errorText	Used in error statements when the conversion fails, for example, errorText might be "untar" so that the error message, `Cannot %s the file`, reads appropriately

The section about ftpaccess in the next chapter discusses the option field in greater detail.

Let's look at a sample entry in the ftpconversions file:

```
: : :.Z:/pathName/compress -c
➥%s:T_REG:O_COMPRESS:compress
```

In the preceding example, a regular file is compressed whenever the user adds the extension .Z to a file name.

The doc/examples directory in the software distribution provides the following example of ftpconversions:

```
warp 318% more ftpconversions
 :.Z: : :/bin/compress -d -c
➡%s:T_REG¦T_ASCII:O_UNCOMPRESS:UNCOMPRESS
 : : :.Z:/bin/compress -c
➡%s:T_REG:O_COMPRESS:COMPRESS
 :.gz: : :/bin/gzip -cd
➡%s:T_REG¦T_ASCII:O_UNCOMPRESS:GUNZIP
 : : :.gz:/bin/gzip -9 -c %s:T_REG:O_COMPRESS:GZIP
 : : :.tar:/bin/tar -c -f -
➡%s:T_REG¦T_DIR:O_TAR:TAR
 : : :.tar.Z:/bin/tar -c -Z -f -
➡%s:T_REG¦T_DIR:O_COMPRESS¦O_TAR:TAR+COMPRESS
 : : :.tar.gz:/bin/tar -c -z -f -
➡%s:T_REG¦T_DIR:O_COMPRESS¦O_TAR:TAR+GZIP
```

New Command-Line Options

The WU version of ftpd recognizes the following command-line options:

➜ **-A.** Disables the ftpaccess file.

➜ **-a.** Enables the ftpaccess file.

➜ **-d.** Enables debugging.

➜ **-i.** Enables logging (in xferlog) of all files uploaded.

➜ **-L.** Enables logging of any attempt to modify a user name.

➜ **-o.** Enables logging (in xferlog) of all files downloaded.

Using the ftpaccess file is enabled by default.

All the other command-line options available with the regular version of FTP, such as -l, -t, and -T, are also available with the WU version of FTP.

Summary

This chapter discusses the setup of an FTP service that is more secure than the generic FTP service the preceding chapter covers. This chapter includes a review of the configuration changes you have to make according to the computer platform you use.

The WU version of FTP offers the following additional items:

➜ Control over user access based on group ID and class.

➜ Automatic compression (or decompression) and tar of files on the server just before they are FTP'd.

➜ Sophisticated tracking of uploads and downloads in log files.

➜ Automated service shutdown.

The following chapter, "Managing an FTP Service," discusses each of these enhancements in greater detail.

Managing an FTP Service

Now that you have created a wonderful FTP service, it is time to look at the tasks you need to accomplish to maintain and manage the service. This chapter discusses all the tasks related to managing the service. These tasks are described in terms of the job of the FTP system administrator.

The Internet system operator is charged with the following tasks:

→ Putting archive files into the system

→ Creating and updating README files that describe the files in each directory

→ Facilitating navigation between the files

→ Linking one archive to another

→ Updating files in the archive

→ Removing old files

→ Creating, renaming, and eliminating subdirectories

→ Monitoring the files for security breaches and checking for computer viruses

→ Answering user questions

→ Reviewing files uploaded to the /upload directory for possible elimination or inclusion in /pub

→ Interacting with company personnel to keep in touch with product and service revisions

→ Understanding product and service revisions

→ Keeping the FTP service up-to-date in terms of revisions to the service code and the availability of better service software

To perform these tasks, FTP system administrators do not need superuser access to the server host; they only need access to the directories they are going to change, such as the /pub and /dist directories.

If your company has many products, or your products and services are of such a difficult, technical nature that it is impossible for one person to keep up with all the revisions of all the products, some companies might choose to farm out some of the FTP system administrator jobs to appropriate company personnel. If one engineer in the company is responsible for one of the software products offered by the company, for example, you might put that person in charge of updating the FTP archive files relating to that engineers product. In this case, you might consider changing the ownership of the directories to someone who is able to keep them current. You use the chown() command to change the ownership of the directories.

If you plan to distribute the job of the FTP system administrator among a variety of people in your company, it's best to set up a group, called something like ftpadmin, and add all the people administering the FTP service to that group. After you do that, you have to change the group ownership (to the ftpadmingroup) of all the files and directories on which these people need to work. Finally, you have to change the permission set on these files so that group members can write to the files.

Organizing Your Archive Files

In order to organize the archive files, the FTP system administrator needs to understand the contents of the files. At the highest level, it is easy to organize the files by subject matter; if your company has 30 products, you should create 30 subdirectories under /pub (or /dist). There might be lower levels of subdivision that make sense, but creating those subdivisions requires more specialized knowledge of the product. It is crucial, however, that subdivisions be accurate and descriptive of the product. If the FTP system administrator cannot break the subject matter into these smaller divisions, you might ask someone else to aid the FTP system administrator in making those divisions.

Nothing on the Internet has come down as written in stone. Administering your archives is no exception. However, it is worth paying attention to the *de facto* file extensions that give the user a clue as to the contents of the file. You should use the following typical file extensions when naming your archive files:

Extension	Description
bw	Image in black and white
c	C code
c++	C++ code
gif	Image in gif format
gz	Compressed file using gzip
idl	idl code
jpeg	Image in jpeg format
mpeg	Image in mpeg format
pit	Compressed file using PackIt
ps	PostScript
rgb	Image in rgb format
Sit	Compressed file using StuffIt
tif	Image in tif format
txt	Text
Z	Compressed file using Unix compress program
zip	Compressed file using PKZIP

Providing Navigational Aids

You can have some of the greatest archives in the world in your service, but if people cannot easily find them, they will remain buried treasures forever.

FTP system administrators need to be vigilant in helping users effortlessly find appropriate FTP archive files. Because FTP is a text-based service, the tools you have to advertise files are limited. It is important, however, to use every tool at your disposal. These tools include the following:

→ README files in each directory describing the files in the directory

→ Aliases

→ Search paths

→ Symbolic links

→ ls-lR files

→ Archie

The following sections look at each of these tools.

Using README Files

In every directory, even at the login directory level, there should be a README file describing the files and subdirectories in the directory. Although this is a good principle, there are a few exceptions.

At the login directory level, the user's root, you should include (at least) the following information in a README file:

→ The e-mail address (or alias—for example, FTP-administrator) of the FTP system administrator for users to use in case of problems

→ General company information providing a list of available products and services and a corresponding list of directories where such archives reside

→ Copyright information

→ Aliases you use in administering the company's service

➔ Hot topics

➔ Disclaimer information renouncing your company's responsibility for any damage any archive files might cause to the user's machine

These topics get legal issues out of the way up front and provide navigation information.

 note The Washington University (WU) version of ftpd enables you to print this kind of information whenever a user accesses an FTP service. Messages longer than 24 lines scroll off the screen, so keep the messages short.

Just below the directory login level is the product or service level—one directory for each. In these README files, include (at least) the following information:

➔ Product or service description (assume that the user knows nothing about your product or service)

➔ Version number

➔ Information revision date

➔ Copyright information

➔ Disclaimer information

It's worth repeating the copyright and disclaimer information at this level so that there is no confusion about what is redistributable and what is not.

Using Aliases

Aliases give you the ability to call one file by more than one name. You generally use aliases to circumvent multiple layers of the file system—a necessary evil in hierarchical file systems. If a popular tool is buried under the directories /pub/

productName/debug/tools/toolName, for example, you can provide an alias so that users easily can use the cd command to move to the tools directory by adding the following entry to the ftpaccess file:

```
alias toolName: /pub/productName/debug/tools
```

The only way you can use an alias is to use the cd command to move to the directory you want.

The only problem with using aliases is that you have to advertise them because they do not advertise themselves. You can do that by listing the aliases you use in your README files, and by asking the user to execute the following command:

```
quote site alias
```

The WU version of ftpd allows you to use aliases, not the vanilla version of ftpd.

The WU version of ftpd uses a file called ftpaccess to hold alias entries. The syntax of the entries follows:

```
alias  aliasName:  pathnameToRealFilesDirectory
```

For example,

```
alias FAQ:  /pub/productName/doc/troubleShooting
```

in which /`troubleShooting` is a directory that contains the FAQ file that the user wants to access. You can provide an absolute path name (relative to the login directory) as shown, or use a relative path name, depending on the location of the files.

For example,

```
alias FAQ: ../../doc/troubleShooting
```

Defining Paths

Another way of accomplishing what an alias does is to define search paths. Unfortunately, only services using the WU version of ftpd have this option.

Search paths are directories that are searched automatically when a user performs an operation on a file. If, for example, the user changes to a directory named distant,

```
ftp> cd distant
```

the current directory is searched first for the file (`distant`) and, if it is not found, the directories specified as paths are searched for the file.

To set up a search path, add a line to the ftpaccess file similar to the following:

```
cdpath  /pub/productName/tools
```

This line alleviates the need for the user to type the absolute path name to get to a file in the /tools directory, that is, instead of typing

```
ftp> cd /pub/productName/tools
```

you can just type

```
ftp> cd tools
```

You easily might have more than one of these lines, one for each buried, but often requested, document.

The order in which the file system is searched for a file follows:

1. ftpd checks the current working directory for the requested subdirectory.

2. ftpaccess is checked to see whether an alias exists for the requested subdirectory.

3. The search paths listed in ftpaccess are used (in the order in which they are listed) to look for the requested subdirectory.

Using Symbolic Links

Symbolic links provide easy access to other parts of your file structure. A symbolic link file contains the name of another file to which it is linked. Symbolic links connect ideas as well as files. If one file describes a tool, for example, provide a symbolic link to the tool's file:

```
# ln -s /pub/productName/docs/tool  /pub/
➥productName/tools/toolLibrary
```

This lines links the file with the subdirectory—toolLibrary—where the tool resides. This approach maintains the logic of the file hierarchy that locates the documents under /**docs** and tools under /**tools**, while anticipating user interest by facilitating easy access between the different branches of the file hierarchy.

These absolute path names are relative to the login directory (the user's root), so /**pub** is, at the system level, really /usr/ftp/pub (or whatever the login directory is).

You also can use relative path names to set up links, as in the following example:

```
# ln -s tool  ../../tools/toolLibrary
```

Using relative or absolute path names is a matter of personal taste. Whenever the file system changes, you have to review carefully all links.

 About the last thing you want to do is to provide a link from the user's work area into your general file system. Be careful when defining links not to defeat chroot().

Using ls-lR Files

A ls-lR file contains a list of all the files and directories within a branch of a tree. The file appears similar to the output of the ls command with the lR option, hence the customary name of the file. If you went to the top of the tree—perhaps to the /productName directory—and did a recursive listing in long format of the files below /productName, you would get the appropriate list of files for the ls-lR file.

You should create the ls-lR file in the following way:

```
# ls -lR > ls-lR
```

This line does a recursive listing in long format and redirects the output to a file called ls-lR.

 If your file system changes regularly, you might automate the creation of the ls-lR file by making its creation an automatic cron job. A *cron job* is an operation that executes at a specific time, perhaps the same time every night. The following example shows a line added to the roots crontab:

```
0 1 * * *  cd /usr/ftp ; su ftp -c  ls -lR > ls-lR
```

In this line, the `ls-lR` file is created only after changing to the `/usr/ftp` directory, changing the user to the ftp user (`su -c`), and then running `ls`. You really don't want to run `ls` as root, because there might be files in the directory accessible to root but not a user of the FTP service.

Examine the permission set of the ls-lR file. Make sure it is readable but not writeable for FTP users.

If the file structure is large and creates a corresponding large ls-lR file, you can compress the ls-lR file using the standard compress utility, as in the following example:

```
0 1 * * *  cd /usr/ftp; su ftp -c  ls -lR |
➥compress  > ls-lR.Z
```

Using Archie

Archie is a search tool that uses keywords or phrases to find related documents. You can make your FTP archive searchable to Archie by sending a message to archie-updates@bunyip.com saying that your FTP service is running and that the ls-lR file contains a recursive listing of files and directories in your FTP archive. In order to provide maximum exposure for your service, you must create the ls-lR file at the top of your hierarchical tree.

After your FTP service is registered, your ls-lR file is polled automatically at regular intervals. All the words and phrases in ls-lR then become the content matter searched when a user uses Archie to find all files relating to a keyword or phrase. For example, the command

```
% archie myProduct
```

might produce the following output:

```
Host  sizzle.asd.sgi.com
      Location: /dist/ship/2.1
        FILE  -rwxr-xr-x 2346  Feb  16  11:42
➥myProduct
```

It then is easy for users to take this information and ftp to the file, myProduct.

 For more information about using Archie, send the following e-mail to mailserv@is.internic.net, leaving the subject field empty:

```
send  using-Internet/searches/archie/using-archie
```

Before you connect your FTP service to an Archie service, make sure that you do not have either of the following problems:

→ Unresolvable symbolic links

→ Permission problems using ls

Checking syslog Files

syslog files contain important information describing how much your FTP archive is used daily. The only problem is that the data is buried under anonymity. A program called xferstats, which is included with the WU version of ftpd, fleshes out this information and puts it in a readable form, as the following example shows.

```
TOTALS FOR SUMMARY PERIOD  Fri  Feb 17  1995  to Fri Feb  17  1995

Files Transmitted During Summary Period        8
Bytes Transmitted During Summary Period      92216
Systems Using Archives                         0

Average Files Transmitted Daily                8
Average Bytes Transmitted Daily              92216
```

Daily Transmission Statistics

Date Sent	Number of Files Sent	Number of Bytes Sent	Average Xmit Rate	Percent of Files Sent	Percent of Bytes Sent
....	....	....	....	....	....
Fri Feb 17 1995	8	92216	54.4 KB/s	100.00	100.00

Total Transfers from each Archive Section (By bytes)

```
                              -- Percent of --
```

Archive Section	Files Sent	Bytes Sent	Files Sent	Bytes Sent
....	....	....	....	....
/upload	4	46792	50.00	52.37
/pub	3	42395	37.50	46.11
/Index/Info files	1	3029	37.50	1.62

Hourly Transmission Statistics

Time	Number of Files Sent	Number of Bytes	Average Xmit Rate	Percent Of Files Sent	Percent Of Bytes
....	....	....	....	....	....
00	8	92216	53.7 KB/s	100.00	100.00

This report shows that eight files were sent containing 92,216 bytes from three subdirectories.

You can change the duration of the report to look at weekly and monthly statistics. You can use this information to see whether parts of your FTP archive are used on a regular basis. If parts of your archive are not used regularly, you might reconsider the pertinence of the files or revise the navigational aids that direct users through those directories.

You also can use this information to monitor hardware needs. You initially might have set up your Internet service with a minimum of machinery. These statistics give you a good idea about pub load. If you plot the growth of your service over time with a simple usage versus time graph, you can anticipate when you will need additional disk storage.

Checking ftpadmin E-Mail

If you set up an alias for yourself, you have the daily chore of checking the ftpadmin e-mail. If you require that users send you e-mail when they upload files, the first thing you should do is match newly uploaded software in /upload with corresponding e-mail. If you find software without e-mail, consider the uploaded file suspicious. Actually, consider all uploaded files as potential threats to your system. Even though you took the trouble to isolate uploaded files in one directory, they still can do harm.

You also can direct other error messages to this address. If you use a cron job to create the ls-lR file, for example, send errors to ftpadmin.

The remainder of the mail is a combination of user complaints, questions, and requests. Remember that you are the first line of customer contact

(through the Internet) for your company. Potential customers appreciate timely feedback, curious answers to questions, and references to additional information.

 note The remainder of this chapter discusses system administration of the WU version of ftpd.

Configuring the WU Version of ftpd

The WU version of ftpd, which is what is supplied with Linux, uses the ftpaccess file as the holding place for configuration information. You can do any of the following things:

→ Restrict user access to the FTP service by user type

→ Restrict user access according to CPU load

→ Restrict user access by group

→ Automatically display information to users

→ Log information about service usage

→ Provide shortcuts for file access

→ Control uploading of files

The control files for the server that are discussed in the following sections—ftpaccess, ftphosts, ftpconversions, ftpgroups, and ftpusers—are located in the /etc directory for the Slackware distribution of Linux.

The following sections describe how to accomplish each of these tasks.

Restricting User Access

As an FTP system administrator, you need some ammunition to fight people who misuse your service. The WU version of ftpd enables you to deny access to your FTP service; the vanilla version of ftpd does not.

ftpd cannot single out specific users to deny access to; it can only deny access to the entire FTP client host. To deny access to host rusty.nail.com, for example, you create a file called /etc/ftphosts and put in it the following entry:

```
deny ftp  rusty.nail.com
deny anonymous rusty.nail.com
```

Notice that with the /etc/ftphosts file, you must deny access to both the ftp and anonymous users because the ftpd server sees these users as different, even though to us they are synonymous. What these entries do is deny access to the FTP server if the remote user attempts to log in using either of the specified user names. Denying anonymous ftp access is illustrated in the following:

```
WINSOCK.DLL: Microsoft Windows Sockets Version 1.1.
WS_FTP 95.04.27, Copyright © 1994-1995 John A.
➥Junod. All rights reserved.
- -
connecting to 204.191.3.150 ...
Connected to 204.191.3.150 port 21
[7] from 204.191.3.147 port 1041
220 pc FTP server (Version wu-2.4(1) Sun Jul 31
➥21:15:56 CDT 1994) ready.
USER anonymous
530 User anonymous access denied.
logon failure, so quitting
[7] Socket closed.
```

The preceding example illustrates a remote user being denied access through the anonymous user, as a result of the changes in the /etc/ftphosts file. To deny access to the entire archive, you use the deny command in the /etc/ftpaccess file:

```
deny host.com   /etc/doc/refuse
```

in which host.com is the name of the host machine whose users you want to deny access, and refuse is a text file that prints when users from host.com try to ftp into the archive. Or, instead of domain names, you can use IP addresses to define hosts.

You even can deny access to entire domains by using wild cards, as in the following example:

```
deny ftp *.nail.com
```

You can restrict host access by allowing only specified hosts to access the FTP service. For example:

```
allow ftp *.nail.com
```

means that only users from nail.com can access the FTP service anonymously.

In the ftphosts file, if you have more than one deny or allow entry, make the order of the entries proceed from most to least specific. Otherwise, the general case, if read first, will obliterate a specific case, as in the following example:

```
deny *.nail.com
allow  forge.engr.nail.com
```

Although the second entry grants access to forge.engr.nail.com, the first entry overrides the second entry.

n o t e The ftpaccess file is used to define classes of users and their access to the archive. It also controls which messages are displayed when and other intricacies of wu-ftpds behavior.

The ftphosts file is used to define hosts from which you will not accept anonymous logins. This is like the ftpusers file: if the host name is found in ftphosts, access is denied.

You can limit user access by defining classes in ftpaccess. A *class* is a combination of a user type and a domain name (or IP address). For ftpd, there are three types of users:

User Type	Description
Anonymous	Users restricted by chroot() to a subset of the file system
Guest	Users with IDs and passwords that have been restricted to a subset of the file system
Real	Users, usually company employees, who have full access to the file system

The class construct assigns users from specific hosts to a particular user type, using the following syntax:

```
class    className    userType    user.host.com
```

For example,

```
class    friend  guest  *.sgi.com
```

defines all users in sgi.com accesses as user type guest; the class of these users is friend. If a user is not defined as part of a class, he has no access to the system. If he is defined by more than one line in ftpaccess, his user type and class membership are defined by the first class whose specifications he satisfies. If a user is both class friend, user type guest; and class everyone, user type anonymous; for example, and if class friend is listed before class everyone in ftpaccess, his user type is defined as type guest. For this reason, you list the narrowly defined class definitions first, and the general class definitions last. If you were to put class everyone first whose domain name were all users (*), all users would be defined as class friend, regardless of what followed in the listing of classes.

To give anonymous FTP users access to the public archives, you have to define them in the following way:

```
class    everyone    anonymous    *
```

Restricting User Access Based on CPU Load

Whenever there is an ftp request, inetd spawns a new copy of ftpd to handle the request. As more and more requests come in, more and more ftpd processes are spawned. The more people using the FTP service, the greater the CPU load. At some point, depending on the speed of the computer, the CPU cannot handle the workload, and service to all FTP clients slows.

You can cure that problem automatically by restricting the number of users of a specific user type at any one time. You can do that by using the limit command with the following syntax:

```
limit  className    maxNumber  dayTime
overloadMessage
```

For example,

```
limit   friend   150   SaSu700-1800   /usr/doc/
overload
limit   friend   100   Any            /usr/doc/
overload
```

limits the number of users of class friend to 150 on Saturday and Sunday between 7 a.m. and 6 p.m., or 100 users at any other time. All FTP clients that try to log on that exceed the number of maximum users receive the `I'm sorry...` message defined in /overLoad.

The format of the time field is that the day of the week is represented by the first two letters of the day (Su, Mo, Tu, and We, for example), and you use a 24-hour clock. You can use a series of times for the same limit specification by using the OR (l) operator. Mo800–1300 l Fr900–1400, for example, means Monday 8 a.m. to 1 p.m. or Friday 9 a.m. to 2 p.m.

Notice that you put your most restrictive limit clauses first and proceed to the least restrictive. If you put the Any limit statement before the SaSu700–1800, for example, the Saturday-Sunday statement would have no effect.

ftpd reads the limit information and denies FTP connections before doing the chroot().

Restricting Access for Security Reasons

An FTP client, by default, has five chances to log onto ftpd before getting a kind "See you later" message. You can change the number of login attempts by using the loginfails command in the ftpaccess file:

```
loginfails 3
```

This limits the number of failed attempts to three.

If it is important to you that you get an e-mail address as the password when a user logs in, the WU version of ftpd enables you to check the format of the entered password.

Remember, this version does not check the authentication of the password—just the format. To check the format, you use the passwd-check command in ftpaccess, as follows:

```
passwd-check   formatCheck   reaction
```

in which `formatCheck` can be one of three values:

none	Does not provide password format checking
trivial	Checks to see whether there is an at (@) sign in the entered password
rfc822	Checks to see whether the entered password has a domain part and a local part (meaning that it complies with RFC 822)

The reaction field can have one of two values:

warn	Sends a warning to use the correct format when entering passwords
enforce	Terminates the FTP client's login if the password is formatted incorrectly

The passwd-check parameter is illustrated in the following:

```
220-
220-                     Welcome to the Unilabs Research
➥Group Archive
220-
220-Please login using your e-mail address as your
➥password.  This practice
220-is strictly enforced.
220-
220-You are connected to pc.unilabs.org
220-The current local time is Sun Jul 16 18:54:22
➥1995.
220-
220-To report problems with this FTP archive,
➥please send mail to ftp@unilabs.org.
220-
220-
220 pc FTP server (Version wu-2.4(1) Sun Jul 31
➥21:15:56 CDT 1994) ready.
USER anonymous
331 Guest login ok, send your complete e-mail
➥address as password.
PASS xxxxxx
530-The response 'guest' is not valid
530-Please use your e-mail address as your password
530-    for example: joe@stargazer.unilabs.org or
➥joe@
530-[stargazer.unilabs.org will be added if
➥password ends with @]
530 Login incorrect.
```

In addition, it is also possible to deny archive site access to clients who do not have a working nameserver. Normally, the IP Address of the client is transmitted to the server. If the IP address cannot be converted into a name, the connection generally is accepted anyway.

By adding the line

```
deny !nameserved message-file
```

to the ftpaccess file, any client whose IP Address cannot be converted into a name is denied access. This means any entries in the log that would have been only an IP address no longer have to be manually traced in the event of a problem.

The message-file is the name of a file containing the text that would be displayed to the user if there is no nameserver for that machine. This is illustrated in the following:

```
220-
220-                     Welcome to the Unilabs Research
➥Group Archive
220-
220-Please login using your e-mail address as your
➥password.  This practice
220-is strictly enforced.
220-
220-You are connected to pc.
220-The current local time is Sun Jul 16 19:11:45
➥1995.
220-
220-To report problems with this FTP archive,
➥please send mail to ftp@unilabs.org.
220-
220-
220 pc FTP server (Version wu-2.4(1) Sun Jul 31
➥21:15:56 CDT 1994) ready.
USER anonymous
530-
530-Sorry, but access cannot be granted because no
➥DNS has an entry for
530-your IP address.  Contact your DNS
➥administrator and ask them to
530-include your address in the inverse address
➥database.
530-
530 User anonymous access denied.
```

Restricting Users' Actions

Not only can you keep people out of your system, you can keep users and groups of users from taking specific actions.

Restricting the Use of tar and compress

The WU version of ftpd enables you to prevent specified user classes the right to tar or compress files. You do that by adding one or both of the following lines to the ftpaccess file:

```
compress    no    friend
tar         no    friend
```

The second field is yes or no, depending on whether you want the class, defined in the third field, to compress or tar. The default is yes.

Restricting File Functions

You can restrict types—not classes—of users from performing a number of file manipulations. The syntax of the command is similar to the compress and tar expressions—the second field is yes or no, and the third field names the type of user:

```
chmod       no    anonymous
delete      no    anonymous
overwrite   no    anonymous
rename      no    anonymous
umask       no    anonymous
```

These poor users can't do anything, but sometimes that is appropriate.

Creating and Managing Groups of Users

It is possible to restrict a group of users to a different part of the file structure than that of anonymous users. The principle is the same as with anonymous users: you use chroot() to restrict the group to the file system under the login directory, which becomes their root directory. You might want to do that if your company is working jointly with another company. In that case, you want to give employees of the other company access to some of your file structure, but not the entire file structure!

To create a group called guests, you put an entry in /etc/group similar to the following:

```
guests:*:25:type1,type2,type3,type4
```

Then you enter encrypted passwords for each user type (type1, type2, and so on) in the /etc/passwd file. The entry is similar to the following:

```
guests:aTerriblePassword:200:25:guests FTP user: \
    /users/guests/./type1:/bin/false
```

This entry uses chroot() to restrict a type1 user under the login directory /users/guests/, and makes her login directory /type1 (whatever follows the /.), which is a subdirectory of the login directory.

In ftpaccess, you then associate groups and guest users using the guestgroup command:

```
guestgroup guests
```

You can grant specified classes of anonymous users special access rights as well. You do that by making a class of anonymous users a group. If you have defined a class of anonymous users as allies, who are employees of corporation XYZ (XYZ.com), using the entry

```
class allies  anonymous  *.XYZ.com
```

you can create a group for them in /etc/group using an entry like the following:

```
XYZ::25:
```

To assign users of class allies to the group XYZ, you use the autogroup command in /etc/group:

```
autogroup XYZ  allies
```

Now that you have defined a group of users, you can make the files and directories under the login directory readable to the group XYZ only.

Changing Groups

You can allow FTP users to change their group ID using two commands:

```
site group groupName
site gpass groupPassword
```

in which *groupName* is the name of the group the FTP user wants to change to, and *groupPassword* is the password of the group. After logging in as anonymous, for example, the user uses the following commands:

```
ftp> site group engr
350 Request for access to group field accepted.
ftp> site gpass Wjsile23kl23jsic
350 Group access enabled.
ftp>
```

Notice that the password is not hidden in this case.

To allow FTP users to use the site group and site gpass commands, you must set the private option in ftpaccess as in this example:

```
private yes
```

Then you must create the directory, /ftpgroups, under the same directory that /group is under—usually ~ftp/etc. In /ftpgroups, you specify the group, defined in /group, that the site group maps to, and the gpass password, as in the following example:

```
engr:Wjsile23kl23jsic:XYZ
```

In this case, the site group is engr, the gpass password is Wjsile23kl23jsic, and the file access is the same as that granted to group XYZ.

Sending Messages to FTP Users

The WU version of ftpd provides four commands to display messages to logged in FTP users:

➜ banner

➜ message

➜ readme

➜ shutdown

Using the banner Command

The banner command displays a file at user login. You specify, in ftpaccess, the path name to the display file using the banner command, as in the following example:

```
banner /usr/ftp/greetings/bannerMSG
```

This path name is relative to the system root, not the login directory.

The banner message should contain any information you want the FTP users to know before logging in. You might want them to know that they must use their e-mail address as a password to log in or who to contact if there are problems, or you might want them to see a simple greeting. Your banner message can include macros to provide updated information. The following table shows the macros you can use with the banner and message commands.

Macro	Replaced By
%C	Current working directory name
%E	e-mail address (of FTP system administrator) defined by the e-mail entry in ftpaccess
%F	Number of free kilobytes in current working directory
%L	Host name where FTP archive files reside
%M	Maximum number of users of the users class allowed to log in
%N	Current number of users of the current user's class
%R	Current user's host name (name of FTP client)
%T	Time of day, in the format weekday month day hour:minute:seconds year. For example, Sunday Feb 24 8:30:30 1995
%U	User's name, as specified at login

You might use vi to create the following banner message:

```
%U logged in at %T from %R.

For system administration help, email %E.

Maximum number of users: %M
%U, you are number: %N

Welcome!
```

Using the message Command

The message command works much like the banner command; it even uses the same macros. The difference is that the message command controls when the message is displayed. There are two instances in which the message is displayed:

→ At login

→ When the user changes (using the cd command) to a specific directory

To display the message at user login, use an entry in ftpaccess similar to the following:

```
message /usr/ftp/greetings/messageMSG login
```

where /usr/ftp/greetings/messageMSG is the path name and the file of the message to display.

To display a message when a user changes to a specific directory, use an entry in ftpaccess similar to the following:

```
message /usr/ftp/greetings/messageMSG cwd=dirName
```

where dirName is the name of the directory that triggers the display of messageMSG. Instead of a specific directory, you can use the asterisk wild card (*) to specify that any directory trigger the messageMSG.

To display the contents of a file in each directory, name the files the same in each directory (but make the content different). If the name of the file is README, for example, you could use the following entry:

```
message .README cwd=*
```

You might put in the README file a description of the contents of the current directory.

To display a message only to a specified class of users, put the name of the class at the end of the entry, as in the following example:

```
message /usr/ftp/greetings/friendMSG cwd=home
➥friend
```

You can display the same message to more than one class by adding each class name to the end of the entry, separating each class name by a white space. If the messages are for anonymous or guest users, make sure that the messages are in files under the login directory.

Using the readme Command

You use the readme command to alert users that the README file has changed in a directory. The syntax of the entry is the same as that of the message command:

```
readme pathname (login ¦ cwd=dirName) [className
➥...]
```

where `pathname` is relative to the FTP login directory.

The command does not display the README file; it only alerts the user that there has been a change.

If you update all the README files, you can alert the user with the following entry:

```
readme README cwd=*
```

Using the shutdown Command

There are two ways of shutting down the FTP service:

→ Using the shutdown command in ftpaccess

→ Using the utility program ftpshut

The utility program, ftpshut, is discussed in a later section.

The shutdown command uses the following syntax:

```
shutdown   pathname
```

`pathname` is the name of a file that contains shutdown information. ftpd periodically checks for the existence of the file. If you create it, ftpd reads the file for shutdown information in the following format:

```
year month day hour minute denyTime disconnectTime
message
```

The first five fields specify the exact time of the shutdown. `month` is an integer in the range of 0 to 11, and `hour` is an integer between 0 and 23.

`denyTime` is the number of hours and minutes before shutdown time when users will be denied access to the FTP service. `disconnectTime` is the number of minutes before shutdown time when active users are disconnected from the FTP service. Both denyTime and disconnectTime use the following format:

```
HHMM
```

To deny FTP service access 1 hour and 15 minutes before shutdown, for example, denyTime would equal 0115.

The message in the shutdown file can include all the macros used by the banner and message commands, plus the following three:

Macro	Replaced By
%d	disconnectTime
%r	denyTime
%s	shutdown time

People denied access to the FTP service receive a standard `shutdown, call later` message. Current users receive the shutdown message specified in the shutdown file.

Logging User Events

The WU version of ftpd enables you to log user events, such as uploading and downloading files, by using the log commands command. You can do that only for specified user types—real, guest, or anonymous. To turn on logging, you put an entry in ftpaccess using the following syntax:

```
log commands userType [userType ...]
```

where `userType` is real, guest, or anonymous. You can specify more than one user type to log commands. Separate the user types with a white space. You have to have at least one user type to turn on logging.

The log entries appear in the syslog file as RETR and STOR commands for downloads and uploads, respectively.

If you want to log more information than that, you have to use the log transfer command. Like the log command, you can specify the user type that you want to monitor. You also can restrict the log events to downloads or uploads only.

The log transfer command has the following syntax:

```
log transfer userType [userType ...] flow [,flow]
```

where `userType` is the type of user whose actions you want to log, and `flow` is inbound or outbound. You can specify either flow or both inbound and outbound flows.

Instead of putting the logging information in syslog, log transfer puts the log information in the file defined in pathname.h; the default name is xferlog.

Understanding Log Transfer Logs

You used the log transfer command because you wanted more information than that given by the log command. The log data suffers the same fate as anything squeezed into as small a space as possible: the data is cryptic. The following is an example.

Descriptions of these fields are on the next page.

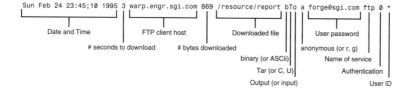

Field	Description
1–5	The first five fields are date and time information in a customary format.
6	The number of seconds it took to download the file: 3.
7	The host of the FTP client: warp.engr.sgi.com.
8	The number of bytes downloaded: 869.
9	The name of the downloaded FTP archive: /pub/report.
10	The a tells you that the downloaded file was in ASCII. The other option, b, signifies that the downloaded file was binary.
11	The T tells you that the file was archived using Tar. The other options are C (compressed) and U (uncompressed).
12	The o stands for outbound, meaning that the file was downloaded. The other option, i, inbound, means that the file was uploaded to the FTP server.
13	The a specifies that the user type is anonymous. Other options include r (real) and g (guest) user types.
14	The user's e-mail address he used as a password when logging into the FTP service: forge@sgi.com.
15–16	The last two fields involve the authentication of the user. The second-to-last field, 0, means that there is no authentication involved; you simply believe the user is who he says he is in the password entry. The asterisk (*) means that the user ID can be anything.
	If the service authenticates the user, the second-to-last field is set to 1 and the last field is the user ID. Authenticating the user involves running an authentication service on the same server as the FTP service.

You can compile this log information into an interesting set of statistics using the Perl script, xferstats, included with the WU version of ftpd. You can tell from the statistics, for example, which files are downloaded most often, or the times when people access the service the most.

Restricting Uploading

As mentioned earlier, if you are going to allow people to upload files at all, you should restrict uploads to a single directory (for this example, suppose that the directory is called /upload). You restrict uploading privileges because you need to douse the glee in hackers' eyes who have specially formulated a Trojan Horse virus designed to incapacitate your system.

To define uploading permissions, you can use the upload command in the ftpaccess file, using the following syntax:

```
upload pathName dirName yes¦no owner group mode
➥[dirs¦nodirs]
```

The yes¦no option gives you the opportunity to allowldisallow, respectively, uploading to the directory, dirName, under the file hierarchy, pathName. If you allow uploading to a specified directory, you can define the owner, group, and mode of the file. The final field, dirs¦nodirs, specifies whether users can create subdirectories in /upload.

To block all uploads to all directories under the login directory, use an entry in ftpaccess similar to the following:

```
upload /usr/ftp * no
```

This entry says that users may not upload to any directory under /usr/ftp (the login directory). To allow uploading to the file /upload, use an entry similar to the following:

```
upload /usr/ftp upload yes root engr 0600
```

This entry allows users to upload files into the /upload directory. Those files become owned by root and group engr. The mode of the file is 0600, which gives the owner read and write permissions on the file, but no permissions to anyone else. Because other users cannot read or write to the file, they cannot view or change it. This prevents users from setting up the hottest porn Internet site on your server.

Restricting Uploading by Nonanonymous Users

The upload command applies only to anonymous users. To restrict the file names that other users can upload, you use the path-filter command, which has the following syntax:

```
path-filter userType pathName expOK [expNotOK]
```

This command specifies that users of type userType may upload files consisting of file names described by regular expressions, expOK, and may not upload files consisting of file names described by the regular expressions, expNotOK.

If a file name does not contain any of the regular expressions, expOK, or it does contain disallowed regular expressions, expNotOK, ftpd does not permit the upload and, instead, displays the message in pathName to the user.

For example,

```
path-filter guest /usr/upload ^[-A-Za-z0-9] ^.
```

allows users of type guest to upload files with file names consisting of alphanumeric characters only, and not, specifically, file names containing periods.

Using the Administrative Tools

The WU version of ftpd provides three administrative tools. One tool, ftpshut, forewarns users of the service shutdown and then it shuts down the service. The other two tools, ftpwho and ftpcount, provide interesting statistics about who is using the service and how many are using it.

Using ftpshut

The ftpshut command warns users that a service is going to shut down, denies access to users because a service is shutting down, and performs the service shutdown. By default, new users are denied access to the FTP service 10 minutes before shutdown; active users are disconnected from the service, by default, five minutes before shutdown.

You can change these default values by using the –l option to set the number of minutes before shutdown that new users will be denied access to the service. You can use –d to set the number of minutes before shutdown that active users will be disconnected from the service.

The syntax of the ftpshut command follows:

```
ftpshut [-l minutes] [-d minutes] shutDownTime
➥[message]
```

where `shutDownTime` is the time the service will be shut down, and `message` is the message displayed to active users just as their connection to the service is terminated. The message can contain any of the macros available to the shutdown command, as described in the section "Using the shutdown Command."

Using ftpwho

The ftpwho command tells you how many people of each user class currently are using the archive, how many are allowed per user class, and some additional information about the service running for each user.

The format for the output of ftpwho is identical to that of your system's ps command. The following is a sample output of ftpwho:

```
%ftpwho
Service class friend:
    0  S  0  634  58  0  198 18 209ebd90 62
➥23849723 ?
        0:00 ftpd
            1 users (2 maximum)
```

Actually, there is a line similar to this one for each defined user class. The meaning of these values varies by system, so you need to check your man pages for the definition of the fields in ps.

Using ftpcount

The ftpcount command tells you the number of users per user class that currently are accessing the FTP service. It also tells you the maximum number of such users allowed at any one time, as defined by the limit command in the ftpaccess file.

The following is an example of the output of ftpcount:

```
%ftpcount
Service class friend       -     5 users ( 25
➥maximum)
```

Again, there would be a line similar to this for each user class.

Summary

In this chapter, you looked at many of the tools you can use to ensure system security, restrict user access, and monitor log files. You also saw how to make the lives of users easier by implementing aliases for files and by defining search paths. You learned how to shut down the service and use other tools to garner usage statistics that can help you anticipate how your service is growing.

As you saw in this chapter and in Chapter 9, FTP is pretty great for downloading files, but not so great at finding files in the first place. To find FTP archive files, a special Internet tool was created called Gopher. The next chapter describes how to set up such a service.

13

Setting Up a freeWAIS Service

I f your service includes an enormous database of information that you want to make available to others, you should offer a Wide Area Information Server (WAIS) service. A WAIS service allows WAIS clients and the latest version of WWW clients to search for keywords and key phrases throughout a database, and then to display the database matches. The database can contain text, binaries, and JPEG images.

WAIS was created as public domain software by Thinking Machines, a company that builds a massively parallel supercomputer called the Connection Machine. Thinking Machines developed WAIS in coordination with Apple Computer, Dow Jones, and KPMG Peat Marwick to prove that a networked information service could be created using TCP/IP (and also, what a great WAIS server a Connection Machine could be). WAIS quickly became the prototype database search engine. It became formally described as protocol Z39.50.

The popularity of WAIS grew so fast that Thinking Machines stopped supporting the public domain version of WAIS and spun off a separate company—called WAIS, Inc.—that provides and maintains a commercial version of the software. The freeware version of the software was picked up by CNIDR (Clearinghouse for Networked Information Discovery and Retrieval). CNIDR folded in enhancements from several versions of WAIS.

Currently, CNIDR maintains a version of WAIS called freeWAIS. This is the version of WAIS that is discussed in this chapter. For more information about the commercial version of WAIS, you can contact WAIS, Inc. at freeWAIS@cnidr.org.

This chapter describes the parts of freeWAIS (the indexer, the service, and the client), how those parts interact, how to compile the software, how to set up the service, and how to test the service.

Understanding the Parts of freeWAIS

freeWAIS is divided into three parts, as shown in figure 13.1:

→ Indexer

→ Service

→ Client

The freeWAIS indexer takes data stored in a database and creates an index from it. It creates, among other things, a list of words that occur in the database documents, and a table that shows where those words occur in the documents.

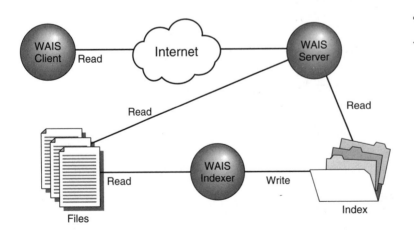

Figure 13.1

The three parts of freeWAIS.

The freeWAIS service uses the index created by the freeWAIS indexer to match data in the database document with the search criteria defined by the user. The service also is responsible for splitting up a user's natural language search criteria, using each word as a keyword, finding documents in the database that contain those words, and keeping a score that suggests to users how pertinent a document might be per given search criteria. If the freeWAIS service finds 10 documents that contain some or all of the search criteria, for example, it lists each document and gives each a score between 0 and 1,000. The higher the number, the better the document matches the search criteria.

freeWAIS clients use the Z39.50 protocol to build search criteria in the appropriate form. Clients also display the list of matching documents found by the service, and allow a user to retrieve any of the matching documents. Document types include simple ASCII text, binaries, audio files, PostScript documents, HTML documents, JPEG files, and GIF files. Figure 13.2 shows a freeWAIS client.

Figure 13.2

A freeWAIS client.

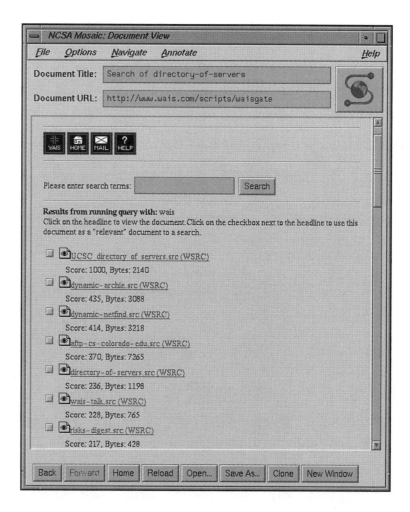

freeWAIS clients originally were available only for the Mac and text-based Unix. Today, you can find freeWAIS clients available for Microsoft Windows and graphical Unix front ends such as Motif. The latest version of WWW clients, such as Mosaic and Netscape, also act directly as a front end to freeWAIS services. The advantage of using a WWW client is that you can use it to find and graphically display information in the database. A FREEWAIS client cannot display an HTML document. Assuming that people will use a WWW client, however, you can use it to populate your WAIS database with multimedia documents. In fact, you can include just about every file format you can think of in the index, including images, sounds, videos, x-rays, PostScript files, SGML-encoded text, e-mail, Usenet news, lexicon lists, and catalogs!

An Overview of freeWAIS

This section shows you how to perform a simple search so that you can get a feeling for how freeWAIS works. Although it might be putting the cart before the horse—you don't have your service running yet—this section offers you some understanding of what freeWAIS is and how it works. The section can help you make sense of some configuration options you will choose when setting up your service.

The following example shows the output of a text-based freeWAIS client searching for documents relating to cryogenics:

```
% waissearch -h warp.engr.sgi.com -d newSource -p
➥cryogenics
```

```
Search Response:
 NumberofRecordsReturned:3
     1:Score 666, lines:      6    `after death´
     2:Score 333, lines: 369    `absolute zero´
     3:Score 333, lines: 231    `outer space´
```

The search reveals three sources of information relating to cryogenics. The scores 666, 333, and 333 are called the relevancy feedback. The higher the number (1000 is the maximum), the more likely the document discusses the search criteria, cryogenics in this case. The last field identifies the document. At this point, you choose a document by entering **1**, **2**, or **3**.

```
View document number [type 0 or q to quit]:1
Headline: after death
Researchers now use the science of cryogenics to
maintain body parts, even entire cadavers, for
weeks, months, and even years after the death of
the person. The Neptune Society maintains vaults of
cryogenic environments in which cadavers are
maintained in the hope they can be revived in the
future.
View document number [type 0 or q to quit]: q
Search for new words [type q to quit]: q
```

This abstract about the document is called a *headline*. You create one for each document in the index. The user now should know whether or not this document is the one he wants.

Following this general introduction to freeWAIS, read on to see how to build the service.

Getting the Software

You can ftp freeWAIS from ftp.cnidr.org in the following directory:

```
/pub/NIDR.tools/freewais/freeWAIS-0.5.tar.Z
```

When you look in the freeWAIS/ subdirectory, you see many versions of the freeWAIS binary. Each version is tailored to a specific platform, as illustrated in the following output:

```
ftp> cd /pub/NIDR.tools/freewais
250 CWD command successful.
ftp> dir
200 PORT command successful.
150 Opening ASCII mode data connection for /bin/ls.
total 31339
-rw-r--r-- 1 root     system    5657033 May 26
➥1993 freeWAIS-0.1.tar.Z
-rw-r--r-- 1 root     system    1580065 Oct  1
➥1993 freeWAIS-0.2.tar.Z
-rw-r--r-- 1 root     system    1583161 Oct  3
➥1993 freeWAIS-0.201.tar.Z
-rw-r--r-- 1 root     system    1580247 Oct  6
➥1993 freeWAIS-0.202.tar.Z
-rw-r--r-- 1 root     system    1956601 Jan 23
➥15:46 freeWAIS-0.3.Solaris.tar.gz
-rw-r--r-- 1 root     system     731597 Mar 21
➥1994 freeWAIS-0.3.tar.gz
-rw-r--r-- 1 root     system    1501607 Jan 23
➥15:46 freeWAIS-0.4-Alpha.tar.gz
-rw-r--r-- 1 root     system     632378 Jan 23
➥15:46 freeWAIS-0.4-Linux.tar.gz
-rw-r--r-- 1 root     system       9183 Jan 23
➥15:46 freeWAIS-0.4-RELEASE-NOTES
-rw-r--r-- 1 root     system    1428633 Jan 23
➥15:46 freeWAIS-0.4-SGI.tar.z
-rw-r--r-- 1 root     system     732808 Jan 23
➥15:46 freeWAIS-0.4-Solaris.tar.gz
-rw-r--r-- 1 root     system     849330 Jan 23
➥15:46 freeWAIS-0.4-SunOS.tar.gz
-rw-r--r-- 1 root     system    1320332 Jan 23
➥15:46 freeWAIS-0.4-Ultrix.tar.gz
-rw-r--r-- 1 root     system    1203170 Jan 23
➥15:46 freeWAIS-0.4.tar.Z
-rw-r--r-- 1 root     system     756841 Jan 23
➥15:46 freeWAIS-0.4.tar.gz
-rw-r--r-- 1 root     system     978105 May  4
➥11:32 freeWAIS-0.5-AIX.tar.Z
-rw-r--r-- 1 root     system    1177502 May  4
➥11:32 freeWAIS-0.5-HPUXv8.tar.gz
-rw-r--r-- 1 root     system    1319110 May  4
➥11:32 freeWAIS-0.5-Irix.tar.gz
-rw-r--r-- 1 root     system     821341 May  4
➥11:32 freeWAIS-0.5-Linux.tar.gz
-rw-r--r-- 1 root     system    1465558 May  4
➥11:32 freeWAIS-0.5-OSF.tar.gz
-rw-r--r-- 1 root     system      10139 May  4
➥11:32 freeWAIS-0.5-RELEASE-NOTES
-rw-r--r-- 1 root     system     712429 May  4
➥11:32 freeWAIS-0.5-Solaris.tar.gz
-rw-r--r-- 1 root     system     775051 May  4
➥11:32 freeWAIS-0.5-SunOS.tar.gz
-rw-r--r-- 1 root     system    1020826 May  4
➥11:32 freeWAIS-0.5-Ultrix.tar.gz
-rw-r--r-- 1 root     system    1231945 May  4
➥11:32 freeWAIS-0.5.tar.Z
-rw-r--r-- 1 root     system     766832 May  4
➥11:32 freeWAIS-0.5.tar.gz
226 Transfer complete.
```

The available code includes freeWAIS-0.4 and freeWAIS-0.5 for Linux, and you can select either. It would be prudent, however, to download the freeWAIS-0.5 version in order to have the lastest patches and service configurations for Linux. Because your service is pre-configured, you can skip most of the discussion of configuring the service.

If your platform is not represented in the preceding output, download the generic binary of the service—freeWAIS-0.5.tar.Z—or download freeWAIS-0.5.tar.gz if you want to use gzip rather than zcat to uncompress the file.

n o t e Version 0.5 of freeWAIS is the last version supported and developed by CNIDR. The next version of the software is called ZDIST 1.0 and, as of this writing, it is in beta form. For more information about ZDIST, see Chapter 15, "Setting Up and Managing ZDIST."

Before you go any further, you might want to check the condition of the source code. To see if there are new patches or known bugs, refer to the newsgroups comp.infosystems.wais, wais-talk@think.com, and zip@cnidr.org, each of which discusses freeWAIS.

The source code comes compressed. So, after ftping it, cd to the directory where you want the code to reside, and uncompress it using the zcat command, as shown:

```
% zcat freeWAIS-0.5.tar.Z ¦ tar xvf -
```

As the file uncompresses, it creates a directory called freeWAIS-0.5 that includes a Makefile, documentation files (including INSTALLATION, many READMEs, and RELEASE-NOTES), and a number of other directories, as shown:

```
warp 106% cd freeWAIS-0.5
warp 107% ls
ANNOUNCEMENT              README-s
➥iubio-wais.readme
COPYRIGHT                 README.gopher_and_v0.4
➥lib
DOCUMENTS                 RELEASE-NOTES
➥man
INSTALLATION             bin
➥sound.readme
INSTALLATION.auto        config.c
➥src
Makefile                 config.c.auto
➥wais-sources
Makefile.auto            doc
```

```
➥wais-test
NEXT-RELEASE             include
README                   iubio-wais.news
```

The following table describes the functions of the directories.

Directory	Description
bin	Contains the binaries you will build
config.c	Contains .c code that implements configuration information
doc	Contains helpful information, including a FAQ, written by Thinking Machines and CNIDR
include	Contains all the header files used by the service and clients
lib	Contains library functions used by freeWAIS
man	Contains man pages
src	Contains the source code for all of the executables, including waisserver, waisindex, waissearch, waisq, freeWAIS client-based on X11, and other freeWAIS clients
wais-sources	Contains the src file for the directory of Internet servers that your WAIS clients can access
wais-test	Contains sample scripts for the indexer and service

Understanding Files in the src Directory

Many important files that you need to customize are in the src directory. The following table explains what these files are.

File	Description
src/indexer	waisindex source code
src/server	waisserver source code
src/ir/	The WAIS toolkit library
src/client/	Client programs source code tree
src/client/ui/	Example routines for user interfaces
src/client/emacs	GNU Emacs client interface
src/client/swais/	Character-based (VT-100 compatible) client
src/client/waisq/	Command-line client
src/client/waissearch/	Command-line client
src/client/x	An X-based (X11R5), Motif client

Now that you have the service software, you need to configure the service by editing the Makefile, config.h, and server.h (and, optionally, the included freeWAIS clients). After editing these files, you run % make default. But let's examine the configuration options first.

Editing the Makefile

The Makefile contains a large list of variables; you will need to set many of them. The first variables you set are standard programs and the locations of Unix commands. The following table describes these settings:

Standard programs or commands	Description
CC	Equals the name of your system's ANSI C compiler: gcc or standard cc.
RANLIB	Set this variable equal to the path name to your system's ranlib command. On SGI and HP machines, because there is no ranlib command, uncomment the line, RANLIB=true.
RM	Set this equal to the absolute path to the rm Unix command on your system (for example, /bin/rm).
MV	Set to Unix move command, mv.
MAKE	Set to standard make program (for example, make).

freeWAIS supports ANSI C. freeWAIS can use GNU CC and non-ANSI C compilers, however, because of the addition of many library routines. If you have a choice, set CC to the ANSI C compiler, CC.

Editing the Directory Paths

You must set the TOP variable equal to the absolute path of the freeWAIS source directory. The other subdirectories get positioned under the TOP directory. *Unless* you are working in SunOS, uncomment the following line in the Makefile:

```
#TOP;sh=pwd
```

The preceding instruction assumes that you build the service in the current directory. Then you should comment out the line marked comment me. If you are using SunOS, do not uncomment the TOP line, because the line following comment me sets TOP correctly. You can change the location of subdirectories, such as INCLUDE, BIN, AND LIB; however, not many good reasons exist for doing so.

Setting Library Variables

Most of the default settings in this part of the Makefile will probably suit your system. You should, however, look at least at the following variables:

→ **RESOLVER.** Set equal to nothing unless your system uses a namespace resolver, in which case you set the variable equal to –Iresolv.

→ **CURSELIB.** Set the version of the curse library.

Setting Compiler Options

The CFLAGS (compiler flags) variable sets the default flags you use when you compile. Table 13.1 describes these options.

The Makefile has CFLAGS defined for many different platforms. If you find a CFLAG for your platform, uncomment it. Otherwise, set your own CFLAGS. An example follows:

```
CFLAGS=-I$ (INCLUDE) -DTELL_USER -DSECURE_SERVER
➡-DRELEVANCE_FEEDBACK -DUSG -DSOUND -DBOOLEANS
```

The Makefile has several other, highly specialized flags that are not of general interest. If you are curious (or work for NASA), look in the Makefile.

Building X and Motif Clients

The Makefile builds the following freeWAIS clients by default:

→ swais

→ waisq

If you want to build an X client—xwais—you must uncomment the following line in the Makefile:

```
#cd x; (env TOP=$(TOP) CC=$(CC) \
    CFLAGS="$(CFLAGS)" MAKE="$(MAKE)" ./makex
```

You can find the preceding under the following line:

```
xwais: libftw libs ui
```

Table 13.1 Compiler Options

Flags	Set This Flag For
	Architecture-Specific Flags
–cckr	Irix version 4+ (SGI)
–DBSD	Pre-4.3 versions of BSD
–DBSD43	4.3+ versions of BSD
–DSYSV	System V Unix (AT&T)
–DUSG	Versions of Unix that include dirent routines in the C library
–M3e–Zi	XENIX
–DNeXT-posix	NEXTSTEP
–A_UX	A/UX
	Indexer and Server Flags
–DBIO	This flag adds indexing for biological symbols and terms. Unless you are in the same business as Darwin, you might pass on this flag.
–DBOOLEANS	When you search for a phrase such as `white night`, the default is to score a hit if `white` OR `night` is found. If you compile waisserver with –DBOOLEANS set, you also can use the Boolean operators AND and NOT. This is a good flag to set.
	Conventional FREEWAIS clients store descriptions about your service options automatically in /wais-sources. Because users can read this file, tell them about the Boolean options available and other significant flags you have set.
–DDUMP_CORE	Setting this flag dumps the core when waisserver aborts. This is a good option to set when you are debugging the server. If your disk space is limited, however, you should recompile with this flag unset when you are done testing the service so that your disk space is not eaten up by core dumps.

continues

Table 13.1, Continued

Flags	Set This Flag For
	Indexer and Server Flags
–DEND_MERGE	Setting this flag makes waisserver wait until the end of its search to merge index files. This flag uses additional disk space compared to the default method, which merges indexes as the service is running. Unless you have a good reason, do not set this flag.
–DLIST_STEMS	Setting this flag instructs the indexer and service log to record the stem of words.
–DLITERAL	Setting this flag enables you to search for strings in a document. The strings must be enclosed in single or double quotation marks. The words `I hope I find this phrase´, for example, must exactly match a phrase in a document for a hit. If you use double quotation marks, you must use escapes with them—for example, \"I hope I find this phrase\". Make sure not to include extra white spaces at the beginning or ending of the phrase unintentionally.
	There are a couple of potential problems when using literals with waisserver. To register a hit, the first word in the phrase must be indexed and not be in the stoplist (described later). The other problem is that waisserver uses stemming, which often conflicts with literal. *Stemming* is the process of removing endings to words, such as *es*, *ing*, and *s*. Stemming is used to generalize a search so that `hoping to see you´ scores a hit when waisserver finds `hope to see you´. If waisserver stems `hoping´, however, to `hop´, it might not score a hit when literal is set and the document contains `hoping´. Ironically, `hoping to see you´ might not hit `hoping to see you´, because it is stemmed to `hop to see you´. You might think twice before setting this flag.
–DNEED_VSYSLOG	If you choose to set the –DUSE_SYSLOG flag and your system does not have the vsyslog() function, you must set this flag.

Flags	Set This Flag For
	Indexer and Server Flags
–DPARTIALWORD	Setting this flag enables users to search using the asterisk (*) wild card. The asterisk can represent zero or more alphanumeric characters, as in the following example: "lad*" matches "lad," "lady," "ladies," "ladel," "ladelling," "ladder," and "latent" (it scores a hit for misspelled words too!). This is a good flag to set.
–DRELEVANCE_FEEDBACK	Setting this flag to On allows FREEWAIS clients to use documents found in previous FREEWAIS searches as search criteria for a new FREEWAIS search. This is a good flag to set.
–DSECURE_SERVER	This flag enables the system administrator to reset the uid under which the service runs using the –u argument after startup.
–DTELL_USER	Using this flag gives the service your user ID at connect time.
–DBIGINDER	Use this flag if you have to index many documents.
–DSTEM_WORDS	Here's that stemming option discussed earlier with –DLITERAL. When the flag is set, waisserver shaves standard endings off words, such as *s*, *ing*, *es*, and *ly* to create, in effect, a wild-card search, so that `surely` scores a hit when finding `sure`. This is a good flag to set.
–DUSE_SYSLOG	Setting this flag makes waisserver log events to syslog rather than using fprintf.

You can use imake to build a Motif version of the freeWAIS client. Look in the Imakefile in /freeWAIS-0.5/src/client/x for the following line and uncomment it:

```
LOCAL_LIBRARIES = $(UI_LIB) -lXm $(XAWLIB)
➡$(XTOOLLIB) $(XMULIB) $(XLIB)
```

The preceding line includes the Motif library (–lXm) in LIBS.

If your C compiler cannot use ANSI prototypes, you need to uncomment the following line in Imakefile:

```
CDEBUGFLAGS = -g -Bstatic -DUSE_ALTFONT -DMOTIF -
➡D_NO_PROTO
```

Look in your C libraries to make sure all of the symbols are defined.

Building the Service

Now that you have finished customizing the build instructions in the Makefiles, make sure you are at the top directory and type the following:

```
% make default
```

If your build does not work, find out whether your operating system does not pass environment variables in Makefiles. If it does not, you have to edit the CFLAGS line in the Makefile.

Also, double-check the Makefile. Many platform-specific settings are commented out. An example follows:

```
# SGIs want this uncommented
# SHELL=/bin/sh
```

It is easy to overlook them. Do a search on your platform name. An example follows:

```
:/sgi
```

If you are reading this section out of frustration because nothing you do seems to make the build work, take solace in the fact that you are not the first to experience build problems. There are many, many specific errors you can get information about by reading the Internet newsgroup comp.infosystems.wais. See whether your problem already has been addressed by the newsgroup. If it has not, pour out your heart on the Internet. Hopefully, someone will come to your aid.

Testing Your freeWAIS Service

Before you open shop on your freeWAIS service, you need to test it. Complete the following two tasks:

1. Use the indexer to index some files.

2. See whether the freeWAIS clients you just built can use the indexes.

The following sections look at each of these steps.

Indexing Files

The first thing you want to do is create directories for the index files, as in the following example:

```
% mkdir /wsindex
```

Index files should be easy to find and manipulate, so locate the index directory at the root or in some logical place.

Also, make a directory for the freeWAIS server log files, as in the following example:

```
% mkdir /usr/local/logfiles
```

Now you need something to index. You need a directory with one or more files in it. You might use, for example, the files in a pubs directory. At this stage of the game, keep the size of the file(s) small—this is just a test, after all.

Run the indexer—waisindex—on your directory of files (to see whether the indexer works):

```
# waisindex -d test -t one_line /usr/resources
```

Use the -d option to define the name of the source test file, and the -t option to specify how you want the file indexed. /usr/resources is the location of sample files.

The –t option has two possible values: one_line and text. The one_line option indexes each line of a document. If waissearch finds a keyword match in a document, it can retrieve the specific line where the match occurred. With the text option, on the other hand, if waissearch finds a keyword match, it must retrieve the entire document. The default is text.

waisindex creates a source file—test—that waissearch can search through for matches with user-specified selection criteria. A freeWAIS source file is an indexed database consisting of a set of files. Chapter 14, "Managing a freeWAIS Service," discusses freeWAIS sources in greater detail.

Using freeWAIS Clients to Find Documents

Included in the software distribution is a directory called wais-test. In it is the script, test.waisindex, which creates the following four WAIS databases:

➜ **test-Bool.** An index of three small documents illustrating the Boolean capability and the use of synonyms. Use the Boolean condition, and, to search for "black and fox." Then, in the document called Bool.syn, search for synonyms; for example, "lazy dog" and "lazy mutt" return the same documents even though the word "mutt" is not in the documents.

➜ **test-Comp.** An index that demonstrates the indexer can handle compressed source files, a compressed mail folder, and document type "mail_or_rmail" in this example.

➜ **test-Docs.** An index of files in the /doc directory, showing the directory recurse switch and plain ASCII document indexing.

➜ **test-Multi.** An index of GIF images and text caption files demonstrating the multi-document-type capabilities of the indexer. Use the X-based freeWAIS client (or a graphical browser, such

as Netscape or Mosaic) to search for "gumby." (The other freeWAIS clients do not support multiple document types.)

Starting and Checking Your Service

As with the other services, you have the option to start your service by itself or to have it started and terminated by inetd. The trade-offs are the same: the consumption of CPU time (if the service runs constantly) versus the slow startup time (because the configuration files must be read) if triggered by inetd. If your service is not used often, let it run under inetd. If your service is contacted frequently, start the service yourself and let it run.

Starting waisserver with inetd

There are several reasons why you might want waisserver to run under inetd:

➜ Without inetd, you must have a waisserver running continuously so that it can listen to port 210.

➜ Some operating systems, like HP-UX, can limit access to services running under inetd.

To start waisserver with inetd, you must perform the following tasks:

1. Add an entry to the /etc/services file or the NIS database that looks similar to the following:

   ```
   z3950    210/tcp  #freeWAIS service
   ```

   This entry just says the service is running on TCP port 210.

2. Add an entry to the inetd.conf file similar to the following:

```
z3950 stream tcp nowait root /usr/local/bin/
➥waisserver\
waisserver.d -u peasant \
-e /usr/local/log/logfile \
-d /usr/local/index_location
```

waisserver is the name of the service, and the –u option designates the service to run as user peasant (with restricted permissions) after it starts. The –e option names the log file—logfile—to use, and the –d option names the default location of the indexes.

After the service is running, you do not want to run it as root, because a software bug might permit a mischievous user access to the system as root. The user peasant is someone who cannot log in; he has permission only to read document and index files, and to write all the log files.

To make the change in the configuration file take effect, first find the process ID (pid) of inetd, as follows:

```
# ps -ef ¦ grep inetd
```

Then, send a hang-up (HUP) signal to the inetd process, as in the following example:

```
# kill -HUP pid
```

pid is the process ID of inetd.

Check the syslog file to make sure that the service was added. The log file should contain an entry similar to the following:

```
inetd[111]: z3950/tcp: Added service, server
    /usr/local/etc/waisserver
```

Starting waisserver without inetd

You might choose to start waisserver from the command line to avoid the delay incurred by inetd as it starts the service.

To start the service from the command line, you use the same command syntax as you used with inetd, except that you have to include the –p option, as in the following example:

```
# waisserver -u peasant -p -l 10 \
    -e /usr/local/log/logfile \
    -d /usr/local/index_location
```

Use the –p option to tell waisserver to listen to a specific port: the one specified after –p, or the one defined in /etc/services (210) if no port number follows –p. Generally, you do not want to follow the option with a port number.

You need to leave the service on port 210 so the rest of the world can access it. You can, however, run different versions of the service on different ports. The software distribution even includes a file called start.myserver; it contains the startup commands for the service to run on port 1024.

All port numbers less than 1023 require root privileges to run. If you change the port to a number greater than 1023, you can let an engineer who is extending the functionality of the service start and stop the service without root access.

After testing your service (described in the next section), you might choose to start the service automatically at system startup.

Testing waisserver

Now that you have waisserver installed and running, it's time to test it. You can do that by creating a new source (src) file with waisindex with the export command, and then using waissearch to search the source. But first, remove the test.src file created earlier:

```
$ rm test.src
```

Create the index file using waisindex, as in the following example:

```
$ waisindex -d /etc/hosts -t one_line -export test
```

The export option adds the domain name and the IP address of the freeWAIS server, and the port number on which the freeWAIS service runs.

Now run waissearch on the file and test for the occurrence of a word—in this case, "found":

```
$ waissearch -p 210 -d test found
```

```
Search Response:
NumberOfRecordsReturned: 1
1: Score: 666, lines: 20 `23.43.241.32 found´
```

```
View document number [type 0 or q to quit]:
```

If you look at the syslog file, and if you are running the service under inetd, you should see an entry like the following:

```
Connection from warp (23.43.241.32) at Fri Mar 3
➡18:32:42      1995
```

This entry shows that your freeWAIS client—running on the machine, warp—is connected to your service over the Internet. That's good news!

If you do not see a message like this, make sure that you have defined the correct path name to the service in inetd.conf. You also might try using telnet to connect to port 210. If you do not get a connection, the service is not starting.

After you confirm that the service is working, you are ready to move it to its permanent position in your file structure and let people in your company try it out.

Letting the World Know about Your Service

Once you are confident that your service is stable, you should let everyone know it is up and running. You do that by sending an entry to the Directory of Servers, at quake.think.com and cnidr.org. The following command indexes your service's files, yourFiles, and registers the index with the Directory of Servers.

```
# waisindex -export -register yourFiles
```

Before you make your service available, however, you might first read in the next chapter about making your service secure.

Altering the Service and Clients

The software distribution enables you to alter the service and the clients, should you want to. The file, ir.c, is a service toolkit. The file, ui.c, is a client toolkit. These files allow you to customize the service and clients to your needs.

Summary

This chapter takes you all the way from defining freeWAIS to configuring a freeWAIS service. Along the way, you find out where to get the source code for the service, indexer, and clients; how to build the service; how to run it; and how to test it. Finally, you see how to let others know that your service is up and running.

Now that you have a freeWAIS service running, you need to manage it and create freeWAIS sources. The next chapter describes how to do those tasks.

Managing a freeWAIS Service

Now that you have freeWAIS up and running, you

have some important tasks to perform. You must

make the service as secure as possible. You must

also provide content for indexing and distribution.

This chapter describes all the waisindex options

and all the document types that it can index.

Making waisserver Secure

Chapter 8, "Making Your LAN Secure," discusses security issues in greater detail and suggests industrial-strength security systems. There are several important things you can do with WAIS service directly, however, to increase its level of security.

Changing the User

Because waisserver runs on port 210, a Unix reserved port, you must start the service as root. All processes binding to waisserver must also run as root.

Because devious minds love to gain root access to a system, it is prudent to change the user of waisserver right after it starts. You can do that by using the –u option. You associate a user ID with the option, for example:

```
# waisserver -u engr -l 10 -e /usr/local/wais
➥/server/server.log -d /usr/local/wais
```

To change to the user ID specified by the –u option automatically after service starts up, include the –DSECURE_SERVER option in your CFLAGS definition.

The user ID you use with the –u option should have very restricted permissions. If someone gains access to the system, you do not want them to have root permissions, only the permissions of the user ID. So, set the permissions with the worst-case-scenario in mind.

Restricting Service Access

You can restrict the clients that use waisserver by domain name. You can specify the domain names of hosts you want to service by:

→ Uncommenting the following line in ir.h:

```
#define SERVSECURITYFILE        "SERV_SEC"
```

→ Including the domain names in the file whose name is defined by the SERVSECURITYFILE variable in ir.h; the default is SERV_SEC. You have to create the SERV_SEC file. If it does not exist, the service grants every client access.

Place the SERV_SEC file in the same directory as the index files. Make sure that it is readable by the user waisserver is running as, but modifiable only by root (or the freeWAIS system administrator).

Each entry in SERV_SEC must have the following format:

```
domainName    [IP address]
```

domainName is the domain name of a host. The domainName is required; the IP address is optional. If you provide an optional IP address, clients then can gain access to the service by virtue of their domain name or IP address. If, for some reason, the host name does not match the IP address, access is given to both the domain name and the IP address; freeWAIS does not treat this as an error.

To grant access to your service only by folks at Silicon Graphics and the host warp.engr.mit.edu, for example, your SERV_SEC would look like the following:

```
sgi.com         198.33.422.12
warp.engr.mit.edu
```

Notice that you have to use the entire domain name to identify a host.

If you use an IP address in SERV_SEC, you have to be careful not to inadvertently grant access to more networks than you intend. If you grant access to

198.33.233.1, for example, waisserver permits access to all addresses that have the same prefix, including 198.33.233.10 through 198.33.233.19. Be careful to provide the full address.

Likewise, you can inadvertently grant access to more than one network. If you define the network as 198.23, for example, networks 198.230 through 198.239 gain access to the system. To permit access to the entire network 198.23 but not 198.230 through 198.239, use a trailing period—for example, 198.23.

Controlling Access to Sources

You can restrict the clients that use the database by domain name. You can specify the domain names of hosts you want to service by:

→ Uncommenting the following line in ir.h:

```
#define DATASECURITYFILE        "DATA_SEC"
```

→ Including the domain names in the file whose name is defined by the DATASECURITYFILE variable in ir.h; the default is DATA_SEC. You have to create the DATA_SEC file. If the file does not exist, every host has access to every source. If the file does exist and a source is not named in the file, no one has access to the database.

Place the DATA_SEC file in the same directory as the index files. Make sure that it is readable by the user waisserver is running as, but modifiable only by root (or the freeWAIS system administrator).

The entries in the DATA_SEC file must have the following format:

```
dataBaseName     domainName      [IP address]
```

Only domainName and [IP address] have access to dataBaseName. The domain name is required; the IP address is optional.

waisserver enables you to use the asterisk (*) wild card to make your life easier. For example,

```
welcome       *       *
```

grants all hosts access to the database welcome.

If you provide an optional IP address, clients then can gain access to the database source by virtue of their domain name *or* IP address. If, for some reason, the host name does not match the IP address, access is given to both the domain name and the IP address; freeWAIS does not treat this as an error.

To grant access to your database source only by folks at Silicon Graphics and the host warp.engr.mit.edu, for example, your DATA_SEC would look like the following:

```
welcome     sgi.com            198.33.422.12
welcome     warp.engr.mit.edu
```

Notice that you have to use the entire domain name to identify a host.

If you use an IP address in DATA_SEC, you have to be careful not to inadvertently grant access to more networks than you intend. If you grant access to 198.33.233.1, for example, freeWAIS permits access to all addresses that have the same prefix, including 198.33.233.10 through 198.33.233.19. Be careful to provide the full address.

Likewise, you can inadvertently grant access to more than one network. If you define the network as 198.23, for example, networks 198.230 through 198.239 gain access to the system. To permit access to the entire network 198.23 but not 198.230 through 198.239, use a trailing period—for example, 198.23.

A Security Caveat

As mentioned before, the industrial-strength security comes from constructing a firewall that separates your local network from the Internet. Firewalls prevent Internet requests from reaching you directly. That means that returns from a freeWAIS service cannot reach your machine on the local network. (ftp requests fail for the same reason.)

To get around this problem, you have to set up the computer that functions as your company's gateway to the Internet (that contains the firewall) as a forwarding freeWAIS server. The following two steps enable you to do that:

→ Change the ui/source.c code.

→ Modify the source description files used by your freeWAIS clients.

In ui/source.c, there is a commented-out line that starts with

```
/* #define FORWARDER_SERVER
```

That is just what you want to define. Uncomment the line and follow it with the domain name of the Internet gateway machine. Call it fire.bus.com, for example:

```
/* #define FORWARDER_SERVER "fire.bus.com"
```

The source description files for your freeWAIS client start something like the following:

```
(:source
    :version 3
```

```
    :ip-address "198.33.22.11"
    :ip-name "rocket.science.edu"
    :tcp-port 210
    :database-name "rockets"
    .
    .
    .
```

Change the `ip-address` and `ip-name` definitions to that of the Internet gateway machine, and modify the entry for the `database-name`, as in the following example:

```
(:source
    :version 3
    :ip-address "198.55.44.33"
    :ip-name "fire.bus.com"
    :tcp-port 210
    :database-name "rockets@rocket.science.edu"
    .
    .
    .
```

After you make these changes, it appears that the freeWAIS client has direct access to the Internet when, in fact, it is using the Internet host as an intermediary.

Providing Content

Now that you have a running, secure service, it is a good idea to offer some content, at least a little more than the files generated by the waisindex.test script described in the preceding chapter. The job of populating the database with source material is an ongoing one. It requires an understanding of the subject matter and the means by which it might be searched.

The primary tool used to create free sources is *waisindex*. The terminology surrounding waisindex is a bit tricky. waisindex takes data files of all types and creates seven or more index files that contain, for example, a list of each unique word used in a document. These index files are combined into one database called *WAIS source*, or just *source*. The waisserver compares the WAIS source with search criteria supplied by the WAIS client requests to see if there is a match.

Understanding What waisindex Does

waisindex extracts from the raw data files (that WAIS is indexing) all the pertinent data it needs to fill multiple index files used by waisserver to match search criteria to data files.

 In this chapter, *data file* is used as a generic term to represent all file types, such as text and GIF.

Parsing the data files before a WAIS client makes a request reduces the amount of time it takes waisserver to determine to what extent there is a match between search criteria and the data files. The only downside is that the WAIS sources consume a significant amount of disk space, often equaling the size of the raw data files.

The command-line options you can use with waisindex follow:

Command-Line Option	Description
−a	Appends to existing index
−contents	Indexes file contents
−d	Specifies the base file name for the index files
−e filename	Specifies log file for error information; default is stderr, or /dev/null if −s is selected
−export	Adds host name and tcp port to the source description to enable Internet access
−l	Specifies log level
−M	Links data files of multiple types
−mem	Restricts memory usage during indexing; the higher the number, the faster the indexing
−nocontents	Prevents the indexing of file contents
−nopairs	Prevents adjacent, capitalized words from being indexed together

continues

Command-Line Option	Description
–nopos	Prevents proximity of keywords in data file from influencing relevance feedback
–pairs	Indexes adjacent, capitalized words together
–pos	Uses proximity of keywords in data file to influence relevance feedback
–r	Indexes subdirectories recursively
–register	Registers your sources with the Directory of Services
–stdin	Enables you to enter file names from the keyboard (standard input)
–stop	Specifies a file that contains stopwords
–t	Specifies data file type
–T type	Sets the type of data file to *type*

You should use the –a option when you just want to update the index files. This saves the time it would take to regenerate all of the files. If a file that was indexed is changed, and the update contains the new index entries, however, the old index entries remain. These old entries both take up space and may lead to erroneous results. Periodically, you must reindex all of the files.

To save disk space, you can exclude the contents of files from being indexed by using the –nocontents option. Even with this option, the header and file name are still indexed. The default is –contents, include the contents of the file in the index.

The –d option specifies the base file name of the index files. For example, if you use

```
-d /usr/local/common
```

the index files are called /usr/local/common.dct, /usr/local/common.fn, and so on.

The only logging levels that have meaning are as follows:

0   do not log

1   log errors and warnings of very high priority

5   log medium priority events, including indexing filename information

10   log every event

WAIS Index Files

Let's look in more detail at the seven index files that waisindex creates from raw data files. Six of the seven are not human readable. The Source Description (.src) file is meant to be read by people.

Inverted File (index.inv)
The Inverted file contains a table that associates the following elements:

➜ Every unique word found in all the data files

➜ A pointer to all the data files a word is in

➜ The importance of the word in the data file, based on how close the word is to the beginning of the data file, and the number of times the word occurs in the data file divided by the number of words in the data file. The higher the percentage, the more likely the word describes the subject matter of the data file.

Document File (index.doc)

The Document file contains a table associating the following elements:

➜ **filename_id.** Specifies which database file the data file is in (there can be more than one database file of data files)

➜ **headline_id.** A pointer to the associated headline for the data file

➜ **start_character.** The location of the start of a data file in the database file

➜ **end_character.** The location of the end of a data file in the database file

➜ **document_length.** The number of characters in a document

➜ **number_of_lines.** The number of lines in a document

➜ **date.** The date the document was created

➜ **time_t.** The time the document was created

Filename File (index.fn)

The Filename file contains a table that lists the file names of the database along with their write-dates and the type of file each is.

Headline File (index.hl)

The Headline file is a table that contains a list of all the headlines of all the documents in the source. A *headline* is a short description of the data file that is returned to the WAIS client when the data file appears to satisfy the search criteria.

Dictionary File (index.dct)

The Dictionary file contains a list of every unique word in the data files. These words are arranged alphabetically. Each word is matched with a pointer to the Inverted file so that, when the search criteria matches one of the words in the Dictionary file, waisserver can tell which data file the word is part of.

Source Description File (index.src)

The Source Description file contains basic descriptions of the source information, including the following:

➜ The name and IP address of the host on which it runs

➜ The port the service monitors

➜ The source's name

➜ Cost information for using the source

➜ The e-mail address of the person maintaining the source

➜ The headline

➜ A description of the source

If a source description file already exists, waisindex does not create a new one unless you have edited it enough so that waisindex considers it significantly different from the original version. If you change basic information about the source, like the host it runs on, you can delete the file and rerun waisindex to make sure the changes are reflected in the source file. If you choose to add a description of the source, you must maintain that manually.

waisindex does not really supply much of a description of the source. Because this is a file designed to be read by others, you might want to beef up the source description. You also might specify a different e-mail address for people to consult if you know who is charged with maintaining the source.

Here's an example of a source file:

```
(:source
     :version 2
     :ip-address "198.32.121.3"
     :ip-name "kiln.asd.sgi.com"
     :tcp-port 210
     :database-name "graphics libraries"
     :cost 0.00
     :cost-unit :free
     :maintainer "librarian@kiln.asd.sgi.com"
     :subjects "major graphics libraries"
     :description
"Server created with WAIS-8 on Mon Mar 5 04:45:32
➥by warp@sgi.com"
```

As you can see, the description section is a little wanting. It would be worth your while to add to it.

You also might supply an alias for a source maintainer to avoid the problem of trying to keep in each source file who maintains the source.

Status File (index.status)

The Status file has a table that contains user-defined parameters.

Determining the Relevance Ranking

waisindex uses an algorithm to determine, as best it can, how closely a source matches the search criteria supplied by the WAIS client. The algorithm returns a number between 0 and 1,000, with 1,000 being a perfect match, based on the following factors:

→ **Word location.** waisindex uses the position of the word in the source to assign it a high, medium, or low value. If the word appears in the headline, the data file receives the highest value. If the word is capitalized in the data file, the data file receives a medium value. If the word simply occurs in the body of the data file, it receives the lowest value.

→ **Word occurrence.** waisindex divides the number of times a word occurs by the number of words in a data file. The higher the fraction, the more likely the search criteria describes the subject matter of the data file, and the higher the relevance ranking.

→ **Word commonality.** If waisindex finds a word in many documents, the word is given less value in determining the relevance ranking than if the word had been found in only one document. The idea behind this calculation is that if 100 data files use a word, probably none of them are about the word; whereas, if only a few data files contain a particular word, chances are higher that those data files actually are about the word. If waisindex finds the word "entomology" in 1,000 data files, for example, it's hard to know which, if any, of the data files really are about entomology. If, however, only two data files contain the word, chances are better that the main theme of one or both of the data files is entomology.

→ **Word groupings.** If the selection criteria is a group of words, waisindex assigns a data file a higher relevance ranking if the words occur together than if they occur far apart in the data file. If the search criteria is "cost of living," for example, finding that phrase or "of living costs" is more likely to satisfy the search requirements than if the words were spread throughout a data file.

Stopwords are words that are too common to warrant indexing. Common stopwords are "and," "a," and "the." freeWAIS version 0.4 comes with 389 predefined stopwords in the src/ir/stoplist.c file. If you want to add more stopwords for all documents, simply add to the stoplist.c file.

If you want to add more stopwords for specific documents only, create your own stopword file that includes all the words in /stoplist.c plus your additions. To use this file, use the –stop *<filename>* option with waisindex, where *filename* is the name of the stopword file.

You must include in your file all the stopwords in /stoplist.c, because waisindex does not use /stoplist.c if another stop file is named on the command line with the –stop option.

Indexing Different Data File Types

You have to tell waisindex what kind of information is contained in a data file so that it can index it correctly. Currently, waisindex can handle more than 30 data file types. To see all of the supported types, execute the waisindex command with no arguments, as follows:

```
# waisindex
```

The types describe the following:

→ The content of the data file

→ What to use as the headline

→ Whether to index the contents of a file

→ How a data file is divided

If a data file consists of a TIFF image, for example, you probably do not want the binary code indexed. Usually, one document is in one data file. However, waisindex can index separately many documents in one file if they are separated by at least 20 dashes.

To define a data type when indexing a data file, use the –t option, as in the following example:

```
% waisindex -d newSource -t text -r /usr/resources/*
```

This line indexes all the subdirectories under /usr /resources as type text.

The most common data file types follow:

Data File Type	Description
dash	Tells waisindex that more than one document is in each file, and that the documents are separated by 20 or more dashes. Each dash-delimited document is indexed separately, and the first line of each document is used as a headline.
dvi and ps	Indicate printer-oriented formats (device-independent TeX and PostScript). waisindex assumes that there is one document in each file, so it indexes each file separately, and uses the file name for the headline.
filename	Handled identically to the text type, except that the file name, instead of the path name, is used as the headline.
first_line	Handled identically to text, except that the first line of the data file, instead of the path name, is used as the headline.
ftp	Contains ftp code so that users can ftp from another server. waisindex indexes the README and INDEX files on remote servers. WAIS clients can search this index and then ftp the file automatically if there is a match. This is an uncommon file type, but a very powerful one.
GIF, PICT, and TIFF	Used with files of images in their respective formats. waisindex assumes that one image is in each file, but it does not index the contents of the file. It simply uses the file name as the headline so that users can search by image name (or, at least, by file name).
mail_digest	Takes standard Internet mail and indexes them as individual messages. The subject field of each message is used as a headline.
mail_or_rmail	Takes standard Unix mailbox files (mbox) and indexes them as individual messages. The subject field of each mailbox file is used as a headline.
netnews	Enables waisindex to index each standard Internet News file separately. For headlines, waisindex uses the subject field of each file.
one_line	Splits up a file into sentences; each sentence is indexed separately. The sentence is its own headline. Because this data file is indexed line by line, waissearch can be very specific about locating the search criteria in a document. This data file type, however, is memory intensive.
text	Indexes the entire file as though it were one document. The path name is used as the headline. This type is the most common.

URL   Enables waisindex to use, as headlines for files, valid URLs by stripping off part of a path name and replacing that part with another path-like description. For example,

```
% waisindex -d newSource -t URL /usr/resources ftp://kiln.asd.sgi.com -r /usr
➥/resources/*
```

indexes the files in all the subdirectories under /usr/resources. It provides as a headline for each file its path name, stripped of /usr/resources, and replaced by http://kiln.asd.sgi.com. So, if waissearch found that file /usr/resources/alpha/beta matched the selection requirements, waissearch would display the headline as `http://kiln.asd.sgi.com/alpha/beta`. This format enables your WAIS service to support WWW browsers. The only downside to the URL data file type is that older WAIS clients also return URL-valid headlines. If users are unfamiliar with URLs, they might be confused by the path name.

Be careful to use the correct data file format when indexing your files. Indexing files incorrectly can prevent them from being viewed. Some WAIS clients, such as xwais, use the data file format to determine what kind of viewer to use to display a data file. If you format a GIF file as PICT, for example, GIF viewers cannot view the GIF file because it is indexed as a PICT file.

everything works fine as long as the WAIS client understands the format. waisserver sends the data file to the client as if it were a binary file.

If a data file type is indexed by default and you do not want the content of the file to be indexed, use the –nocontent option.

Indexing Undefined Data File Types

waisindex can index just about every kind of file that exists. There are some file formats that it cannot index, however, such as MIME files. For such a condition, you use the –T option (instead of –t) to declare the format of the file. The default action is not to index the contents of the file and to use the file name as the headline. If you want the contents indexed, you add the –contents option (it has no argument) to the waisindex command. Even though waisindex does not understand the data file format,

Making Data Files Available to WWW Browsers

You can make your WAIS source files searchable by multimedia WWW browsers, such as Mosaic or Netscape. To do so, execute waisindex with the –T option. For example:

```
% waisindex -d WWW -T HTML -contents -export /usr
➥/resources/*html
```

Now WAIS clients can do keyword searches on HTML documents.

Indexing Multiple Files for WWW Browsers

Sometimes it is nice to give users a little more than they asked for. If the user does a search on the words "Tasmanian Devil," for example, it might be nice to let the user know that not only does your source have a document about the devil, but it also has a video clip and still image of the devil. To associate each of these files with one another, you have to format the names of the files correctly.

To associate files, all the *base names* (the part of the name before the period and the extension) must be the same, and the extensions must be in all capitals. Your directory might look like the following:

```
% ls
Devil.TEXT
Devil.GIF
DeviL.MPEG
```

You use the –M option to associate the files, as in the following example:

```
% waisindex -d Tasmanian -M TEXT,GIF,MPEG  -export *
```

Now when one of the files is selected, the WWW browser displays buttons that lead to the other, associated files.

Linking Files

You also can use the –a option to append files—especially files of different types. When people get your file about rockets, for example, you also might want them to get a nifty image in a GIF file. Generally, sources contain one data file type specified by the –t option. So how do you link files of different types?

You cannot actually mix the data file types, but you can append one data file type to another. In this case, you might index the text files about rockets and then append the image files, using –a, as in the following example:

```
# waisindex -d rockets -t text -r /usr/resources
➡/aerospace
# waisindex -d rockets -t gif -a -r /usr/resources
➡/aerospace/images
```

Using the –a option in this way enables text to be displayed as text and images to be displayed as images; and the source, rockets, contains both text and images.

Using Synonyms

Another way to lead users to related files is by setting up synonyms. Synonyms alleviate several problems, such as when a user looks up "stars," but not "astronomy," or the user looks up "TV" when your documents only use the term "television." When a user specifies a keyword, waisserver automatically looks up the synonyms as well, as defined in SOURCE.syn, which is located in the same directory as the other source files, such as SOURCE.cat.

Each entry in the SOURCE.syn file has the following syntax:

```
reference_word synonym [synonym...]
```

For example, you might have the following entry:

```
work job occupation employment joke
```

As a conscientious Internet system administrator, you want to take a look at the log files for waisserver. If you have the log setting at 10, you can see what words people are using as search criteria. If you see that the service did not return any documents for a keyword, you might consider whether there is a synonym that would have satisfied the search criteria.

Specifying Source Options

There are several things you can do with source files:

→ Name them with the –d *<name>* option

→ Export them with the –export option

→ Register them with the –register option

→ Update them with the –a option

Throughout this chapter, the examples have used –d to name the source file that is created by waisindex. The –export option adds the name of the host and the TCP port on which the service is running to the source file. The clients use this information. If the –export option is not used, the service can only be used for local searches.

One service that everyone uses is called the *directory of services*. It lists all the source files (src) submitted to it. If anyone wants to find out what is new on the Internet, this is a logical place to look. The –register option automatically sends all your source files to the directory of services.

The system administrators of the directory of services reserve the right to delete your offering from the service if they find that your service often is down, or that it is not updated on a regular basis.

After you create source files, you need to update them when the files they represent change. You can update the source files in several ways, as follows:

→ Reindex all the files using waisindex

→ Reindex a subset of the files

→ Append changes to the end of the source file using the –a option

Reindexing all the data files could be quite time-consuming, depending on the number and size of the data files. Periodically, you have to bite the bullet and perform this function, but it is not something you want to do every time one of the data files changes a little.

If you put all your changes to the data files in one file, you can reindex just that file. Otherwise, you can add the changes to the end of the current source file by using the –a option with the waisindex command.

The larger your source, the larger the problem reindexing is. When you reindex, your service is unavailable to users. So, if your indexing takes an hour or more, you might want to consider alternatives to turning off your system. You have the following two options:

→ Create the new source in a different directory and then move or rename the new source so that it replaces the old one

→ Add on to the end of the file using the –a option

The first option is nice only if you have disk space to hold multiple copies of your source—a luxury that some cannot afford. You can create a simple cron job that executes waisindex in a directory other than your production directory. When it finishes, simply mv the new source to the production directory and remove the source in the nonproduction directory.

To add source information to the current source for a new set of files, use the –a option, as in the following example:

```
# waisindex -d Cats -t URL -a -r /usr/resources
➥/felines/newSpecies
```

Logging Messages During Indexing

waisindex can send status messages to a log file if you use the –e and –l options, where the argument of –e is the path and name of the log file, and the –l option defines the logging level.

Logging levels range from 0 to 10. Following –l with 0 turns off logging. Level 1 logs only high-priority messages, level 5 also logs medium-prioity messages, and level 10 logs all messages. The log messages just relate the status of the indexing process.

Indexing Controls

You might have directories that you do not want waisindex to index—for example, image files and files in the /tmp directory. To exclude the files in a directory from being indexed, include that directory's name in the command line:

```
% waisindex -d presidents /tmp
```

If, on the other hand, you want waisindex to recursively index directories, use the –r <directoryName> option:

```
% waisindex -d Devils -r /usr/resources/Tasmanian
```

This line indexes all the files under /Tasmanian and creates a source file called Devils.

Relative Position of Words

When the search criteria contains more than one word, it is possible to take into account how close the words are in a document when computing the relevancy score. The default, however, is not to use that information in the relevancy score. To override the default value, use the –pos option. (The reverse option is –nopos.)

If two capitalized words are adjacent, waisindex adds them together to the dict file. If you know that this is inappropriate for your document, use the –nopairs option.

Freeing Memory and Disk Space

WAIS source files find a way to ravenously eat up disk space, and waisindex loves to consume CPU cycles. If you find that your disk space is low or your system performance is poor, you can use two options with waisindex to conserve disk space: –mem and –nocat.

The mem <numberMbytes> option enables you to specify the maximum number of megabytes of memory you want waisindex to use. Of course, when you restrict the amount of memory waisindex can use, you slow down its execution. If you have to run waisindex in the background, consider using this option.

Summary

This chapter discussed how documents were assigned relevance rankings. You learned about some of the 30 data file formats that waisindex can handle automatically. You also found out how to accomplish a variety of other tasks, including how to link files, use synonyms, update the indexes, register your service with the directory of services, and conserve memory and disk space.

15

Setting Up and Managing ZDIST

When Thinking Machines created WAIS, they standardized their work on the Z39.50 protocol. Because the protocol was limited, however, Thinking Machines added a set of extensions to the protocol, which was renamed Z39.50-1988 (reflecting the year the extensions were added). This protocol, then, is what is used in WAIS.

While WAIS clients and servers gained popularity, work was done to enhance the Z39.50 protocol. The robust version of the protocol was named Z39.50-1992. This protocol has become nationally and internationally accepted as the new standard for networked information search and retrieval protocols. Unfortunately, the two protocols, Z39.50-1988 and Z39.50-1992, are not interoperable. For example, a WAIS client cannot communicate with a service based on the Z39.50-1992 protocol.

 CNIDR's goal is to make future versions of ZDIST backward-compatible with WAIS—but that could take years.

CNIDR, the organization that maintains freeWAIS, decided to switch to the 1992 protocol because of its enhanced features. In so doing, they had to write new service software because the incompatible protocols prevented the new service from using any of the freeWAIS code. Instead of naming the new service freeWAIS 1.0, they chose a new name, *ZDIST* (from the Z39.50 protocol name), to reflect its disassociation from the freeWAIS code.

 As of this writing, ZDIST is in beta testing. Although you can download the service software, you might be better off to wait for the product to mature. To keep abreast of developments, explore the URL, http://cnidr.org/welcome.html.

ZDIST Distribution Software

The ZDIST service, by CNIDR, complies with ANSI/NISO Z39.50-1992, including the following software:

→ ZDIST service (ZServer is a Unix server daemon)

→ Unix client (ZClient doubles as an HTTP gateway)

→ HTTP to Z39.50-1992 gateway

→ E-MAIL to Z39.50-1992 gateway

→ Search Application Programmers Interface (SAPI)

ZServer

ZServer is a small, fast service that mounts database systems to provide ANSI/NISO Z39.50-1992 standardized access to those database systems. ZServer provides robust search and retrieval tools to "deep search" databases not offered by services based on other protocols.

You can run ZServer in standalone mode or under inetd. In both cases, you can limit the number of simultaneous sessions.

ZServer works on the most popular flavors of Unix.

Overview of the ZServer Installation

To install and configure ZServer, use the following procedure.

1. Download the software through CNIDR's WWW document, or ftp it directly using the same name:

   ```
   ftp://ftp.cnidr.org/pub/NIDR.tools/
   zdist/zdist102b1-1.tar.Z
   ```

 As of this writing, the current beta version of the software, beta 1.1, is called zdist102b1-1.

2. Uncompress the software using the uncompress command, as follows:

```
% uncompress zdist102b1-1.tar.Z
```

3. Dearchive the file with the tar command, as follows:

```
% tar xvf zdistX.X.tar
```

4. Change to the zdist1.0 directory, as follows:

```
% cd zdist102b1-1
```

5. Read the README file.

6. Edit the Makefile.

7. Type the following:

```
% make
```

8. Edit (or create) the service configuration file zserver.ini.

Configuring ZServer

After building ZServer, you should use your favorite editor to edit (or create) ZServer's configuration file, zserver.ini. (I'll give you a sample configuration file a bit later.)

The zserver.ini file has two kinds of entries: directives and group names. Group names are enclosed in square brackets. The following list of directives belong in that group, and represent related functionality, for example:

```
[default]
ServerType=
MaxSessions=
Port=
```

In the preceding example, the Server Information Group called default contains three directives.

The configuration file has two groups:

→ Server Information Group

→ Database Information Group

You must have a Database Information Group for every database listed in the DBList directive.

ZServer Configuration Directives

When you edit the configuration file, you must use the directives exactly as shown in the following table. When you give the directives values, you cannot leave a space between the equals sign and the value.

The following sections define the meaning of the directives.

ServerType ServerType can have one of two values: INETD or STANDALONE. This variable controls how ZDIST is run on the server. If you choose INETD, INETD is responsible for starting the service whenever a service request comes to the server, as well as spawning a new service process for each concurrent service request. Each process exits after it services the request.

If you choose STANDALONE, ZDIST spawns a service process for each concurrent request. MaxSessions specifies the maximum number of concurrent requests that can be serviced. Generally, you should use STANDALONE for its superior efficiency to INETD. If, however, you debug the service, you should set the ServerType directive to INETD.

MaxSessions The value of the MaxSessions variable represents the maximum number of concurrent sessions that ZDIST can service. The default value is 10. This value has no effect if ServerType is set to INETD.

Port The port value specifies the port to which the server listens. The default value is 210. This value has no effect if ServerType is set to INETD.

TimeOut The TimeOut value specifies the number of seconds ZDIST should wait for a new request before exiting the session. The default value is 3,600.

Trace Trace can have two values: ON or OFF. This option turns on or off logging of debugging information to the file specified by TraceLog.

TraceLog TraceLog specifies the file where you want to keep debugging information. The default filename is zserver_trace.log. This value only has meaning if the Trace directive is turned on.

AccessLog AccessLog specifies the file in which you want to keep client access information. The default file name is zserver_access.log.

ServerPath ServerPath specifies the pathname to zserver.ini. ZDIST occasionally rereads the configuration information and uses the value in this directive to find it. The default value is the current working directory.

DBList Set DBList equal to a comma-separated list of all databases available on your server. Do not include any white spaces in the list. Make sure to update this list if you add new databases to your service.

Type The Type directive can have two values: SCRIPT or NTSS, depending on the type of database. You must have a Type directive in each database group (and not in the default group). The default value is NTSS.

Location The syntax of the Location directive depends on the value of the Type directive. If the Type value is NTSS, the Location directive should equal the path to the NTSS database. If the Type value is SCRIPT, the Location directive should equal the path to the shell script (or application) that conforms to the requirements of the SCRIPT search engine. You must include this directive in every database group.

Results The Results directive has meaning only if you set the Type directive to SCRIPT. It defines the absolute pathname to a temporary file needed by the SCRIPT search engine.

Sample Configuration File

The following configuration file, zserver.ini, is the sample provided by CNIDR at the following URL: `http://vinca.cnidr.org/software/zserver/zserver_ini.html`.

```
This configuration file, zserver.ini, configures
the server to operate as a forking daemon accepting
no more than 50 simultaneous connections. The
server listens for client connections on port 2210
and writes debugging information to the file /tmp
/zserver_trace.log. Two databases are available
for searching by clients: MyNewServer and ManPages.
Both of these databases are indexed by the SCRIPT
type search engine and each has its own Location
(script) and Results file location
(temporary file needed by the SCRIPT type search
engine).
# This is the Server Information Group
[Default]
ServerType=STANDALONE
MaxSessions=50
Port=2210
Trace=ON
TraceLog=/tmp/zserver_trace.log
ServerPath=/usr/users/zdist1.02/bin
# Each name listed below should have a
➡corresponding Database Information Group
DBList=MyNewServer,ManPages
# This is one of the two Database Information
➡Groups
[MyNewServer]
```

```
Type=SCRIPT
Location=/usr/users/zdist1.02/bin/MyNewServer.sh
Results=/tmp/MyNewServer
# This is the second of the two Database Informa-
➥tion Groups
[ManPages]
Type=SCRIPT
Location=/usr/users/zdist1.02/bin/ManPages.sh
Results=/tmp/ManPages
# This is a special diagnostic group. If you want
➥the error messages
# changed, do so here.
[1.2.840.10003.3.1]
1=Permanent system error
2=Temporary system error
3=Unsupported search
4=Terms only exclusion (stop) words
5=Too many argument words
6=Too many boolean operators
7=Too many truncated words
8=Too many incomplete subfields
9=Truncated words too short
10=Invalid format for record number (search term)
11=Too many characters in search statement
12=Too many records retrieved
13=Present request out of range
14=System error in presenting records
15=Record no authorized to be sent intersystem
16=Record exceeds Preferred-message-size
17=Record exceeds Maximum-record-size
18=Result set not supported as a search term
19=Only single result set as search term supported
20=Only ANDing of a single result set as search
➥term supported
21=Result set exists and replace indicator off
22=Result set naming not supported
23=Combination of specified databases not supported
24=Element set names not supported
25=Specified element set name not valid for
➥specified database
26=Only a single element set name supported
27=Result set no longer exists - unilaterally
➥deleted by target
28=Result set is in use
29=One of the specified databases is locked
30=Specified result set does not exist
31=Resources exhausted - no results available
32=Resources exhausted - unpredictable partial
➥results available
33=Resources exhausted - valid subset of results
➥available
100=Unspecified error
101=Access-control failure
102=Security challenge required but could not be
➥issued - request terminated
103=Security challenge required but could not be
➥issued - record not included
104=Security challenge failed - record not included
105=Terminated by negative continue response
106=No abstract syntaxes agreed to for this record
107=Query type not supported
108=Malformed query
109=Database unavailable
110=Operator unsupported
111=Too many databases specified
112=Too many result sets created
113=Unsupported attribute type
114=Unsupported Use attribute
115=Unsupported value for Use attribute
116=Use attribute required but not supplied
117=Unsupported Relation attribute
118=Unsupported Structure attribute
119=Unsupported Position attribute
120=Unsupported Truncation attribute
121=Unsupported Attribute Set
122=Unsupported Completeness attribute
123=Unsupported attribute combination
124=Unsupported coded value for term
125=Malformed search term
126=Illegal term value for attribute
127=Unparsable format for un-normalized value
128=Illegal result set name
129=Proximity search of sets not supported
130=Illegal result set in proximity search
131=Unsupported proximity relation
132=Unsupported proximity unit code
```

Currently Supported Search Engines

ZDIST currently supports two search engines: ISEARCH, an NTSS search engine, which is the default engine; and SCRIPT, which offers similar functionality to ISEARCH, but is more kludgy. Both engines are included in the software and written by CNIDR. SCRIPT tests the Search API. Patches are for bug fixes and enhanced functionality when you create a less-than-elegant application. ISEARCH supersedes SCRIPT.

For more information about ISEARCH, see the following URL:

```
http://vinca.cnidr.org/software/isearch
➥/isearch.html.
```

For more information about SCRIPT, see the following URL:

```
http://vinca.cnidr.org/software/sapi/engines.html.
```

 If you want to use a custom search engine with the Search API, you must write a database driver that communicates between your system and the Search API. Although a Search API makes that task easier, the only documentation is the code itself, libsapi/sapi.c, in the sapi distribution.

Starting ZServer

You can start ZServer from the command line (if the Type directive is STANDALONE) or from inetd.

To start ZServer from the command line, use the following syntax, where *pathName* is the absolute pathname to zserver.ini, and *SIG* specifies a Server Information Group to use rather than [default]:

```
% zserver [-ipathName/zserver.ini[,SIG] \
    [-odirectiveName=value]]
```

Here are several examples:

To start ZServer with default values, type the following:

```
% zserver
```

To use a Server Information Group other than [default], type a command similar to the following, where *infoGroupName* is the name of the Server Information Group:

```
% zserver -i/pathName/zserver.ini,infoGroupName
```

To specify a non-default value for a directive, type a command similar to the following, where *directiveName* is the name of the directive and value is its value:

```
% zserver -i/pathName/zserver.ini
➥-odirectiveName=value
```

If you want to start ZServer using inetd, add the following entry to your /etc/services file:

```
zserver 210/tcp # CNIDR ZServer
```

and add the following entry to /etc/inetd.conf:

```
zserver stream tcpnowait root \
    /home/zdistX.X/bin/zserver zserver -i/home
➥zdistX.X
```

If you have trouble, make sure you have defined the path to zserver.ini correctly.

Testing ZServer

After you build and configure ZServer, CNIDR provides a test search page so that you can check the functionality of your installation. The test search page is at the following URL:

```
http://vinca.cnidr.org/software/zdist/zserver
➡/servercheck.html.
```

Summary

CNIDR decided to take advantage of the enhanced functionality described in Z39.50-1992. By making that choice, they divorced their code from the original WAIS code written by Thinking Machines.

This chapter showed how to install, configure, start, and test ZServer. The software, as of this writing, is still in beta form. Before switching from freeWAIS 0.4 to ZDIST 1.0, consult the newsgroups to see if the software is bug free.

16

Setting Up a Gopher Service

If you have ever run around a file system using simple Unix commands, such as ls and cd, you are familiar with the model Gopher uses to display files and directories on Gopher services. When you log onto a Gopher service and do not specify a directory to look at, the Gopher service automatically sends you a directory listing (like ls) of the root directory of the Gopher service, as shown on the next page.

```
     Internet Gopher Information Client v2.0.16

          Home Gopher server: corp.sgi.com
-->    1. Introduction
       2. Preface
       3. New Developments/
       4. Special Effects/
       5. Magic Carpet/


Press ? for Help, q to Quit              Page:1/1
```

The preceding shows a combination of files and directories, just like a Unix listing. If you want to retrieve a file or move to a different directory, you simply select the one you want.

Although there are similarities between Gopher and basic Unix directory navigation, there are important differences:

→ The Gopher listing contains headers and footers and an arrow that shows the entry you selected to retrieve. ls, on the other hand, only lists names of files and directories.

→ The names of files and directories displayed by Gopher are long and descriptive, whereas Unix file and directory names are generally not as long.

→ Files (and directories) in Gopher lists can reside on different machines, whereas files in a Unix directory are generally on the same machine.

→ When you select a file on a Gopher service, it downloads to the (Gopher) client machine. On a Unix system, you never download from a directory listing.

→ The commands you use to access files and directories often are displayed at the bottom of the screen (which eliminates the burden of

remembering Gopher commands), whereas Unix commands go only on the current command line.

The descriptive file (and directory) names give users some indication of what they can expect to find in a file. This is a nice feature; however, the limitations on the length of the name often pose problems and create confusion. Gopher+ solves this problem.

Gopher provides a transparent interface between services residing on different machines, so the user appears to access files from only one machine when, in reality, each file listed might reside on a different machine. These files can be offered by other Gopher services or other services altogether, such as an FTP service. This transparency eliminates the mental baggage imposed by FTP that forces you to consider the machine a document resides on.

Gopher services take care of other details automatically. If you download a compressed text file, for example, Gopher uncompresses it. If the file is archived, Gopher can untar it. If you download an image, Gopher generates an external viewer to display the image.

Gopher provides other features that make it as different from ls and cd as a seed is from a full-grown plant. For example, Unix Gopher can do the following:

→ Search local WAIS indexes

→ Send queries to remote WAIS services and return results to Gopher clients

→ Send queries to remote FTP services and return results to Gopher clients

→ Answer queries sent by WWW clients that use HTTP or built-in Gopher querying methods

Other software supports Gopher; some of the more interesting products are listed in Appendix B, "Free Software on the Internet." Here are some highlights:

Program	Description
Fwgstat	Creates a usage report of the service.
Glass	Produces 22 different service reports.
GLOG	Analyzes Gopher log files.
gopherdist	Returns the contents of any directory or file in Gopher-space.
Gophreport	Generates reports based on a variety of factors.
jughead	Stands for *Jonzy's universal Gopher hierarchy excavation and display*. Retrieves menu information from Gopher services.
Linkmerge	Merges directories from a selected set of Gopher services to which you can add your own Gopher resources.
veronica	Stands for *very easy rodent-oriented net-wide index to computerized archives*. Provides the capability to search, by keyword, most Gopher-service menu titles in all the Internet-connected Gopher services.

The location of the source code for these programs is presented in Appendix B. As you can see, Gopher is well supported.

Versions of Gopher

There are two versions of Gopher that you can use:

→ Gopher

→ Gopher+

Gopher is freeware; Gopher+ is not. This chapter discusses the installation of Gopher+, because its added functionality makes it worth the licensing fees. If you choose to install Gopher, however, because Gopher+ is a superset of Gopher functionality, many of the installation options are the same. When in doubt, look at the INSTALL file that comes with the source code.

The following section presents an overview of Gopher+. Because Gopher+ contains all the functionality of Gopher, those functions are not repeated in the Gopher+ section.

A section at the end of this chapter describes the future of Gopher: GopherVR. Yes, virtual reality! It's a 3D version of Gopher. GopherVR is in the alpha stage of development, so it is not quite ready to use as a service yet. By the beginning of 1996, however, you should think about replacing Gopher or Gopher+ with GopherVR.

Introducing Gopher+

Even a good thing can get better; such is the case with Gopher. Gopher+ incorporates all of Gopher's features and enables you to perform additional tasks:

→ Retrieve extended information, called *file attributes*, about a Gopher file

→ Return several files when selecting just one menu item—for example, a plain text and a PostScript version of the same text

→ Retrieve a description of the file, called a *file abstract*

→ Retrieve documents based on forms filled out by the user

These Gopher+ features only work with Gopher+ clients (and WWW browsers). Gopher clients can access Gopher+ services, but Gopher clients cannot use any of the advanced features. Likewise, Gopher+ clients can access Gopher services.

Understanding Gopher and Gopher+ File Attributes

File attributes provide valuable information about files. Gopher file attributes include the following:

Attribute	Description
Host	Name or IP address of the service host
Name	Name of the file as shown in the menu
Path	Path and name of the file—for example, top/intro
Port	Port number (usually 70) associated with the Gopher service
Type	Type of document file
URL	WWW URL path name

The Type attribute identifies what a menu item is in a Gopher listing. Gopher recognizes a variety of menu item types, including the following:

Type Reference Number	Type of Document
0	File
1	Directory
2	CSO (qi) phone-book server
3	Error
4	BinHexed Macintosh file
5	DOS binary archive of some sort
6	Unix uuencoded file
7	Index-Search server
8	Points to a text-based telnet session
9	Binary file
g	GIF type
h	html type
I	Image type
I	Inline text type
M	MIME type; item contains MIME
P	Adobe Portable Document Format (PDF)
s	Sound type; data stream is a mulaw sound
T	TN3270 connection

Gopher+ adds the following attributes to the Gopher list:

Attribute	Description
Admin	Name and e-mail address of the system administrator responsible for the file or directory
Document Type	Description of the file type—for example, text/plain
Language	Language in which the document is written
ModDate	Date file or directory was updated last
Size	Size of file in bytes

In addition, the abstract of the file provides valuable information for people trying to find topics without having to download the file and read it. You can get this information by pressing the equal sign (=) when the Gopher arrow is pointing at a menu item. The following printout shows what you get with a Gopher client when you push the equal sign when "Introduction" is selected.

```
Link Info (ok)                              100%
+--------------------------------------------+
#
Type=1
Name=Introduction
Path=top/intro
Host=corp.sgi.com
Port=70
URL: gopher://corp.sgi.com:70/top/intro
A Gopher+ display looks more like the following:
Link Info (ok)                              100%
```

The following is a display of a Gopher+ client for the same file, "Introduction." Compare the Gopher and the Gopher+ displays to see the differences.

```
+-------------------------------------------+
#
Type=1
Name=Introduction
Path=top/intro
Host=corp.sgi.com
Port=70
Admin=Rick <gopherAdmin@corp.sgi.com
ModDate=Sat Apr 9 09:18:53 1995 <19950410091853>
URL: gopher://corp.sgi.com:70/top/intro

ABSTRACT
-------------------------------------------+
```

```
The introduction describes the layout of resources
on this Gopher service. This file can save you time
in searching for documents.
```

Size	Language	Document Type
— —	— — — —	— — — — —
8k	English (USA)	text/plain
14k	English (USA)	application/ ➡FrameMaker

```
+-------------------------------------------+
[Help: ?]  [Exit: u]
```

The Gopher+ attribute listing shows that the Introduction comes in two formats: one is in plain text, and the other is in the FrameMaker format. If you select the Introduction, which version of the Introduction you get depends on the Gopher client. The simple Gopher client enables you to choose between the two versions.

Using Gopher+ Forms

In Gopher+ menu listings, menu items followed by <??> indicate that they display forms after you select them. The following shows an example of such a listing.

```
       Internet Gopher Information Client v2.0.16


            Home Gopher server: corp.sgi.com


 -->     1. Introduction
         2. Newsletter Sign-up <??>
         3. New Developments/


Press ? for Help, q to Quit           Page:1/1
```

If you select menu item 2, the Gopher service returns a form for the user to complete (see fig. 16.1).

Choosing the Service Software

There are three major sources for Gopher service software:

→ University of Minnesota (freeware version 1.3) Gopher

→ University of Minnesota version 2.13 Gopher+

→ GN Public License

The University of Minnesota is the major development site for Gopher service software. The earlier version of the service software, 1.13, is free to all. However, the University is no longer adding functionality to Gopher. Their effort is going into Gopher+.

The later version of the software, 2.1.3, is free if you are creating a Gopher service for an educational institution. There is, however, a licensing fee for businesses using the service. The fee structure is described in the next section. The 2.1.3 version of the software has had additional enhancements applied and is now in beta test under the revision level of 2.1.4beta.

The GN version of Gopher is similar to the freeware version of the University of Minnesota's. This software doubles as a WWW service. It is a nice combination and deserves your attention.

 GN's WWW service, at present, is not robust. It does not, for example, support the Common Gateway Interface (CGI).

 Most of the installation and configuration information for Gopher is identical to that for Gopher+. When in doubt, refer to the INSTALL file that comes with the software.

```
┌──────── Mailing List Sign-up ────────┐
│          Magic Carpet Newsletter       │
│                                         │
│  Name: _____  │
│  E-Mail: _____   │
│  Phone #: _____   │
│  Street: _____   │
│  City, State: _____   │
│  Zip, Country: _____   │
└─────────────────────────────────────┘
```

Figure 16.1

A Gopher+ form.

Licensing Gopher+

The Gopher+ team at the University of Minnesota felt it necessary to start charging for the service software because of the exigencies of being a cost center at the university.

There are three general classes of Gopher+ service providers:

➜ Government and educational institutions

➜ Businesses that produce a gross income of less than $3.5 million per year

➜ All other businesses

All licenses expire one year after the effective date of the agreement.

Small Business Fee Structure

The Gopher+ license fee is $100 if the following conditions are met:

➜ The service does not offer products or services for sale.

➜ There is no charge for access to or information retrieved from the service.

The Gopher+ license fee is $500 if the following conditions are met:

➜ The service is accessible from the Internet.

➜ Products and services are offered for sale through the service.

➜ There is no charge for access to or information retrieved from the service.

The Gopher+ license fee is $500 or 2.5 percent of the total amount charged to Gopher service users (whichever is larger) if the following condition is met:

➜ There is no charge for access to or information retrieved from the service.

Standard Fee Structure

The Gopher+ license fee is $100 per service if the following conditions are met:

➜ The service does not offer products or services for sale.

➜ There is no charge for access to or information retrieved from the service.

The Gopher+ license fee is $2,500 per service if the following conditions are met:

➜ The service is accessible from the Internet.

➜ Products and services are offered for sale through the service.

➜ There is no charge for access to or information retrieved from the service.

The Gopher+ license fee is $2,500 or 2.5 percent of the total amount charged to Gopher service users (whichever is larger) if the following conditions are met:

➜ There is no charge for access to or information retrieved from the service.

➜ The business is not an educational or governmental institution, and it earns over $3.5 million per year.

Getting the Service Software

To get the software for Gopher+, use ftp to get the source from the following host:

```
% ftp boombox.micro.umn.edu /pub/gopher/Unix
```

I had trouble with this address, but the IP address worked fine:

```
% ftp 134.84.132.2
```

You also can point your WWW browser at URL:

```
ftp://boombox.micro.umn.edu/pub/gopher;
```

To contact the University of Minnesota, you can send e-mail to gopher@boombox.micro.umn.edu. Or, send a letter to this address:

> Internet Gopher Developers
> 100 Union St. SE #190
> Minneapolis, MN 55455
> Fax: (612) 625-6817

After connecting and logging into boombox, which, because of its popularity, is no small feat, you should change to the correct directory (Unix), list the contents, and pick out the latest version of the software. Because the 2.1.3 version is the most popular at this time, our discussion focuses on this implementation. You might want to use the 2.1.4beta, and the instructions here are equally applicable. The following shows what appears on-screen during the file transfer.

```
ftp> cd pub/gopher/Unix
250 CWD command successful.
ftp> ls
200 PORT command successful.
150 Opening ASCII mode data connection for /bin/ls.
total 10194
-rw-rw-r— 1 1147 bin 29865 Feb 26 08:32
➥2_1_2to2_1_3.patch
drwxr-xr-x 9 1147 bin 1536 Mar 24 08:22 GopherTools
-rw-r—r— 1 1147 bin 648 Aug 24 1994 MIRROR.LOG
-rw-r—r— 1 1147 bin 972547 Oct 7 1991
➥NeXTtext.tar.Z
drwxr-xr-x 2 root bin 512 Sep 2 1994 ask-examples
...
```

```
-rw-r—r— 1 1147 bin 306508 Mar 8 1994
➥gopher1.13.tar.Z
drwxr-xr-x 2 1147 bin 512 May 31 1994 gopher2.0-
➥patches
-rw-r—r— 1 1147 bin 426337 Jun 30 1994
➥gopher2.016.tar.Z
-rw-rw-r— 1 1147 bin 579000 Feb 26 08:26
➥gopher2_1_3.tar.Z
...
226 Transfer complete.
```

Use the FTP get command to download the service software, as shown in the following.

```
ftp> get gopher2_1_3.tar.Z
local: gopher2_1_3.tar.Z remote: gopher2_1_3.tar.Z
200 PORT command successful.
150 Opening BINARY mode data connection for
➥gopher2_1_3.tar.Z (579000 bytes).
226 Transfer complete.
579000 bytes received in 32.30 seconds (17.51
➥Kbytes/s)
```

You find the source code listed in your current directory as the following:

```
gopher2_1_3.tar.Z
```

You need to uncompress and tar this file by using the following command:

```
warp 149% zcat gopher2_1_3.tar.Z ¦ tar -xvf -
```

Your workstation then very happily spits out gobs of update information that you do not have to pay attention to unless you see error messages.

```
warp 149% zcat gopher2_1_3.tar.Z ¦ tar -xvf -
tar: blocksize = 16
x gopher2_1_3/doc/INSTALL, 4311 bytes, 9 blocks
x gopher2_1_3/doc/Makefile, 534 bytes, 2 blocks
x gopher2_1_3/doc/TODO, 686 bytes, 2 blocks
x gopher2_1_3/doc/admit1.setup, 759 bytes, 2 blocks
x gopher2_1_3/doc/client.changes, 38996 bytes, 77
➥blocks
```

```
x gopher2_1_3/doc/clientlogging.vms, 9612 bytes, 19
➥blocks
x gopher2_1_3/doc/gindexd.changes, 2819 bytes, 6
➥blocks
x gopher2_1_3/doc/gindexd.doc, 6666 bytes, 14
➥blocks
x gopher2_1_3/doc/gopher.1, 7440 bytes, 15 blocks
...
```

If you list your current directory, you see that a new directory was created:

```
%ls
gopher2_1_3
gopher2_1_3.tar.Z
```

When you change to the new directory, gopher2_1_3, and list the contents, you see the files and directories, shown as follows:

```
Copyright    Makefile.config.dist  doc       make.com
MANIFEST               README        gopher    object
Makefile               conf.h        gopherd   patchlevel.h
Makefile.config        copyright     gophfilt  test
```

The contents of these files follow:

Directory	Description
conf.h	A list of service and client configuration options.
doc	A directory that contains the documentation for all parts of the software distribution, including the Gopher service, the Gopher client, revision notes (*.changes), installation (INSTALL), and configuration notes.
gopher	A Gopher, text-based client application.
gopherd	The Gopher+ service application.
gophfilt	A Gopher filter program.
make.com	Some routines that make uses when running on a VMS machine.
Makefile	The Makefile you use to build the service and client applications.
Makefile.config	The list of compile-time variables you can configure before running Makefile. You should edit this file and conf.h, not the Makefile file, when specifying configuration options.
Makefile.config.dist	A reference copy of Makefile.config so that you always can revert to it.
MANIFEST	A list of all the files in all the directories in gopher2_1_3.
object	A directory of, among other things, libraries, sockets, and arrays used by the service and client applications.
patchlevel.h	#defines of the version numbers of the service and client applications.
README	The file that describes some of the directories in the distribution and recognizes individuals for their contributions.
test	A directory that contains, among other things, sample data.

Gazing into the Future of Gopher Services

The next release of Gopher will be a complete re-write of the code, called GopherVR. It uses 3D scenes as a user interface for surfing the Internet and displaying relationships between documents. The alpha version of Unix GopherVR clients is available by using Gopher and anonymous FTP from

boombox.micro.umn.edu

in /gopher/Unix/GopherVR. You can retrieve the code by using the following URLs:

GOPHER://boombox.micro.umn.edu/11/gopher/Unix/
GopherVR
FTP://boombox.micro.umn.edu/pub/gopher/Unix/
➥GopherVR/

GopherVR binaries (only) are currently available for SUN Sparc, SGI, DEC Alpha OSF/1, IRIX, Linux, Solaris x86, and IBM AIX RS-6000 platforms.

In this alpha-test release, you can do the following:

➜ Browse through Gopher directories by driving around Gopherspace

➜ Move between Gopher services by driving through 3D scenes

➜ Open objects by clicking them

➜ Retrieve information about the neighborhood you are in

➜ Retrieve descriptive information about objects

The GopherVR client requires that the system be running X-Windows and have a color display. It is still very much in the experimental stages at this time. For the latest information about GopherVR, subscribe to gopher-news by e-mailing to this address:

gopher-news-request@boombox.micro.umn.edu

Major Gopher software releases are announced on gopher-announce. To subscribe to gopher-announce, send e-mail to this address:

gopher-announce-request@boombox.micro.umn.edu

The Future of GopherVR

Future versions of GopherVR will incorporate the following features:

➜ Definition of 3D icons for objects in Gopherspace

➜ Placement of objects in 3D scenes

➜ Additional navigation features that enable users to browse in the 3D scenes

Summary

This chapter introduced you to Gopher and Gopher+. It highlighted the differences between them. You learned how to download the source code for Gopher+. You then saw how to compile the code, install it, and publicize the service. The chapter finished with a crystal-ball look into the near future when Gopher clients take on a new look—where the search for documents in Gopherspace becomes a journey through a 3D virtual reality.

Managing a Gopher Service

Managing a Gopher service is crucial to its success.
As a system administrator, you are responsible for
the architecture of the file system and the naming
of files and directories. The choices you make, in
this regard, determine the usability of the service
interface—no small responsibility!

Your job also includes reviewing the log files to see
how often your service is being used, and to see
which files and directories are used. Also, you need
to set a number of configuration variables.

Editing the gopherd.conf File

The gopherd.conf file sets configuration options for the Gopher service. The settings are straightforward. You might not need to change any settings from their default values. In this section, you examine all the options. Remember, changing the configuration can be as simple as uncommenting or commenting out a line in the configuration file. Don't delete lines; that action can come back to haunt you.

Creating an Alias for the Service

It is not a good idea to tie a specific machine to your Gopher service. There are times when you might replace the machine or split the Gopher service across machines. Instead, you should create an alias for the machine. Then, when you move your service to a new machine, you simply point the alias at it.

To create an alias, you use the hostalias keyword:

```
hostalias: host_alias
```

where `host_alias` is the alias for your server that is returned to Gopher/Gopher+ clients. Before a client can access a Gopher/Gopher+ service using the host_alias name, you must create an entry in your Domain Name Service (DNS).

Setting Cache Times

You can set the length of time a cache file remains valid by using the Cachetime keyword:

```
Cachetime: time_seconds
```

where `time_seconds` is the duration in seconds of the cache file. To hold a file for 180 seconds, for example, use this entry:

```
Cachetime: 180
```

Checking File Decoders

When users request a file, they can add an extension to it, such as .Z or .gz. Gopher recognizes these extensions and, in this case, compresses the file using zcat before sending it to the client. The file decoder section of the configuration file links extensions to associated programs.

gopherd.conf, by default, has two file decoders enabled and two commented out (with the pound sign).

```
decoder: .Z /usr/ucb/zcat
decoder: .gz /usr/gnu/bin/zcat
#decoder: .adpcm /usr/openwin/bin/adpcm_dec
#decoder: .z /usr/gnu/bin/zcat
```

In this example, the .Z extension accesses the compression program, zcat, located in /usr/ucb. You might find other extensions to include in this section—for example, tar.

Limiting Concurrent Sessions

The PIDS_Directory variable identifies the location of the file that specifies the maximum number of concurrent service requests the service will handle. The more requests, the slower the performance. The fewer the requests the service accepts, the more frustrated users get who cannot access the service. You must find your own middle ground between system performance and satisfying user demand.

This part of the service, as of this writing, is still under major revision. You might want to ignore this variable until it becomes more stable.

The default in the configuration file is

```
#PIDS_Directory: /pids
```

As you can see, it is commented out by default. If you choose to uncomment it, make sure the file that contains the information, /pids in this example, is in part of the file system restricted by chroot().

Setting Maximum Number of Clients

You can use the MaxConnections keyword to define the maximum number of clients you want your service to handle. To have a maximum of 20 concurrent users, for example, use the entry:

```
MaxConnections: 20
```

Figuring Out File Contents

Gopher must know the correspondence between file extensions and gopher formats. The mapping, defined in gopherd.conf, establishes a standard notation so that Gopher clients know whether they need to generate an external viewer to display Gopher information. The format for the mapping follows:

```
viewext: ext go-type pfx gopher+type ISO_language
```

in which **viewext** is the keyword that establishes the mapping. Explanations of this syntax follow:

Elements of viewext Entry	Description
ext	File extension
go-type	Gopher type number, as defined in the previous chapter
pfx	A prefix for the service's selector string
gopher+type	MIME document type
ISO_language	ISO abbreviation for the language of the document

For example,

```
viewext: .txt 0 0 Text/plain En_US
```

shows that the file extension, .txt, is equivalent to Gopher type 0, Text/plain, written in English.

The Gopher type number is one of the following:

Gopher type Number	Description
0	File
1	Directory
2	CSO (qi) phone-book server
3	Error
4	BinHexed Macintosh file
5	DOS binary archive of some sort

continues

Gopher type Number	Description
6	Unix uuencoded file
7	Index-Search server
8	Points to a text-based telnet session
9	Binary file
g	GIF type
h	html type
I	Image type
i	inline text type
M	MIME type—item contains MIME data
P	Adobe Portable Document Format (PDF)
s	Sound type—data stream is a mulaw sound
T	TN3270 connection

The prefix used for the service's selector, pfx, is used as a quick way of parsing user requests. Generally, the value is set to 0, for text files, or 9, for binary files.

The Gopher+-type field is based on the definitions used for MIME. This information is important because it helps the Gopher client determine which application to begin so the document can be viewed. An image might start an xview window, for example.

The last field in the format is optional. It specifies the language the document is in. This field, of course, does not make much sense for image files. The convention is to use a two-letter (ISO-compliant) language code, followed by an underscore, followed by a two-letter country code (for example, Es_ES means Spanish from Spain).

There are many viewext definitions. The following is just a sample to give you a flavor:

```
# Different Languages
viewext: .txt.spanish 0 0 Text/plain Es_ES
viewext: .txt.portuguese 0 0 Text/plain Pt_PT

# Graphics file formats
viewext: .gif I 9 image/gif
viewext: .jpg I 9 image/JPEG
viewext: .tif I 9 image/tiff

# Sounds
viewext: .snd s s audio/basic
viewext: .wav s s audio/microsoft-wave

# Movies
viewext: .mov ; 9 video/quicktime
viewext: .mpg ; 9 video/mpeg

# Binary files..
viewext: .zip 5 9 application/zip
viewext: .tar 9 9 application/x-tar
viewext: .ps 0 9 application/postscript

# These are defined by IANA..
viewext: .rtf 0 0 application/rtf
viewext: .word 0 0 application/MSWord
```

There is also the promise that Gopher automatically will recognize the file type, as shown by the following definitions:

```
#magic 0 GIF 9 I Gif
#magic 0 snd s s audio/basic
```

Those definitions are not yet implemented, however.

You might find that you have document types not included in any viewext definition. You will have to define the new document type at that time. If you define a new document type, start the Gopher+ type field with an application. If you want to define a type for FrameMaker files, for example, you can use the following definition:

```
viewext: .frm 0 0 application/framemaker
```

Hiding Files Based on File Types

No doubt, there are files that you do not want visible to Gopher clients. You can use the keyword, ignore, to specify file extensions for such files. The extensions are not case sensitive.

The following sample list shows you the file extensions included by default with the ignore keyword in gopherd.conf:

```
ignore: lost+found
ignore: lib
ignore: bin
ignore: etc
ignore: dev
ignore: ~
ignore: .cache
ignore: .cache+
ignore: .forward
ignore: .message
ignore: .hushlogin
ignore: .kermrc
ignore: .notar
ignore: .where
```

Many of these file extensions refer to system files that are not for general consumption.

You might add or subtract to this list according to the needs of your system. You should take care when adding to the list, however, that you do not currently have any file names ending with the string you specify with the ignore keyword. If you add the following line, for example, any file name ending with that string (Making Money, for example) would be invisible to Gopher clients:

```
ignore: money
```

Using Character Patterns to Hide Files

The ignore keyword hides files from Gopher clients based on the ending of file names. The ignore_patt keyword hides files whenever a pattern of letters occurs (anywhere) in a file name. The pattern of letters is case sensitive.

Here are some example patterns:

```
ignore_patt: ^core$
ignore_patt: ^usr$
ignore_patt: ^tmp$
```

Again, if you choose to add to this list, be careful not to hide files unintentionally.

Splitting Files into Multiple Parts

There might be times when you want to combine files and send them all at once to the Gopher client. This saves time and, perhaps, suggests an association between the group of files.

To distinguish separate documents that appear as one, you can use the filesep keyword to define characters that separate the documents. For example, you could use the following separator:

```
filesep: ^----------------------------------------
```

Editing gopherdlocal.conf

There really are only a couple of lines that you must edit in the gopherdlocal.conf file. If you do not, however, it automatically publishes nasty little notes about your system administrator!

Identifying System Administrators

There are two keywords in gopherdlocal.conf that gopherd uses when it needs to identify system administrators:

➜ Admin

➜ AdminEmail

Follow the Admin keyword with the alias for the system administrator and any other contact information you want to include, such as a phone number or address.

Follow the AdminEmail keyword with the e-mail address of the system administrator alias.

The defaults follow:

```
Admin: blank
AdminEmail: blank
```

You therefore have little choice but to complete these lines, unless your system administrator's name is "blank," and their email address is "blank."

Adding an Abstract

The keyword Abstract identifies a sentence as an abstract, or a concise description of what your service provides. The entire description needs to be on one line, so connect sentence fragments broken over a number of lines by using the backslash (\).

The default message follows:

```
Abstract: blank\
The server administrator has not set an abstract \
for this machine. Please ask them to do so!
```

Ouch! Better make sure not to skip this step.

Including Gopher Site Information

The next section of gopherdlocal.conf asks for general information about the Gopher site. By default, the following information headings are listed without content (except the last field):

```
Site: blank
Org: blank
Loc: blank
Geog: blank

Language: En_US
```

Descriptions of these headings follow:

Heading	Description
Site	Name of service
Org	Name of institution supporting service
Loc	City, state, and country where institution resides
Geog	Latitude and longitude of institution
Language	Language in which documents are written
TZ	Timezone in Greenwich Mean Time offset (the timezone field is not displayed by default)

Defining User Messages

The keyword BummerMsg specifies the reply that is dispatched automatically when users try to access the service inappropriately, or the service *load* (or number of users) is already at its maximum. Here is the default:

```
BummerMsg: We're sorry, we don't allow off-site
access to this server
```

Defining Access Permission

The keyword access defines what users are allowed to do with Gopher data, and how many users can be working on the service at the same time.

The format of the keyword follows:

```
access: hostName_IPAddress  permissions  #users
```

where hostName_IPAddress is the name of the host or its IP address, respectively; **permissions** specifies the permission set of service users; and **#users** specifies the maximum number of users that can be connected to the service at any one time.

The permissions follow:

➜ **Browse.** Denying someone the right to browse means that users cannot query directory contents; they can, however, access nondirectory items.

➜ **Read.** Denying someone the right to read a file means that they receive the BummerMsg instead of the file when they ask to retrieve it.

➜ **Search.** Denying someone the right to search means that users cannot access indexes (Gopher type 7) that you have made available through Gopher+.

➜ **ftp.** Denying someone the right to ftp means that Gopher+ cannot act as a gateway to ftp services.

Consider this example:

```
access: sgi.corp.com  search !browse read !ftp  5
```

In this example, folks at sgi.corp.com can search and read files, but not browse and ftp them. Also, a maximum of five users at any time from sgi.corp.com can access the service.

You restrict a user from using these permissions by preceding the permission with an exclamation point (!). To deny someone the right to browse, for example, you can use this code:

```
access: 192.23.423.12 !browse
```

You also can use a partial IP address to limit everyone on a particular network to the defined access permissions:

```
access: 192.23. !browse
```

Be sure to include the period (.) after the **23**. Otherwise, any IP address starting with **192.23** would have the same permissions—for example, 192.234.67.25 and everyone in 192.235 network.

Also, instead of an IP address or full host name, you can use the word default. The default access permissions pertain to all hosts accessing the service that do not have specific access permissions defined for them. For example, you might make the default permissions the following:

```
access: default !browse, read, search, !ftp, 15
```

These default permissions allow hosts to search and read Gopher directories, but not to browse or ftp them.

The default access permission set becomes the base from which you vary. Given the default definition, the following permission set allows up to 15 concurrent users at sgi.corp.com to ftp, read, and search Gopher directories:

```
access:   sgi.corp.com  ftp
```

Likewise, the permission set

```
access:   sgi.corp.com !read, !search
```

prevents sgi.corp.com users from doing anything with Gopher directories, because this permission set cancels the only access allowed by the default access permissions.

Authenticating Users

It has been the goal of many service creators to identify who is accessing their service so that if the user is up to no good, a system administrator can put the finger on someone. This goal has not yet been reached for a variety of reasons. If Joe Schmo finds out a login name and password, or if a workstation is not password protected, Joe Schmo's identity is hidden behind the login name.

Still, there is the desire to make authentication a reality. The gopherd.conf file contains two keywords to that end:

➜ Authitem

➜ Serverpw

The Authitem keyword specifies a file or directory that requires a password and user authentication before it can be accessed. The format of Authitem is

```
Authitem:  authMethod
➜/file_dirName_regularExpression
```

where authMethod is the method of authentication, and /file_dirName_regularExpression identifies the file, directory, or regular expression that is to be protected. Currently, there are two methods of authentication:

➜ **Unix.** Uses the Unix passwd file.

➜ **Unixfile.** Uses a passwd file in the /etc directory under the dataRoot directory.

For example,

```
Authitem: unix /hippos
```

protects the directory, hippos, by requiring a password based on the Unix passwd file.

You also can specify a password to gain access to the service by defining the keyword Serverpw (server password), for example:

```
Serverpw: 0ver_the_ra1nb0w
```

You need to change these values from their default settings:

```
Authitem: unixfile /secure
Serverpw: super_secret_squirrel
```

Configuring the Compile-Time Options

The two files where you configure compile-time options are Makefile.config and conf.h. Some of the options are platform-specific. So, in addition to considering the tasks discussed in this section, look at the comments in the configuration files to see whether there are other configuration options you should edit.

Editing Makefile.config

The Makefile is the description file that helps build your service. The Makefile.config file provides configuration definitions that Makefile uses.

The Makefile.config file is quite long. This section only looks at those parts that are generic to all platforms. Following the configuration information, however, enables you to compile the Gopher 2.1.3 and 2.1.4beta server and clients without a problem. In fact, a successful compile can be achieved without changing any parameters!

About five pages into the configuration file, you see the following options:

```
# Where shall we install stuff?
#
PREFIX = /usr/local
CLIENTDIR = $(PREFIX)/bin
CLIENTLIB = $(PREFIX)/lib
SERVERDIR = $(PREFIX)/etc
# On SCO manuals are in /usr/man but its easiest to do a
# symbolic link from /usr/local/man to /usr/man for this and other packages
MAN1DIR = $(PREFIX)/man/man1
MAN5DIR = $(PREFIX)/man/man5
MAN8DIR = $(PREFIX)/man/man8
```

These options specify where all the Gopher files are installed. Descriptions of these options follow:

Option	Description
CLIENTDIR	Directory for the client application and gophfilt
CLIENTLIB	Directory of the client Help file, gopher.hlp
MAN1DIR	Directory of the man pages for the gopher client and gophfilt
MAN8DIR	Directory in which the man pages for gopherd are installed
PREFIX	Base path name that defines where everything is installed
SERVERDIR	Directory of the service (gopherd) and the server configuration file (gopher.conf)

The locations of these files, as specified in the Makefile, are standard and do not require modification.

Configuring the Service

In addition to SERVERDIR, there are four other variables that configure the Gopher service: DOMAIN, SERVERPORT, SERVERDATA, and SERVEROPTS.

The DOMAIN variable sets the domain name of the service host:

```
DOMAIN = .micro.umn.edu
```

Note that the leading period is required.

If the hostname command returns a fully qualified domain name on your system, as in this example,

```
% hostname
engr.sgi.com
```

set DOMAIN to NULL:

```
DOMAIN =
```

Otherwise, set it to the part of the domain name that the hostname command does not return.

The SERVERPORT variable, as you might expect, defines the port to which the service listens. The default is 70. Change this port number only if you do not want to make the service available to Internet users. If you are modifying the service, for example, you might want to put the developmental version of the Gopher service on a high port number (between 1024 and 9999).

The SERVERDATA variable defines the starting location of the data provided by your Gopher service. You must change it from its default form:

```
SERVERDATA = /gopher-data
```

The values of both variables, SERVERPORT and SERVERDATA, can be overridden at the command line. If you do not define them, however, you have to enter their values when you execute the service. To save keystrokes and lost time caused by simple mistakes, it is a good idea to define the defaults of these variables.

The other line that sets service options looks similar to the following:

```
SERVEROPTS = -DSETPROCTITLE -DCAPFILES #-DBIO -DDL
      -DLOADRESTRICT
```

The options following the equal sign (=) and before the pound sign (#) represent source code that is compiled into the Gopher service. All the options after the pound sign are ignored during Gopher's compilation.

The options you can use in this line are shown in the table at the bottom of this page.

To use –DLOADRESTRICT, set the user access restriction in the conf.h file and uncomment the LOADLIBS line in the Makefile:

```
#LOADLIBS = -lkvm
```

 note It is important to note that the configuration file indicates that the LOADRESTRICT option has only been tested with SunOS 4.1.1. By enabling this option for a Linux installation, the compile fails. Consequently, use of this option should be avoided on Linux systems.

To get Don Gilbert's version of WAIS, ftp to

```
ftp.bio.indiana.edu
```

Option	Description
–DADD_DATE_AND_TIME	Adds dates and time to Gopher titles
–DBIO	Use only if you use Don Gilbert's version of WAIS (wais8b5) to enable searching by symbols; not recommended for other usage
–DDL	Supports Tim Cook's dl database program
–DCAPFILES	Provides backward compatibility with the cap directory
–DLOADRESTRICT	Restricts user access based on the number of active users; also adds –lkvm in SERVERLIBS
–DSETPROCTITLE	Sets the name displayed by the ps command; for bsdish systems only

To use the –DDL option, you must have the source code, getdesc.o and enddesc.o, in the directory specified by DLPATH. You also need to uncomment the DLOBJS line in the Makefile:

```
DLPATH = /home/mudhoney/lindner/src/describe
#DLOBJS = $(DLPATH)/getdesc.o $(DLPATH)/enddesc.o
```

You can get the source code for the program Describe, which creates the dl databases from

```
ftp.deakin.edu.au
```

where you get

```
pub/describe/describe-1.8.tar.Z
```

Configuring the Gopher Client

You also can set Gopher client options by using the following line:

```
CLIENTOPTS = #-DNOMAIL -DAUTOEXITONU
```

Just as with the SERVEROPTS variable, all options after the pound sign are ignored. The options available for client configuration follow:

Option	Description
–DNOMAIL	Prevents remote users from mailing documents (for use with the Gopher client)
–DAUTOEXITONU	Exits Gopher client using u (as well as q)

The DREMOTEUSER option is no longer used.

Controlling Debugging

You might choose to include debugging source code when you first install your Gopher service to help track problems. After you have it working, however, you might like to reduce the size of the Gopher executable and slightly improve performance by eliminating the debugging source code.

To eliminate the debugging source code, comment out the following line in the Makefile:

```
DEBUGGING = -DDEBUGGING
```

Providing WAIS Indexes

If you want your Gopher service to be accessible by WAIS indexes, you must perform the following steps:

1. Download freeWAIS by ftping it from

   ```
   % ftp gopher.boombox.micro.umn.edu
   ```

   Retrieve the source in the following file:

   ```
   /pub/gopher/Unix/freeWAIS-0.3.tar.gz
   ```

    Even though the version of freeWAIS is currently 0.5, boombox.micro.umn.edu does not currently have either freeWAIS-0.4 or freeWAIS-0.5. If you want to include the current version of freeWAIS, you need to obtain it from ftp.cnidr.org, as discussed in Chapter 13. It is recommended that, if you can, you should use the latest version of freeWAIS.

2. Dearchive and decompress the WAIS file and edit the Makefile according to your system.

3. Change to the top WAIS directory and run make:

   ```
   % make
   ```

note Alternatively, you can make just part of the source by executing one of these commands:

```
% make lib
% make ir
% make bin
```

4. Recompile freeWAIS by running make in the top directory of freeWAIS.

5. In the Makefile.config file, make sure the WAISTYPE variable is set correctly, as in the following code:

```
WAISTYPE = #-DFREEWAIS_0_4
```

 note Even if you choose to use the freeWAIS-0.5 release, you must set the WAISTYPE value to FREEWAIS_0_4. If you set it to FREEWAIS_0_5, the compile fails.

6. Link the freeWAIS and Gopher services by typing the following lines:

```
% cd GopherSrc
% ln -s WaisTop/include ./ir
% ln -s WaisTop/src/client/ui .
% ln -s WaisTop/bin .
```

in which `GopherSrc` is the directory of the Gopher source code—for example, /usr/local/etc/gopher1.14—and `WaisTop` is the directory of the freeWAIS source code—for example, /usr/local/etc/freeWAIS-0.5.

 If you chose to pull the pre-built version of freeWAIS from ftp.cnidr.org, then you are not able to link Gopher and WAIS together because you do not have the required source files. Consequently, you need to obtain the complete source distribution and build it for Linux.

When you compile the Gopher service, these links automatically allow freeWAIS and Gopher to interact.

 note Providing full-text indexing for NeXT computers requires a different procedure. For instructions, look in the INSTALL file.

Editing conf.h

The conf.h file contains configuration information for the service and the included Gopher client. Because the scope of this book is essentially the service, only the highlights of the Gopher client configuration options are discussed here.

Configuring the Service

The very /end of the conf.h file contains the variables that relate to the Gopher service operation. Although the variables cover many topics, most relate to load and limitations of service execution.

The WAISMAXHITS variable defines the maximum number of returns a query to a WAIS index can generate, as in this example:

```
#define WAISMAXHITS 40
```

This code limits Gopher services from supplying more than 40 WAIS-generated matches to a query. Forty is a reasonable number to start with.

If you turned on the LOADRESTRICT definition earlier, the MAXLOAD variable defines the maximum load the Gopher service will bear before refusing to serve documents to users, as this code shows:

```
#define MAXLOAD 10.0
```

You can override this variable on the command line when you invoke the service.

Read the man page for the signal() command on your system. Confirm that the return type is void. If it is not, you need to define the SIGRETTYPE variable to the correct type. The default type is void:

```
#define SIGRETTYPE void
```

The READTIMEOUT variable defines the time the service waits for a network read before timing out. The default is one minute:

```
#define READTIMEOUT (1 * 60)
```

The WRITETIMEOUT variable defines the time the service waits for a network write before timing out. The default is three minutes:

```
#define WRITETIMEOUT (3 * 60)
```

There is a problem with running Gopher under inetd: it can handle only a limited number of arguments. As you can see from the variables so far that can be overridden on the command line, the Gopher service potentially can use many command-line arguments. To handle this problem, gopherd builds a file of arguments, called gopherd.conf; its location is specified by the CONF_FILE variable, as shown in this code:

```
#if !defined(CONF_FILE)
#   define CONF_FILE      "/usr/local/etc/
➥gopherd.conf"
#endif
```

Configuring the Client

You define the default language the Gopher service uses for system messages with the variable DEFAULT_LANG:

```
#define DEFAULT_LANG "En_US" /* English (US)
```

Gopher can use a variety of other languages, including the following:

```
/* #define DEFAULT_LANG "Da_DK" /* Danish */
/* #define DEFAULT_LANG "De_DE" /* German */
/* #define DEFAULT_LANG "En_GB" /* English (UK) */
/* #define DEFAULT_LANG "Es_ES" /* Spanish */
/* #define DEFAULT_LANG "Fr_FR" /* French */
/* #define DEFAULT_LANG "It_IT" /* Italian */
/* #define DEFAULT_LANG "Jp_JP" /* Japanese */
/* #define DEFAULT_LANG "No_NO" /* Norwegian */
/* #define DEFAULT_LANG "Sv_SE" /* Swedish */
```

object/Views.c has more examples of foreign language definitions.

You can define two Gopher services that Gopher clients automatically contact when invoked by using the CLIENT1_HOST and CLIENT2_HOST variables:

```
#define CLIENT1_HOST "gopher.company.corp.com"
#define CLIENT2_HOST "gopher2.company.corp.com"
```

Which service of the two the Gopher client contacts is arbitrary. The idea is to have two servers running the Gopher service so they can load balance user requests. Load balancing is the process of distributing user request equally across servers. When loads are balanced, system performance is maximized.

You also can set the Gopher client to look for a Gopher service on a different port number by setting the CLIENT1_PORT and CLIENT2_PORT variables:

```
#define CLIENT1_PORT 70
#define CLIENT2_PORT 70
```

If you only want one root machine, set `CLIENT2_PORT` to 0.

You change these port numbers only if you have put a special version of your Gopher service on a different port. For general Internet access, keep your Gopher client requesting information on port 70.

International Options

If you are installing Gopher clients to be used by people who do not speak English, you should enable the –DGINTERNATIONAL option in the Makefile.config. The current offerings include help systems in German, Spanish, French, and Italian; and system messages in German, Spanish, Swedish, Italian, and piglatin(!).

To use these languages, you must perform the following steps:

1. Run make in the gopher2_1_3/gopher/locales directory to change the foreign language files into binary catalogs.

2. Install the message files in the location specified by NLSPATH. Customary locations include /usr/lib/locales, and /usr/lib/nls.

   If NSLPATH is not specified, the default path for the message files is defined by the DEF_NLSPATH variable in the nl_types header file.

 n o t e For more information on NSLPATH, read the man page for catopen().

3. Set the LANG or LC_MESSAGES environment variables to the appropriate message file. For example,

```
LANG=Es
```

or

```
setenv LC_MESSAGES fr
```

If you have trouble making the messages work, the problem might be that the proper files are not in the /usr/lib/nls directory. In such a case, run

```
% make install
```

in which **make** creates a directory that contains all the message catalogs that a Gopher client checks if it cannot find message catalogs any other way.

Installing Programs for the Gopher Client

The Gopher client uses many external programs common to Unix systems. If you are providing a Gopher client, you should check the following list to make sure that your system has these programs:

→ To run telnet 3270 connections, you need tn3270 or a version of telnet that understands tn3270.

→ To enable the Gopher client to download files, your system must have kermit and zmodem. The corresponding binaries are kermit, sz, sb, and sx.

→ To use documents in metamail, your system needs mm.tar.Z, which you get from thumper.bellcore.com.

→ To display images, your system needs a generic graphics program—for example, xv or xloadimage.

Compiling the Gopher Service and Client

When you finish setting all the configuration variables, it is time to compile the source and install image. You have several options, including whether you want to build just the service, just the client, or both.

To compile the client only, type

```
% make client
```

To compile the service only, type

```
% make server
```

To compile the client and the service, type

```
% make
```

Installing the Gopher Client and Service

After building the applications, you need to install them.

To install the client only, type

```
% cd gopher
% make install
```

To install the service only, type

```
% cd gopherd
% make install
```

To install everything, type

```
make install
```

The biggest problem that you might run into results from not having created all the directories defined in your configuration files.

The install command used in the build is the BSD version. If you have problems, or your system does not have the BSD version of install, you need to install the program manually, using the following procedure:

1. Move any old version of gopherd to another directory.

2. Copy (cp) gopherd to /usr/local/bin.

Whether or not you can run the automated install, you have to manually install the man page. Use the following code, for example:

```
# cd doc
# cp gopherd.conf.8 /usr/local/man/man8
```

Your service is ready.

Starting Your Gopher+ Service

You can start the Gopher+ service using or not using chroot() to limit users' access to your file system. Just like FTP, Gopher+ can restrict users to a subdirectory of your system using chroot(). The other option is to start the service with the –c option, which does not chroot() the user. The option does, however, make gopherd use secure versions of file-opening system calls.

Although the –c option works reasonably well and enables you to put symbolic links in the Gopher+ data directory, chroot() is still more secure.

To start the Gopher+ service using chroot(), type a line similar to the following:

```
% /usr/local/etc/gopherd  /home/gopher-data 70
```

in which home/gopher-data is the directory where the Gopher data resides.

To start the Gopher+ service without using chroot(), type a line similar to the following:

```
/usr/local/etc/gopherd -c /home/gopher-data 70
```

If you want to start the service automatically with the server, you can insert an entry into your rc.local file (or equivalent) similar to the following:

```
if [ -f /usr/local/etc/gopherd ]; then
 /usr/local/etc/gopherd /home/hostName/dataRoot 70
 fi
```

Using Other Command-Line Options

The following options are available to you with the gopherd command:

Option	Function
–C	Disables directory caching; default is to cache them
–c	Runs without chroot() restrictions; default is to run with restrictions
–D	Enables debugging; default is off
–I	inetd invokes service; default is off
–L avgLoad	Sets maximum load average
–l logFileName	Creates log file where connections are recorded
–o fileName	Uses fileName as the configuration file instead of gopherd.conf
–u name	Sets name as the owner running gopherd
directory_for_data	Uses directory_for_data as the data directory for Gopher
port#	Uses port# as the port number for the service

For more information about the security benefits of having your service run under a subdirectory access-restricted by chroot(), see Chapter 11, "Managing an FTP Service."

To reduce response time, gopherd caches directories while fulfilling requests for them. When a second request for the directory is received, the service looks for a file named .cache in the directory. If the cached directory is less than the number of seconds specified by Cachetime in gopherd.conf, the cached directory is sent to the requester. If the directory is older (or if there is no .cache file), the cached version of the file is not used. The directory is fetched from the disk, sent to the requester, and cached for the sake of the next request.

You should enable debugging (–D) only while you are testing the service. You should turn off debugging when the service is online, because debugging hurts performance.

If you choose to run your service under inetd (and you probably should not), you must use the –I option so that gopherd knows not to run as a daemon, but as a service that fulfills one request and then terminates. It also is important to put this option first in the list of options; otherwise, the Gopher client gets start-up messages inappropriately.

Log files specify the activity performed by the service. They list what topics were searched for, and they list the documents sent to Gopher clients, for example. Log files are valuable because they show you what terms users employ to find documents. You might consider adding aliases, for example, if people use the search criterion *plane* with no result when your documents use the word *airplane*. Log files are examined more closely in "Using Log Files," later in this chapter.

If you use the file name cwsyslog, gopherd sends the log information to syslog. It does not make much sense, however, to mix log information into other syslog information. Trying to see the large picture when everything is mixed together is difficult. Keep log data in its own file.

In order for the –L argument to work, gopherd must be compiled with the LOADRESTRICT option turned on. When the maximum load average is reached, the service stops sending data to clients; instead, it sends the message `System Load Too High`. This option supersedes the MAXLOAD variable defined in conf.h.

n o t e Remember that, for Linux systems, this option is not currently supported.

In Makefile.config, the file that is set equal to SERVERDIR is the default location of the configuration file, gopherd.conf. You can choose to use a different configuration file by following the –o option with a file name. If you are testing the service,

perhaps you need an alternate configuration file. It is much easier to change from one configuration file to another at the command line rather than in a configuration file.

You always want to use the –u option to run gopherd as an unprivileged user. If clever hackers find a bug in gophered that they can exploit, you want them running around the file system as unprivileged users, not as root!

n o t e Running the service is different from starting the service. Determining who should be the owner of each action is confusing. The rule is that you want to run the service as a nonprivileged user, but you want to start the service as root so that chroot() can take effect. For more information about chroot(), see Chapter 12.

The directory_for_data option sets a new default directory for Gopher data; it supersedes the default defined in the configuration file.

There are not too many reasons why you would change the port number of the service from 70. If you are testing a new version of the service on another port number, you can start it with that port number by using the –U option. Make sure, however, that you also use the directory_for_data argument on the command line.

Starting gopherd with inetd

Up to this point, this chapter has assumed that you want to start gopherd in stand-alone mode. In this mode, gopherd runs constantly (as a daemon) on the server and forks off a copy of itself whenever a request for Gopher (on port 70) comes in. The good aspect of running gopherd in stand-alone mode is that start-up time for a new service is very quick. The downside is that running gopherd as a daemon consumes considerable CPU cycles. If you are running a dedicated server for the service, this is not a problem. If you are trying to run other programs, perhaps other services, as well from your server, you have to judge whether you can afford to run gopherd as a daemon. If it turns out that running gopherd in stand-alone mode consumes too much CPU time, at least you know that you can run the service using inetd. This option saves CPU time, assuming that the service is not accessed every other minute. If this assumption is true, restarting the service for every request probably consumes more CPU time than running it as a daemon. At that point, you need to make some decisions about buying more hardware or severely restricting access to the service by using MaxSessions and LOADRESTRICT, for example.

Running gopherd under inetd has the advantage of freeing up CPU time by shutting down the service between service requests. The *caveat*, as just mentioned, is that this advantage becomes a disadvantage if the service is accessed on a regular basis. This is because gopherd must reread all the configuration files as it starts up. With fast machines, this performance hit is minimized, but it is not eliminated.

Whether your service runs under inetd depends mainly on the popularity of your service. If your service is being accessed five times a day, you want it running under inetd in order to free up the CPU. If, on the other hand, the service is being accessed five times per minute, gopherd almost certainly should run in stand-alone mode.

To run gopherd under inetd, you must edit two files. The first file you must edit is /etc/services. To add a Gopher service, add to the file a line similar to the following:

```
gopher    70/tcp    #This is our gopher service
➡(port 70)
```

This line says the Gopher service listens to requests on port 70 and it uses TCP. Everything after the pound sign (#) is a comment.

You also must edit the /etc/inetd.conf file by adding a line similar to the following:

```
gopher    stream    tcp    nowait    root    /usr/local/
➡etc/gopherd          gopherd -I -l logfile  -u
➡restricted
```

Every field separated by tabs in this example is standard, except the last field, where the optional arguments are given that you want to use to start the service. Because you are starting the service under inetd, you must use the –I option and it must be the first argument in the list to prevent aberrant messages from reaching the Gopher client. In this example, gopherd uses a log file, named logfile, and it runs as user restricted. These users should have very limited permissions so that, in case gopherd has a bug and hackers gain access to the system through the bug, they will have only the permissions of restricted users.

This example shows that the service is started as root. This is necessary in order to restrict users to a subdirectory of the file system (–c was not used) defined by chroot(). Although gopherd starts up as root to take advantage of chroot(), it runs as user restricted. You therefore have the best of both worlds: users restricted to a chroot()'d subset of the file system and limited to the permission set of a restricted user.

/usr/local/etc is the standard location of gopherd. If you have placed it in a different directory, substitute the correct path to the service.

When you change a configuration file, remember to restart the service so the configuration files are reread and the changes can take effect. You use the hang-up signal to do this:

```
# kill -HUP pid
```

in which **pid** is the process ID of the inetd, which you can obtain by using the following commands:

```
# ps -ax ¦ grep inetd
 2463  ??  Is    0:00.31 inetd
29438  p0  RV    0:00.7 grep inetd (tcsh)
```

In this case, **2463** is the process ID of inetd.

Testing Your Service

Before you tell everyone that your service is working, it is a good idea to test it. The first way to test the service is by starting a Gopher+ client and connecting to the Gopher+ service.

After you connect to your service, press Enter. The service should respond by displaying the top directory of the Gopher resources.

Using telnet

In addition to using your Gopher+ client to test your service, you can use telnet. If your service is working correctly, your telnet session should look something like the following:

```
warp[8:21pm]-=> telnet gopher 70
Trying 128.101.95.29 ...
Connected to gopher.micro.umn.edu.
Escape character is '^]'.

0About Gopher /.about gopher.micro.umn.edu 150
7Search Micro Consultant asd joeboy.micro.umn.edu
➡156
7Search everywhere kdkdkd ashpool.micro.umn.edu 158
1Search parts of the gopher world /Search parts of
➡the gopher world gopher.micro.umn.edu 150
.
Connection closed by foreign host.
warp[8:40pm]-=>
```

Using gopherls

If you do not want to go through the hassle of running telnet, you can run gopherls, which is linked to gopherd. gopherls takes only one argument, but the argument is mandatory. The argument is the path name to a directory. gopherls processes this directory as though it were a Gopher+ client request and displays the message that normally would be sent to the Gopher+ client.

```
# gopherls /usr/local/dataRoot
0About Gopher  0/about gopher.  micro.umn.edu 150
7Search  Micro Consultant asd
joeboy.micro.umn.edu 156
7Search  everywhere kdkdkd ashpool.  micro.umn.edu
158
1Search parts of the gopher world  /Search parts of
the gopher world gopher.  micro.umn.edu 150
```

You can do a quick check of all your directories by using gopherls.

Publicizing Your Gopher Service

To get your Gopher service listed in Gopher menus, send mail to

gopher@boombox.micro.umn.edu

If you are in Europe, send mail to

gopher@ebone.net

Include the following information in your mail:

→ Service's name (as it appears on the menu)

→ Full host's name

→ Port number (hopefully, 70)

→ System administrator's name (use an alias) and e-mail address

→ Short paragraph describing the contents of the service (include that you are running Gopher+ to distinguish your service from a Gopher service)

→ Selector string (optional)

The *selector string* is a path name where you want people to start in your data directory. Generally, you leave this option blank so that people start, by default, at the root of your data files. One exception is a server that runs services for multiple companies; each company wants people to start in their data files (not those of other companies).

Although none of these pieces of information takes great brain work to complete, you should be absolutely sure that what you submit is absolutely correct, final, and everlasting. You do not want to put the name of your current system administrator for the service in the form, for example, because that

will change over time. After information goes out to thousands, if not millions, of people, it is hard (and can be damaging) to make corrections.

Using Log Files

After you get your service running, you will be interested in learning how (and how many) people are using your service. The Gopher service does not by default use a log file. To enable logging, a log file must be specified on the command line, as shown in the following example:

```
gopherd -u gopher -l /var/log/gopherd
```

This starts the Gopher service to write the log records into the file /var/log/gopherd.

The log file contains connection information about each service request. Here is an excerpt from a log file:

```
Wed Apr 05 11:15:18 1995 19823 sgi.com : retrieved
➥binary /Introduction
Wed Apr 05 11:16:23 1995 18738 192.34.234.33 :
➥search /earnings
Wed Apr 05 11:18:22 1995 16736 sgi.com : retrieved
➥Doc/First Quarter Earnings
Wed Apr 05 11:18:45 1995 18746 sgi.com : retrieved
➥Doc/New Products Guide
Wed Apr 05 11:19:18 1995 11532 jan.sun.com : search
➥/advances
```

Most of the fields in the display are transparent. The first five fields are the time stamp for the service request or reply. The next field is the process ID of the Gopher service working on the request or reply. The field after the process ID gives the IP address or host name of the host that originated the request or reply. The second-to-last field contains a reserved word, such as *retrieved* or *search*, that describes the kind of action the service took. The final fields describe the document type and the document searched for or retrieved by the service.

The following are other reserved words that can appear in log files:

Reserved Word	Action Performed
executed *script arguments*	Ran a script, named *script*, using *arguments*
retrieved binary *fileName*	The service returned a binary file (or image) named *fileName*
retrieved directory *dirName*	The service returned a directory named *dirName*
retrieved file *fileName*	The service returned a file named *fileName*
retrieved ftp: *ftpHost@fileDirName*	Service returned the file or directory, *fileDirName*, using an FTP gateway
retrieved maildir *mailFile*	Service returned an e-mail from *mailFile*
retrieved sound *fileName*	Service returned a sound file named *fileName*
Root Connection	Appears when a user connects as root to the service
search *dBASE* for *criteria*	Service searches the database, *dBASE*, for the search *criteria*

In addition to these reserved words, you might find one of the following error messages:

Error Message	Meaning
Client went away	Client dropped the connection to the service before the service could complete its reply
System Load Too High	When a client tried to connect to the service, it exceeded the maximum average system load, and was refused connection
Malformed hostdata file	The host data in an index was nonsensical
Can't set UID!	System administrator used –U or –u to invoke the service, but the user could not be changed
readline: Time out!	The service disconnected from the client because the client did not send data within the time specified by the conf.h variable, READTIMEOUT
Possible Security Violation	Service detects possible breach of security
Denied access for *hostName*	A host, named *hostName*, was refused service because of access permissions defined in gopherd.conf

Getting the Big Picture

Log records can tell you many things. You can learn what search criteria people often use, you can learn which documents and directories are used and not used, and you can get an indication of the average load your service carries.

When log files get long, however, the big picture is often lost in the details. Many software packages are available on the Internet, some included with Gopher (but not Gopher+), that can give you a broader perspective of the log data. It is not within the scope of this book to describe these programs individually. As you might expect, each program provides some indication of all, or some subset of, the following:

→ Service load by day of the week

→ Peak number of service transactions

→ Most popular directories

→ List of hosts that have accessed the service

→ List of all files requested

→ Number of files requested

→ List of all searches conducted

→ Number of searches conducted

→ List of all menus requested—the root menu or the subdirectories

→ Total number of service requests and replies

→ Number of text files retrieved

Table 17.1 lists the software that provides some of these functions.

Table 17.1 Gopher Log Interpreting Software

Software	Location	Description
gla	boombox.micro.umn.edu in pub/gopher/Unix/GopherTools	One of the better log analyzer scripts
GLASS	boombox.micro.umn.edu in pub/gopher/Unix/GopherTools	Produces 22 reports
glog	boombox.micro.umn.edu in pub/gopher/Unix/GopherTools/ glog directory	Log analyzer that came with Gopher 1.x
Gopherreport	feenix.metronet.com in /pub/perl/scripts/gopher/ tools	Reports Gopher Usage based on days, time, files, hosts, errors
Logger	boombox.micro.umn.edu in pub/gopher/Unix/GopherTools	An older log analyzer

Updating Log Files

The longer a service runs, the longer the log file. At some point, you should archive the contents of the log file (and eventually remove the file). This is not exactly advanced system administration.

There is a script, however, that can help you automate your chores. Logger rotates files and keeps basic statistics about the service as inferred from the log file. You can use ftp to get Logger from

boombox.micro.umn.edu in pub/gopher/Unix/
GopherTools

Constructing Your Menu System

Creating your directory and file structure is one of your most challenging jobs. It requires that you be familiar with the documents so that you can place them correctly in the file system and write abstracts for the documents.

This section describes the steps you take to add files and directories under your data root directory.

Creating Directories and Files

If you have ever laid your hands on a Unix workstation, you no doubt already know the (very) uncomplicated Unix commands it takes to copy files and create directories and files. Actually, that's the beauty of it: You do not have to learn the newest scripting language, Einsteinium, in order to create your Gopher menus and populate your database. The familiarity of the commands goes a long way toward reducing errors.

To create a Gopher menu (a directory), change to the directory in which you want to create the new directory and use mkdir:

```
% cd /usr/local
% mkdir hot_topics
```

Within your new directory, you need to create files or copy files. To copy a file, use the cp or rcp command:

```
% cd hot_topics
% rcp guest@warp:/usr/people/geckel/latest .
```

Your last step is to create descriptive file and directory names, such as *Hot Topics*, *Latest Economic Figures*, and *Trends for 1995*. You use the mv command to rename the files:

```
% mv latest 'Hot Topics'
```

There is a limitation on the number of characters (80) you can use. Consequently, you have to be concise and descriptive when you create file names. Remember, those who are using Gopher 1.*x* clients cannot access the abstract associated with the file (which Gopher+ clients receive after pressing the equal sign).

The menu items are the user's interface to your service; they are what the user sees first. You might have documents in your service that make you worthy of the next Nobel prize, but if they are named poorly, they might go unnoticed. Because the menu titles give users their first look at your service, your astuteness in naming the files and directories can directly influence the success of the service. So, avoid slapping on a half-baked file name, such as newDoc2.

Naming Files and Directories

Now that you are prepared to do your best to create descriptive file names, you need to know the correct procedure. You cannot use mv, as in this example:

```
mv hippo  'Sounds of the Great African River Hippo'
```

Instead, you use a .cap directory. Suppose that you have three documents:

```
/usr/local/doc/hippo
/usr/local/doc/africa
/usr/local/doc/rivers/
```

Here's what you do:

```
% cd /usr/local/doc
% mkdir .cap
% cd .cap
% cat > hippo
Name=Sounds of the Great African River Hippo
Numb=2
^D

% cat > africa
Name=Animals in Africa
Numb=1
^D

% cat > rivers
Name=African Animals Living In Rivers
Numb=3
^D
```

Now review the procedure you just used.

1. You created a directory called .cap in the same directory as the documents you are naming.

2. You created files of the same name as the files you are naming.

3. You used the keywords Name and Numb to specify the name of the document as you want it to appear in menus, and the order in which it should be listed in menus. In this example, the Gopher menu would appear as the following:

```
1. Animals in Africa.
2. Sounds of the Great African River Hippo.
3. African Animals Living In Rivers/
```

Using .names Files

An alternative to using the .cap directory is using a .names file. The concept is the same, except that you put in one file what you create separately as three files in the .cap directory. For example, the equivalent of the preceding exercise follows:

```
% cd /usr/local/doc
% cat > .names
# You can add a comment here if you like

Path=./hippo
Name=Sounds of the Great African River Hippo
Numb=2

Path=./africa
Name=Animals in Africa
Numb=1

Path=./rivers
Name=African Animals Living In Rivers
Numb=3
Abstract=Beautiful pictures of animals living in
and around major African rivers and lakes with
accompanying text about the wildlife.
```

As you can see in the last file, you can use other keywords to describe your files in greater detail. The Abstract keyword identifies the concise description of the file the users can see whenever they select a menu item and press the equal sign (=).

Another keyword is Ask, which you use to get user input. The Ask keyword, along with Gopher+ forms, is discussed in this chapter in the section, "Creating Forms."

The dot file does not have to be called .names, although this is the convention. Using .names files saves you the trouble of creating a .cap directory and a separate file for each file to be named.

The only reason you might not want to use .names files is that they are not compatible with Gopher 1.*x* clients.

Creating Links to Other Files and Directories

One of the great features of Gopher is that the source of the Gopher information is hidden from the user. One menu item on the service server can be followed by a menu item that exists on a different Gopher server, and followed by another menu item that links to an FTP service. To the user, everything transpires behind closed doors, and all that matters is the appropriateness of the returned file.

There are two ways to link one service to another. The first and simplest way is to create a file that is linked to another file on a (perhaps) remote server. By convention, all link files begin with periods; the convention is to name them .links files.

A link file contains five lines in the following format:

```
Name=
Type=
Port=
Path=
Host=
```

You also have the option of using the Numb field in your link files to specify the placement of the file in the list of files.

The Name field is the menu item that appears to users. The Type field contains a numerical description of the type of document to which the file is linked. The following are the possible values of the Type field:

Value	Type of Document
0	Text file
1	Directory
2	CSO name server
7	Full text index
8	telnet session
9	Binary file
h	HTML file
I	Image file
M	MIME file
s	Sound file

The Port field identifies the port of the (potentially) remote server to query. The Path field provides the path to the linked file on the remote server. The Host field identifies the (possibly) remote host by IP address or full host name with which you want to link.

.links files are similar to .names files; one difference is that the Path field starts with ./ in .names files, because the .names files always refer to a document in the directory in which the .names file is located.

Here is a simple example:

```
Name=New Product Offerings
Type=0
Port=70
Path=0/local/latest
Host=sgi.corp.com
```

You can retrieve this information for yourself so that you can prepare the .link files by using a Gopher client to find a file you want to link with, selecting it, and then pressing the equal sign. The Gopher service displays all the information needed for each of the fields in the .links files.

The other way to retrieve this information is by telneting into a service. When you do so, the remote server responds with the information in the following format:

```
objectType    Name    Path    HostName    Port#
```

All these fields must remain the same, except for the Name field, which you can change.

By using different values for the Type field, you can access different kinds of objects on servers. Here is a link to a directory:

```
Name=New Product Offerings
Type=1+
Port=70
Path=1/
Host=furnace.sgi.com
```

Notice that the convention is to mark anything in a Gopher+ service with a plus sign (+).

Using .cap Files

The other way of linking files is by using .cap files. Suppose, for example, that you have a sound file called Meow that you want to make available to people. Here is what you would do:

1. In the same directory as Meow, create a new directory called .cap.

2. Create a file in the .cap directory using the same file name as the sound file name, Meow.

The file should contain one or all five of the fields that identify the linked file—including Name, Type, Port, Path, and Host. You only need to put into the file under .cap the fields that are different. All other fields default to the information in the Meow file.

If Meow were in /usr/local/sounds, you would use these commands to make the link:

```
cd /usr/local/sounds
mkdir .cap
cat >Meow
Type=s
Name=Cat Sound
^D
```

In this case, the host supplies the three fields that are missing: Port, Path, and Host.

Linking with Other Services

Up to now, you have been linking to other Gopher services. It is just as easy to link with other services, such as telnet, FTP, WAIS, or a script.

Linking to telnet Services

You can use .link files to start telnet sessions, as in the following code:

```
Name=New Product Offerings
Type=8
Port=23
Path=guest
Host=@furnace.sgi.com
```

note To start a TN3270 link, set the Type field to T.

Linking to Other Services

To link to FTP, WAIS, or a script, you have to use the following format for the Path field:

```
Path=service_link:arguments
```

in which `service_link` is ftp, waissrc, or exec; and `arguments` is additional information needed by the remote service.

To link to an FTP service, use this format:

```
Name=Gopher menu title for FTP resource
Path=ftp:hostName@/pathname/[fileName]
Type=Remote resource type
Port=+
Host=+
```

in which `hostName` is the IP address or fully qualified domain name of the server where the FTP service is running. `fileName` is in brackets in the Path field definition because it is optional. The Path field can specify a directory or file name.

The plus signs in the Port and Host fields tell the remote FTP service to return results to this Gopher service. If you put the full host name of another Gopher into the Host field, the FTP service sends its reply to that host, so that host acts as a gateway to the FTP service and handles the client's request.

The default port number for an FTP service, 21, is always used.

Linking to WAIS Services

You can provide a link to a WAIS service to include its index in your service. To do so, use the following format:

```
Name=Menu title for WAIS resource
Path=waissrc:sourceFile
Type=7
Port=+
Host=+
```

in which `sourceFile` is the full path name of the WAIS source (the src file). For more information about source files, see Chapter 13, "Setting Up a freeWAIS Service."

Using Links to Execute Scripts

All the other services so far return files that are static. Perhaps you want to generate some information on the fly and return it. You might want to extract some information from a database, for example. To offer dynamic information, you must use scripts. *Scripts* are programs that process the information you want your Gopher service to display.

To use a link to execute a script, format the .link file:

```
Name=Gopher menu title
Path=exec: "arguments" : scriptName
Type=type of script's output
Port=+
Host=+
```

in which `arguments` are arguments that you need to pass to the script, and `scriptName` is the full path name, relative to Gopher's data directory, of the script executable. If the script does not require arguments, you still must include the argument's field by placing " " in it, as this example shows:

```
Path=exec:"":myScript
```

The Type field denotes the kind of reply that will be sent—for example, 0, which is text.

Searching Indexes

If you use a link to query an index, the client must specify the search criteria, and your .links file must specify the script as the Path item—not an index, as you would expect by setting Type=7 (index). A sample follows:

```
Name=Search Index for Search Criteria
Path=7/sbin/myScript
Type=7
Port=+
Host=+
```

You can query more than one index at a time by putting the host name, port number, and path name to the index in a file that has the extension .mindex (multiple index). For example,

```
%cat > AirplaneSearch.mindex
furnace.sgi.com  70  7/indexes/airplane_index
oven.sun.com  70  7/indexes/flight_index
^D
```

Structuring Your File System

A great deal of effort often goes into the contents of your service files. They might be programs, images, or documents that your company has crafted at great expense and time. Too often, however, the people who toil so hard to create a product invest less energy in making it clear and presentable to others.

Your menu system is the user interface to the content in your files. Without a clear, concise, and well-thought-out hierarchy of files, file names, file groupings, and directory names, navigating your service can prove more trouble than it is worth. Invest the time it takes to really look at the arrangement of directories, the groupings of files in the directories, and the names of files and directories.

You already have learned that file and directory names have to be descriptive—not shorthand afterthoughts, such as newDoc3. Other good rules for names include avoiding insults ("If you still don't understand, choose me."), being specific (avoid, for example, "civilization"), avoiding technical jargon when possible (not "Polling in Replicated Services"), and remaining simple (not "Restructuring Forecasted Gross Income Figures").

About the worst case of file structuring would be a service without subdirectories—everything in one directory. Less obvious offenders are nearly as bad. Consider this file structure:

```
Finances
     Fiscal Growth
          1st Quarter Growth
     2nd Quarter Growth
          Increasing Profit Margins
               Reducing Expenditures
     3rd Quarter Growth
```

When you begin to structure a file system, it is sometimes hard to figure out what the future portends and how that should influence the file structure. Sometimes it is hard to figure out where to put new files. Are they different enough to warrant the creation of a new directory, or is there enough of a connection with other files in a current directory? You might find that, by mistake, you have parallel subdirectories in different parts of the file hierarchy. At some point, you might feel that the entire hierarchy is like a fortress of cards just waiting to fall down with the addition of one more file.

Reviewing the hierarchy of files is an important job that is hard to do well. Its importance often is obscured by the more technical tasks you are expected to perform. A program called *gophertree* helps you examine your file hierarchy. It lists only the directories in the system, for example, or it enables you to look at only a restricted part of the file hierarchy at one time.

You can obtain gophertree from boombox.micro. umn.edu in /pubs/gopher/Unix/GopherTools.

Using Files Common to Other Services

You already might have a significant number of files outside the subdirectories restricted by chroot(). Some might be easy to move, but others might not be easy to move. Some files might be part of another service you are offering, such as FTP. You might want to avoid duplication of files by using symbolic links. Unfortunately, that does not work because the link points outside of the chroot()'d hierarchy. This leaves you with only one alternative: copy the files into the chroot()'d hierarchy.

Using FTP Files

If your company already has an FTP service, you can leverage the files for use with Gopher. Find out the root for the document files. Make that path equal to the root document path as specified in gopherd.conf.

If there are directories in the FTP file system that you do not want to access through Gopher, use the ignore keyword in gopherd.conf to prevent access to those directories. For more information about the ignore keyword, see the section earlier in this chapter, "Hiding Files Based on File Types."

Creating Forms

If you have ever wanted to get information from a user, you know that it can be tedious if you have to ask questions sequentially. Gopher+ enables you to present forms to users with multiple input points.

These forms also are called *ASK blocks*. You create forms in files that have the extension .ask. They contain keywords that define the contents of the line on which they reside. Here is a very short example:

```
Note:                  WriteIt!
Note:        Information Pamphlet Order Form
Note:
Note:
Ask: Topic:<tab>
Ask: Phone:<tab>
Ask: email: <tab>
Note:
Note:
Choose:Version:English<tab>Spanish<tab>
```

Note that the tabs that end each Ask line are not strictly necessary, but are backward-compatible with older Gopher+ clients.

This form would display as shown in figure 17.1.

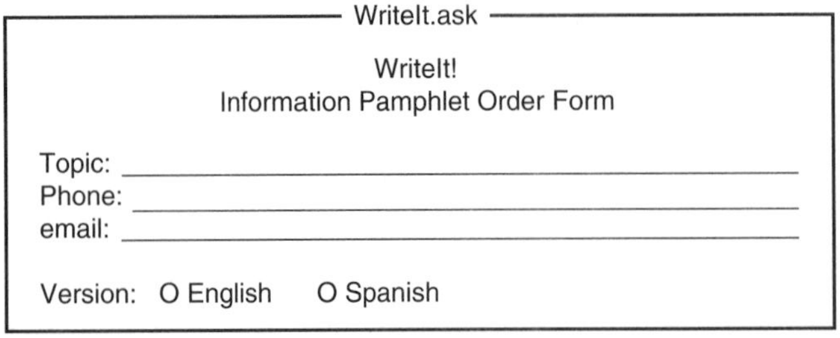

```
┌─────────── WriteIt.ask ───────────┐
│               WriteIt!             │
│    Information Pamphlet Order Form │
│                                    │
│  Topic: _____   │
│  Phone: _____   │
│  email: _____   │
│                                    │
│  Version:  O English    O Spanish  │
└────────────────────────────────────┘
```

Figure 17.1

A Gopher form.

You can see that the keywords created places for user input.

The user-input keywords follow:

Keyword	Function
Ask	Presents question and provides space to fill in the answer
AskL	Presents question and provides multiple lines for the answer
Askp	Presents question and provides space to enter a password
Choose	Presents a question with a set of answers from which the user chooses; many clients display these fields as radio buttons
Note	Prints text on form
Select	Presents Approve/Disapprove question; many clients display check boxes on forms

You can add default values for any of these keywords by typing the default value:

`Ask:Country:<tab>USA`

in which USA is the default value for the Ask question.

The Select keyword works a little differently from the other keywords. Here is a short example:

```
Note: What colors do you want?
Select: Red?:1
Select: Blue?:0
Select: Green?:0
```

These lines create three check boxes under the question in the Note. The numbers following the colon, 0 or 1, specify whether the boxes are on or off by default. In this example, only the red color is on by default. Some Gopher+ clients, however, display to the user true and false or yes and no instead of 0 and 1.

Now that you have created a form, you must write the script to handle the input. For the preceding form, you could write the following PERL script:

```
#!/usr/sbin/forms/pampletOrder

# Retrieve user input
$Topic = <>;
$Phone = <>;
$email = <>;
$Version = <>;

# Strip out unwanted characters

$Topic =~ s/[^A-Za-z0-9. ]//g;
$Phone =~ s/[^A-Za-z0-9. ]//g;
$email =~ s/[^A-Za-z0-9. ]//g;
$Version =~ s/[^A-Za-z0-9. ]//g;

# Return information to client

print << "EOF"
```

The first four lines of the script read the user entries from standard input. The second four lines strip out unwanted characters to prevent any monkey business. The **print** statement returns the information to the Gopher client. Instead of returning the information to the client, you could save it in a file using a statement similar to the following:

```
open (OUTPUT, ">/forms/output/writeit.$$") || die
➡"Can't    file to write in"
```

This script should be in a file that has the same root name as the .ask file—in this case, writeit.

To make all this work, you place the two files, writeit and writeit.ask, in the part of the Gopher service restricted by chroot() and make the script, writeit, executable by the same owner under which gopherd runs.

Finally, you should make a .names file for the script so that the menu title is more descriptive.

Summary

This chapter showed you that you must have a combination of talents to be a Gopher+ service administrator. On one hand, you must have the ability to look at log files and detect the health and usability of the system. On the other hand, you have to understand the content of the Gopher+ service well enough to create a meaningful file hierarchy, and to name files and directories appropriately.

This chapter showed you how your Gopher+ service can connect to other Gopher+ services or other internet service altogether, such as FTP or telnet. Providing invisible access to multiple servers is one of the great features in Gopher+.

Another great feature is the use of forms to input user data. This chapter gave you the basics you need to create forms and write PERL scripts that process the forms.

Setting Up a WWW Service

All the command-line interfaces covered so far in this book are powerful and fast, but have a learning curve and are text based. You can make text look only so good. WWW services present a multimedia interface. If you work at all in a windowing environment, the GUI front end flattens out the curve for learning how to use a WWW browser. The color, sound, images, and video clips provide the flash and excitement that makes "surfing the Internet" so easy and fun.

The real tool that WWW services use to make interfacing with the Internet so easy is *hyperlinks*. To look at a different document, just click on a highlighted word, button, or image. Rather than read the README files or look through reams of files that only might match your search criteria, WWW clients enable you to navigate the Internet with point-and-click ease (see fig 18.1).

I present the WWW service last because it's the newest of the services, and because WWW clients can use many of the services previously presented.

For example, a WWW client can access Gopher, FTP, and (for some clients) WAIS services, in addition to WWW services.

Getting the Client Software

The various WWW browsers all are free, and some will soon be reborn as commercial products. Table 18.1 describes the browsers and tells you where you can get them.

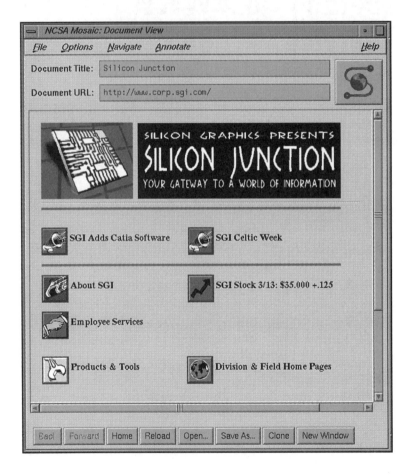

Figure 18.1

A World Wide Web page.

If you haven't already used a WWW browser, no description can substitute for getting your hands on and playing with a browser. Try it out first on the following URL:

http://www.paramount.com

Paramount's home page includes most of the tools you are likely to see in Web pages, including hypertext, buttons, and movie clips.

Table 18.1 WWW Browsers

Name	URL and Description
Lynx	ftp://ftp2.cc.ukans.edu/pub/lynx/
	A full-featured WWW browser developed at the University of Kansas that best displays character-based pages. The Lynx client compiles without difficulty on Linux.
MidasWWW	http://www-midas.slac.stanford.edu/midasv22/introduction.html
	A full-featured WWW browser developed at Stanford Linear Accelerator Center (SLAC) for X Window systems. Similar to Mosaic, but provides better support for inline graphics, including .fig, .jpeg, and .tiff files without having to spawn an external viewer.
Mosaic	ftp://ftp.ncsa.uiuc.edu/Mosaic/
	The most celebrated WWW browser, developed at the National Center for Supercomputer Applications (NCSA) at the University of Illinois, with versions for most Unix platforms, Apple Macintosh, and Microsoft Windows. MPEG movies, JPED images, and sound files automatically spawn external viewers, because Mosaic can only handle GIF or XBM image formats.
Netscape	http://home.netscape.com
	A full-featured, graphical browser created by Netscape Communications Corporation.
Emacs	ftp://moose.cs.indiana.edu/pub/elisp/w3/
	Compatible with Mosaic. Especially good for Mosaic users who also must dial in to the Internet, perhaps from home, on a slower line.
NeXT	ftp://info.cern.ch/pub/www/bin/next/
	Available for NeXT computers only.
perlWWW	ftp://archive.cis.ohio-state.edu/pub/w3browser
	A character-based WWW browser, written in PERL, developed at Ohio State University.

Getting Service Software

Three major WWW services have been written for the Unix platform. This book discusses installing the NCSA version of the Web service. Table 18.2, however, shows you where you can get the binaries for the other services, too.

This book discusses the NCSA Web service for the following reasons:

→ It is small and fast.

→ It can serve many documents simultaneously because the service draws so little on system resources.

→ It can run as a standalone daemon, or under inetd.

→ The service understands both the HTTP/1.0 and HTTP/0.9 protocols.

→ You can limit user actions and connections. You can prevent users from specific hosts from connecting to your service. You can also require user authentication to gain access to your service, if the WWW client supports user authentication.

→ If a browser supports user authentication, you can authenticate browsers with a user name and a password.

→ It enables you to create HTML catalogs of your directories. Catalogs describe what is in the directories.

→ You can write your own service scripts that generate documents on the fly.

→ You can move document files to different directories and different servers without having to rewrite the HTML, and without having to advise users of the move.

→ You can write scripts to handle form requests. Forms are documents that have one or more fill-in text fields that are often used for entering search criteria.

The NCSA Web service has a couple of features not found in the CERN service. Both services, however, are excellent.

Table 18.2   Binaries for Other WWW Services

Service	URL and Description
CERN	`ftp://info.cern.ch/pub/www/bin` From the birthplace of the WWW, comes the public-domain CERN Web service, supporting clickable images, forms, and access authorization.
NCSA	`http://boohoo.ncsa.uiuc.edu` or `ftp.ncsa.edu` Like the CERN service, the NCSA service is in the public-domain and written in C. This small, fast service supports clickable images, searches, HTML forms, and access restrictions.
Plexus	`ftp://austin.bsdi.com/plexus/2.2.1/dist/Plexus.html` This service is written in PERL, so is easy to modify, but heavyweight.

Setting Up the NCSA WWW Service

To get the service, you can either use a WWW client and point your URL at `http://boohoo.ncsa.uiuc.edu`, or use FTP to connect to `ftp.ncsa.uiuc.edu`.

After logging in as an anonymous user, change to the httpd_1.4 directory. The directory path is /Web/httpd/Unix/ncsa_httpd/httpd_1.4.

 note This book discusses the 1.4 version of the service. If a later version of the service exists when you connect to NCSA, you might choose to install it instead. If you do, make sure you check the README file and the installation documentation.

When you list the contents of the service directory, you find that there are two forms of the binary that you can download:

→ Compiled

→ Uncompiled

If your machine is on the following list, you're lucky: you can download a compiled version of the service. If not, you must download hpptd_1.4_source.tar.z and compile it after uncompressing and dearchiving it. NCSA offers the following compiled versions of their WWW service:

→ httpd_1.4.2_aix3.2.5.Z

→ httpd_1.4.2_aix3.2.5.tar.Z

→ httpd_1.4.2_hpux9.0.5.Z

→ httpd_1.4.2_hpux9.0.5.tar.Z

→ httpd_1.4.2_irix5.2.Z

→ httpd_1.4.2_irix5.2.tar.Z

→ httpd_1.4.2_linux.Z

→ httpd_1.4.2_linux.tar.Z

→ httpd_1.4.2_osf3.0.Z

→ httpd_1.4.2_osf3.0.tar.Z

→ httpd_1.4.2_solaris2.4.Z

→ httpd_1.4.2_solaris2.4.tar.Z

→ httpd_1.4.2_sunos4.1.3.Z

→ httpd_1.4.2_sunos4.1.3.tar.Z

All binaries come compressed, so you must uncompress and untar them—but first make sure you move yours to the directory in which you want it to reside, for example, /usr/bin/X11. The files that contain the word tar are the entire distribution, such as all the configuration and support files. The files that do not contain the word tar contain only the binary for the HTTPD server. Then use the following command:

```
% zcat httpd_1.4.2_operatingSystem.tar.Z | tar xvf-
```

in which *operatingSystem* is one of the operating systems listed above, depending on your operating system, or source, if your operating system is not listed in the http_1.4.2 directory.

Executing the preceding command creates an httpd_1.4.2 directory, which contains a README file and the following subdirectories.

Subdirectory	Contains
cgi-bin	(Common gateway interface) Sample gateway binaries and scripts; where you put custom gateway binaries of your own

continues

Subdirectory	Contains
Makefile	Rules and dependencies that build the service
conf	Not surprisingly, service configuration files
icons	Icons for directory indexing
src	All of the .c executables
support	Applications that the passwords users need to access the service

Installation notes are included in a separate, compressed file, Install.txt.z. You must download it separately.

```
ftp> get Install.txt.z
```

To uncompress it, use zcat.

```
% zcat Install.txt.z ¦ more
```

The cgi-bin directory contains the following directores and files:

```
warp 188% cd cgi-bin
warp 189% ls
archie      date      fortune      nph-test-cgi
test-cgi.tcl uptime
calendar    finger    mail         test-cgi
test-env    wais.pl
```

These programs allow your service to connect to other Internet services.

The conf directory contains the following directories and files:

```
warp 243% cd support
warp 244% ls
Makefile            change-passwd.readme
```

```
➡inc2shtml.c
auth            htpasswd.c
➡unescape.c
```

You use these programs to establish the passwords that users need to access the system.

Most likely, you will never have to work at all with the other directories, cgi-src, src, and icons.

Recompiling the Linux WWW Service Binary

If you have decided to reconfigure the default file locations for configuration files, then you must edit the associated files and rebuild the HTTPD service. The process of rebuilding the binary is simplified, however, because you already have the required components, and the Makefile is customized to Linux.

The HTTPD service binary is configured to use a directory under /usr/local/etc/httpd. The httpd binary is installed as httpd in this directory, along with the cgi-bin, support, logs, htdocs, conf, and icons directories.

If you wish to reconfigure where the files are located in the file system, then you must edit the file src/httpd.h. The following is the relevant section that must be changed:

```
/* --------------- config dir ---------------- */

/* Define this to be the default server home dir.
➡Anything later in this file with a relative
➡pathname will have this added.
 */
#define HTTPD_ROOT "/usr/local/etc/httpd"
```

```
/* Root of server */
#define DOCUMENT_LOCATION "/usr/local/etc/httpd/
➥htdocs"
```

Let's assume you want to put your HTTPD service files in /home/httpd. You would change the preceding lines to read:

```
/* ---------------- config dir ------------- */

/* Define this to be the default server home dir.
➥Anything later in this * file with a relative
➥pathname will have this added.
 */
#define HTTPD_ROOT "/home/httpd"

/* Root of server */
#define DOCUMENT_LOCATION "/home/httpd/htdocs"
```

Save the files and run a make to build the new binary. The make is started by running the following command:

```
make linux
```

Once the build is done, copy the new binary and support files into your new directory structure. You now are ready to configure your server.

Configuring the WWW Service

This section describes the minimal number of steps you must perform to configure your WWW service to your platform. The process involves editing three configuration files in the conf directory:

➜ httpd.conf-dist

➜ srm.conf-dist

➜ access.conf-dist

You should leave these configuration files as they are and make copies, perhaps saving without the -dist extension.

 note In all conf files, extra whitespace is ignored and only one directive can go on each line.

Whereas all of the basic configuration information is presented in the next several sections, advanced configuration administration is covered in the next chapter.

Setting Up httpd.conf-dist

The httpd.conf configuration file controls how the service, httpd, runs. Make a copy of httpd.conf-dist, call it httpd.conf, and use it to configure the service. Keep httpd.conf-dist as a reference copy.

Before you can edit the configuration file, you must decide whether you want the service to run under inetd or as a standalone daemon, and whether you want to restrict access to the service. In this section, you set the service to run as a standalone daemon that everyone can access. A later section discusses more involved configuration setups.

To set up httpd.conf, set the values of the directives in the following table.

Directive	Description
AccessConfig *fileName*	*fileName* is either an absolute pathname or a partial pathname relative to ServerRoot that specifies the location of the access.conf configuration file. The default is `AccessConfig conf/access.conf`.
AgentLog *file*	*file* is the file where you want to keep record of the client agent software. This directive is for statistical purposes and the tracing of protocol violations. You can only use this directive in standalone mode. The default is `AgentLog logs/agent_log`.
ErrorLog *fileName*	*fileName* is either an absolute pathname or a partial pathname relative to ServerRoot that specifies the location of the error log file. httpd includes information such as segmentation violations, bus errors, bad scripts, timed out clients, .htaccess files that attempt to defeat access.conf directives. The default is `ErrorLog logs/error_log`.
Group [*groupName* | *groupNumber*]	Specifies the group ID the copies of the service run as when answering client requests. This directive is only pertinent if the ServerType is set to standalone. The group ID can either be a name or user number. If you use a number,you must precede it with a pound sign (#). The default is `Group #-1`.
IdentityCheck [on | off]	Determines if the remote user is logged in as himself. This directive only works if the client application is running an RFC 931-compliant Identity daemon, such as identd. The default is `IdentityCheck off`.
MaxServers *number*	*number* is the maximum number of children for the hunt group.
PidFile *fileName*	*fileName* is a partial pathname relative to ServerRoot where you want httpd to record the process ID of each running copy of httpd. You can only use this directive in standalone mode. The default is `PidFile logs/httpd.pid`.
Port *portNumber*	*portNumber* specifies the port number httpd listens to. Ports below 1024 are reserved by the system. Port numbers cannot be greater than 65536. Unless you do

Setting Up and Managing Internet Services

	not want to make the service available to the Internet community, set the port number to 80. The default is `Port 80`.
ResourceConfig *fileName*	*fileName* is either an absolute pathname or a partial pathname relative to ServerRoot that specifies the location of the srm.conf configuration file. The default is `ResourceConfig conf/srm.conf`.
ServerAdmin *emailAddress*	*emailAddress* specifies the Internet System Administrators address. It is a good idea to use an alias, for example, `ServerAdmin sysAdmin` so that you can change system administrators without changing the e-mail address. This directive does not have a default.
ServerName *hostName*	*hostName* specifies the the domain name of your server or a DNS alias, for example `ServerName www.companyName.com`
ServerRoot *pathName*	*pathName* defines the absolute path of the root of your service above which users cannot trespass. The default is `ServerRoot /usr.local.etc.httpd`.
ServerType [inetd l standalone]	Specifies whether httpd is running under inetd or in standalone mode. The default is `ServerType standalone`.
StartServers *number*	*number* is the number of service processes you want to run concurrently.
TimeOut *seconds*	*seconds* defines the maximum amount of time (in seconds) the service waits for the client to submit a request once it has been connected, and the maximum amount of time the service should wait for the client to accept a request. The default is `TimeOut 1800`.
TransferLog *fileName*	*fileName* is either an absolute pathname or a partial pathname relative to ServerRoot that specifies the location of the log that records data, such as host, date, and file name, of service requests. These entries are described in greater detail following this table. The default is `TransferLog logs/access_log`.

continues

Directive	Description
TypesConfig *fileName*	*fileName* is either an absolute pathname or a partial pathname relative to ServerRoot that specifies the location of the MIME configuration file. The default is `TypesConfig conf/mime.types`.
User [*userName* I *userNumber*]	*userName* or *userNumber* defines the user ID the copies of the service run as when answering client requests. This directive is only pertinent if the ServerType is set to standalone. The user ID can either be a name or user number. If you use a number, you must precede it by a pound sign (#). By default, the copies run as user number one: `User #-1`

Normally, you should run the service in standalone mode (ServerType standalone). If you run it under inetd, each time a service request comes in, inetd must fork off a new process, load the httpd binary, and load and parse all three configuration files. When running in standalone mode, httpd_1.4 just copies itself and the copy handles the new request. As you can see, system performance is improved using the standalone mode. The only exception to this rule is if the service is not often used. Then you have the CPU serving the httpd process even though there are not requests for it to do anything.

Entries in the access_log file, or the file specified by the TransferLog directive, have the following form:

```
host rfc931 authuser [DD/Mon/YYYY:hh:mm:ss]
➥ "request"
   ddd bbbb
```

The elements of the entry are explained in the following table.

Element	Description
host	Either the IP address or the DNS name of the client making the request
rfc931	Any information returned by identd for the client
authuser	The user name that was sent by the client for the purposes of authentication
DD/Mon/YYYY	The day, month, and year the request was received
hh:mm:ss	The hours minutes and seconds of when the request was made
request	First line of the request
ddd	Status code returned by the server
bbbb	The total number of bytes sent by the server

Setting Up srm.conf

The srm.conf-dist (server resource management) configuration file specifies the location in which the service finds your scripts and documents. Make a copy of srm.conf-dist, call it srm.conf, and use it to configure the service. Keep srm.conf-dist as a reference copy.

To set up the configuration file, set the values for the directives listed in the following table.

You set the UserDir directive to the partial path, relative to the user's home directory (as given in /etc/passwd), that leads httpd to personal files. The service adds this partial path to the requested path name to find the user's document, For example, if this directive were set to its default

```
UserDir public_html
```

httpd would translate a request for /~images/first.gif to ~images/public_html/first.gif. You then define the path, public_html.

Because this directive can lead to security problems, you have the option of turning off this directive by using the keyword DISABLED.

```
UserDir DISABLED
```

Directive	Description
AccessFileName *fileName*	*fileName* specifies the name of the file that you can include in any directory that specifies access permissions for that directory. The default is `AccessFileName .htacess`.
AddDescription *text fileID*	Associates descriptive *text* with a type of file defined by extensions, a file name, an absolute path name, or a file name using wild cards (for example AddDescription "image file" *.gif).
AddEncoding *kind ext*	Specifies that files with *ext* are of type *kind* so that appropriate actions can be taken. For example, if the file is compressed, the browser can automatically uncompress it: `AddEncoding compress Z`.
AddIcon *path name1 name2 ...*	Specifies the icon to display with a kind of file; used when browsers display FTP menus.
AddIconbyEncoding *path name1 name2 ...*	Performs the same task as Icon except that the encoded information determines the icon used.
AddIconType *path type1 type2 ...*	Performs the same task as Icon except that the MIME type determines the icon used.
AddType *kind ext*	Supersedes MIME definitions for the specified extensions (*ext*) found in the mime.types file.

continues

Directive	Description
Alias *name path*	Substitutes *path* for *name* in path names. For example, if `Alias books /usr/resources` then books/apples is equivalent to /usr/resources/apples.
DefaultType *type*	Specifies the default MIME type. The default is `DefaultType text/html`.
DefaultIcon *pathName*	*pathName* specifies the default icon to use when FancyIndexing is on. The default is `DefaultIcon /icons/unknown.xbm`.
DirectoryIndex *fileName*	Specifies the *fileName* to return when the URL request is just your service, for example, http://www.sgi.com. The default is `DirectoryIndex index.html`.
DocumentRoot *path*	*path* specifies the absolute path to the directory from which httpd retrieves documents. The default is `DocumentRoot /usr/local/etc/httpd/htdocs`. If you have to serve documents outside of this directory, you can provide symbolic links or an alias from this directory.
FancyIndexing [on l off]	Adds icons, file name data, headers, and footers to lists of files automatically indexed; necessary only for backward compatibility with HTTP V1.0. The default is `FancyIndexing on`.
HeaderName fileName	Specifies the file name to be used at the top of a list of files automatically indexed. The default is `HeaderName HEADER`.
IndexIgnore *kind1 kind2 ...*	Specifies kinds of files to be ignored during file processing. The default is `IndexIgnore */.??* *~ *# */HEADER* */README`.
IndexOptions *option1 option2 ...*	Specifies a variety of indexing parameters, including FancyIndexing, IconsAreLinks, ScanHTMLTitles, SuppressLastModified, SuppressSize, and SuppressDescription.
OldScriptAlias *name path*	Performs the same task as Alias; but provides for backward compatibility to HTTP V1.0.
ReadmeName *fileName*	*fileName* specifies the footer information to attach to automatic directory indexes. The default is `ReadmeName README`.
Redirect *pathname URL*	Remaps *pathname* of document to new *URL*. There is no default for this directive.

ScriptAlias *name path*	Is similar to Alias, but used for scripts. This directive substitutes *path* for *name* in path names, for example

```
Alias collection /usr/cgi-bin/
```

so that `collection/scripts` is equivalent to `/usr/cgi-bin/scripts`. If you move `cgi-bin` from its default location, `/usr/local/etc/httpd/cgi-bin`, you might provide an alias path to it with `ScriptAlias`.

UserDir [path I DISABLED]	Specifies the directory users can make available for httpd access. The default is `UserDir public_html`.

Setting Up access.conf-dist

The access.conf-dist configuration file defines what service features are available to all WWW browsers. The default is to make everything available to all browsers. Make a copy of access.conf-dist, call it access.conf, and use it to configure the service. Keep access.conf-dist as a reference copy.

 note The next chapter describes security measures you can take to protect your WWW service, so I put off an extensive discussion about security until then.

Many of the configuration directives in the access.conf-dist file are sectioning directives. They stand out because they use angle brackets.

Sectioning directives have a beginning and ending delimiter, for example,

```
<Directory>
...
(/Directory>
```

Any directives between the delimiters apply to the listing following the first delimiter. For example,

```
<Limit GET>
order allow, deny
allow from all
</Limit>
```

In this example, the sectioning directive, Limit, determines who can retrieve information from the service, which, in this case, is "allow from all."

To set up the access.conf file, perform the following tasks:

→ Set the first Directory sectioning directive to the path of your cgi-bin directory. The default is

```
<Directory /usr/local/etc/httpd/cgi-bin>
```

→ Remove the Indexes option from the Options directive (in the first Directory sectioning directive) so that users cannot browse through the httpd directory. The default is

```
Options Indexes FollowSymLinks
```

The possible values for the Options directive include the following:

→ **All.** All features are enabled for the directory.

→ **ExecCGI.** cgi scripts can be executed in this directory.

→ **FollowSymLinks.** httpd follows symbolic links.

→ **Includes.** Server-side include files are enabled in this directory.

→ **IncludesNoExec.** Enables server-side includes, but disables the exec option.

→ **Indexes.** httpd allows users to retrieve service-generated indexes of this directory. Precompiled indexes in the directory are always available.

→ **None.** No features are enabled for the directory.

→ **SymLinksIfOwnerMatch.** httpd only follows symbolic links if the target file or directory is owned by the same user ID as the link.

→ Set the second Directory sectioning directive to the path DocumentRoot defines in the srm.conf file. The default is

```
<Directory /usr/local/etc/httpd/htdocs>
```

In this case, allowing the Indexes option in the Option directive (within the second Directory sectioning directive) is fine, because you want people to browse your documents.

→ Set the AllowOverride variable to None to prevent others from changing the settings in this file. This directive controls which access control directives can be overridden in a directory by the .htaccess file. The default is

```
AllowOverride All
```

Other values include the following:

→ **All.** Access control files are unrestricted in this directory.

→ **AuthConfig.** Enables the use of AuthName, AuthType, AuthUserFile, and AuthGroupFile directives.

→ **FileInfo.** Enables the use of AddType and AddEncoding directives.

→ **Limit.** Enables the use of the Limit sectioning directive.

→ **None.** No access control files are allowed in this directory.

→ **Options.** Enables the use of the Options directive.

The directives enabled by AuthConfig are defined as the following:

→ **AuthName.** Sets the authorization name of the directory, for example,

```
AuthName CompProject
```

→ **AuthType.** Sets the authorization type of this directory. Currently, there is only one type: Basic.

→ **AuthUserFile.** Specifies the file to use that contains the list of users and passwords used in user authentication, for example,

```
AuthUserFile /usr/local/etc/httpd/
conf/.htpasswd
```

→ **AuthGroupFile.** Specifies the file that lists user groups for user authentication, for example,

```
AuthGroupFile /usr/local/etc/httpd/
↳conf/.htgroup
```

→ Set the Limit sectioning directive to the appropriate values. The directives that can come in Limit sectioning directive include the following:

→ **allow** *hostName*. Enables specified hosts from accessing the service.

→ **deny** *hostName*. Prevents specified hosts from accessing the service.

→ **order** *ordering*. Determines the order in which the allow and deny directives are evaluated. Customary values are "deny,allow" and "allow,deny."

→ **require *entity1 entity2 ...*** Entity values can be user, group, or valid-user. These are the authenticated users or groups that can access the system. valid-user are users identified by AuthUserFile.

The only method that can currently follow the first Limit directive is GET, which allows clients to retrieve documents and execute scripts.

The default for the Limit sectioning directive is

```
<Limit GET>
order allow, deny
allow from all
</Limit>
```

In the default condition, the order directive defines the order in which allow and deny are evaluated, and everyone is allowed to retrieve documents.

Installing httpd

After you make basic changes to the configuration files, you can move httpd to the correct location in your file system.

 n o t e Remember that the HTTPD binary assumes it will find things in the default location of /usr/local/etc/httpd. If you out the files somewhere else, the binary still expects to look in the default directory for its configuration files. This can be altered by changing the HTTPD service configuration files or through a command line option.

Use the mkdir command to create a directory—call it httpd—in a location specified by ServerRoot. Then copy httpd and all the subdirectories, conf, logs, icons, and cgi-bin to the new directory, httpd, using the following command line:

```
% cp -r httpd logs conf icons cgi-bin <pathName>/
➥httpd
```

Use chown to make the logs directory writeable by the user ID under which the service runs.

Starting Your WWW Service

Your service is ready to start! You now need to decide whether you want httpd to run under inetd or as a standalone daemon. If your service gets little use (I hope not!) or you are testing your service, you can minimize the impact of httpd on your system by starting your WWW service under inetd. However, if your service is accessed regularly, you should run httpd as a standalone daemon, because every time inetd starts up and shuts down the service (which it does for each service request) causes a delay.

The following three command-line options, however, are common to both run-time environments:

Option	Description
-d directoryName	Specifies the absolute path to the httpd binary if it's not in the default location; this path matches the path specified by ServerRoot in httpd.conf
-f file	Name Specifies a configuration file to read instead of httpd.conf
-v	Displays the version number of the service

Running httpd Under inetd

inetd starts and stops services according to the requests the server receives: each service request starts an instance of the service, which terminates after sending a reply to the request. Each request specifies a port number; port numbers correspond to services running on the server. The standard port number for a WWW service is 80. You can change the Port variable in httpd.conf if you want the service to run on a different port. You would do that only to run a different version of the service for internal personnel, otherwise, all WWW services should run on port 80.

To make httpd run under inetd, complete the following tasks:

→ Add a line to /etc/services similar to the following:

```
http portNumber/tcp
```

http is the name of the service and *portNumber* is normally 80.

→ Add a line to /etc/inetd.conf similar to the following:

```
http stream tcp nowait nobody /pathName/httpd
httpd
```

where *pathName* is the pathname to the httpd binary. You can add any necessary command-line options after httpd.

→ Use the following command to restart inetd to make it read the configuration file, inetd.conf:

```
% kill -HUP <pid>
```

pid is the process ID of the service. The WWW service then starts whenever a request comes to port 80.

To stop the service, comment out the line you just added to inetd.conf.

Running httpd as a Daemon

The downside of running httpd as a standalone daemon is that it is always running. Of course, if your service is well liked, your service is going to run all the time anyway. The service runs faster in standalone mode because it does not need to repeatedly start, stop, and read the configuration files.

To start the service daemon using the defaults, type the following:

```
# httpd &
```

The ampersand (&) makes the service run in the background. You start the service as root so that the service can bind to port 80. After reading the configuration files, it changes the user ID and group ID to that specified in the httpd.conf configuration file.

Remember that, for example, if you have moved httpd from its default location, to start the executable with options.

You probably do not want to do this every time you restart the server. To automatically start the service during server startup, edit the /etc/rc0 file, for example:

```
if [ -x /usr/bin/X11/httpd ]

then

/usr/bin/X11/httpd
fi
```

When you need to restart the service, find the pid of httpd. If httpd has more than one, which it probably does, be sure to kill the parent by finding the process that has the lowest ID and a parent process ID of 1.

You can rest assured that the service is working well if the httpd server error log (logs/error_log, by default) says the following:

```
httpd: successful restart.
```

To restart httpd, execute the following on the command line:

```
# kill -1 'cat pidfile'
```

in which `pidfile` is the setting of PidFile for your service.

Alternatively, you can use the ps command to grep for httpd's process ID and send it a HUP signal.

To stop the service, execute the following on the command line:

```
# kill 'cat pidfile'
```

Testing httpd

Even if you have not yet populated your resources/ directory with data files, you at least can use a WWW browser to access the service adding the following to the URL field:

```
http://serverName
```

If your receive the contents of ServerRoot/ index.html or a directory index, hooray!—your service works. If you don't, look at the access and error logs for some clues about what is wrong.

Another way to determine whether the service is running is telneting into it, as the following example demonstrates:

```
warp 106% telnet www.corp.sgi.com 80
Trying 192.26.51.29...
Connected to palladium.corp.sgi.com.
Escape character is '^]'.
HEAD / HTTP/1.0
HTTP/1.0 200 OK
Server: Netsite-Communications/1.0
Date: Saturday, 11-Mar-95 02:25:58 GMT
Content-type: text/html
Connection closed by foreign host.
warp 107%
```

The preceding display shows the name of the server and the version of the service software.

Letting Others Know

All this effort goes for naught unless you let the Internet community know about your service. Chapter 3, "Advertising on the Internet," provides a comprehensive guide for getting out the word. There are, however, some WWW-specific avenues of announcing your service, including sending a message to the following addresses:

➔ www-request@info.cern.ch

➔ www-announce@www0.cern.ch

➔ whats-new@ncsa.uiuc.edu

 Make doubly sure that your announcement contains correct information. Correcting incorrect information after you send it out is difficult. Make sure, for example, that you set your URL off by itself. If you make it part of a sentence, users can confuse sentence punctuation with the URL; for example, an ending period.

Summary

It's time to open the gates and let the outside world in on the riches of your WWW service. In this chapter you completed a variety of tasks, including downloading the software, building and installing it, configuring the service, and editing the Makefile. After testing the service and creating a home page, you are at the jump point: if you send the announcements, they will come.

But wait! The security measures discussed in this chapter were very basic. If your service requires more sophisticated security, you need to read the next chapter, "Managing a WWW Service," before opening the flood gates. And, as the title of the next chapter implies, your job as Internet System Administrator is not complete. Although WWW services are easy to maintain, there are important chores that require your attention.

19

Managing a WWW Service

After you get your WWW service up and running, your job as Internet system administrator is far from done. You still have to do your common, everyday tasks, in addition to major tasks, such as revising the document tree.

Part of your managerial task involves maintaining your service's security. If you want your service to be open to everyone, the basic security measures presented in Chapter 18 might be enough for your company. If, however, your security requirements are more stringent, this chapter provides a little more octane for your service's security system.

Constructing URLs

Now you have a running service. Great! Let's make sure that people can find something to browse.

The search path for data files is called an URL (Uniform Resource Locator). To find your service, you need only the following URL:

```
http://serverName[:portNumber]
```

in which `serverName` is the name of your server and `portNumber` is specified only if you have your service running on a port other than 80.

If that's all the browser provides, httpd returns the contents of ServerRoot/index.html, if it is defined. If it's not, it returns a directory index that looks like what you get when you do a ls -l.

When browsers want specific documents, they use an expanded URL of the following form:

```
http://serverName/[Alias \
      (or ScriptAlias)/][pathName/]fileName
```

Both `Alias` and `ScriptAlias` are path names defined in srm.conf. For example, to define WWW to represent /usr/resources/WWW, you would make the following entry in srm.conf:

```
Alias /www/ /usr/resources/WWW/
```

httpd substitutes the path name defined in srm.conf for Alias or ScriptAlias. For example,

```
http://www.documentName
```

is resolved as

```
http://usr/resources/WWW/documentName
```

If httpd does not find an Alias (or ScriptAlias) in the URL, it checks to see if there is a prefix of the form

```
/~userName
```

If httpd finds this prefix, it substitutes for the prefix the user's public HTML subdirectory, public_html. httpd does not look for this prefix if, in srm.conf, you set UserDir to DISABLED.

If neither an Alias (or ScriptAlias) nor user prefix is in the URL, httpd inserts the path defined by DocumentRoot in srm.conf.

Creating a Home Page

Your company does not need a home page, but it is nice to have one. Many users may never see your home page because they may go straight to one of the many data files in your source tree. If for no other reason, however, it is nice to have a point of entry for users who have decided that it would be interesting to learn more about your company. You might also provide a hyperlink in each Web page to the home page so that users can start over easily.

The standard name of the home page is home.html. You put it at the top of your source tree, for example: http://www.corp.sgi.com/home.html. It is also a good idea to copy home.html into index.html or to set DirectoryIndex in srm.conf to home.html. These provisions send out your company's home page with even the most minimal URL address.

You use the home page, first, to make people go, "Wow!," and second, to give people an index to what is going on at your company. You should take a look at a wide variety of home pages already on the Internet before designing your own. Find several you like and use the stylistic elements in them that you like most.

If your company has multiple divisions, each might like to maintain their own home page. You might like to have a company home page that points users to the home pages of each company division.

There are no conventions for home pages; however, users have come to expect several elements, as follows:

→ "What's Hot" hyperlink, with the date it was last revised, publicizing your company's latest and greatest

→ Hyperlink to the system administrator, often called the WebMaster, for user feedback

→ Hyperlinks to major topics on the service, for easy navigation and an overview of your idea of what your company does best

→ The date the home page was last updated

Writing Your Home Page

The file format for WWW pages is HTML. It is beyond the scope of this book to teach you HTML. After you see a Web page, you get a clear idea what HTML lets you do: hypertext links, interactive buttons (which are links), and clickable, inline pictures.

There are a number of free HTML editors available for X Windows, for example, htmltext, which you can learn about from the following URL:

```
http://web.cs.city.ac.uk/homes/njw/htmltext
➥/htmltext.html
```

You also can embed HTML tags into documents using your favorite text editor. Learning the tags is easy, but there is some ramp up time involved.

 t i p Take a look at the HTML mode available for Emacs, URL:

```
ftp://ftp.ncsa.uiuc.edu/Web
➥html/elisp/html-mode.el
```

This extension to Emacs enables you to use keyboard commands to enter HTML tags easily.

Commercial HTML editors are emerging, such as HoTMetal, URL:

```
ftp://ftp.ncsa.uiuc.edu/Web/html/hotmetal
```

or send e-mail to

```
hotmetal@sq.com.
```

You also can use a variety of filters to convert files to HTML. Avalanche Development, makers of HoTMetaL, for example, has tools that convert WordPerfect and Microsoft Word documents to HTML.

The following gives you some other filters for documents you might like to convert:

FrameMaker to HTML

```
http://info.cern.ch/hypertext/WWW/Frame/fminit2.0
➥/www_and_frame.html
```

```
http://ww1.cern.ch/WebMaker/WEBMAKER.html
```

```
ftp://bang.nta.no/pub/
```

```
ftp://ftp.alumni.caltech.edu/pub/mcbeath/web
➥/miftran/
```

```
http://www.seas.upenn.edu/~mengwong/txt2html.html
```

BibTeX to HTML

```
ftp://gaia.cs.umass.edu/pub/hgschulz/windex-
➥1.2.tar.Z
```

```
http://www.reasearch.att.com/biblio.html
```

Interleaf to HTML

```
http://info.cern.ch/hypertext/WWW/Tools
➥/il2html.html
```

```
http://info.cern.ch/hypertext/WWW/Tools
➥/interleaf.html
```

PostScript to HTML

```
http://stasi.bradley.edu/ftp/pub/ps2html/ps2html-
➥v2.html
```

Troff to HTML

```
http://cui_www.unige.ch/ftp/PUBLIC/oscar/scripts
➥/ms2html
```

Managing Log Files

The WWW service has two log files: the *error log*, which contains error messages, and the *transfer log*, which contains information about who's using the service. You use the ErrorLog and TransferLog directives, respectively, to set the locations for these logs in the httpd.conf configuration file. The default locations of the files are /logs/error_log and logs/access/log, respectively, relative to the directory in which the httpd binary resides. The ServerRoot directive in the http.conf configuration file specifies the binary's residence.

The transfer log contains entries that adhere to the following format:

```
hostName userCheck authUser dateTime request
code numBytes
```

For example:

```
palladium.corp.sgi.com  -  -  [12/Mar/1995:09:12:18
-0900]  "GET/What's-Hot.html  HTTP/1.0"  200  68742
```

The following describes each field in the entry:

→ **hostName.** The name of the host machine.

→ **userCheck.** If the IdentityCheck directive in httpd.conf is off, a dash appears in this field; if the IdentityCheck directive is on, httpd tries to connect to a RFC 931-compliant daemon on the machine running the WWW browser to get the user's name. If the browser machine has such a daemon, the user's name appears in the field; if the daemon is not running (usually the case), a dash (-) appears in the field.

→ **dateTime.** The time the request was made in the browser's local time including the number of hours difference from GMT, nine hours, in this example.

→ **request.** The service request sent by the WWW browser.

→ **code.** Transaction's HTTP/1.0 status code (200 in this example).

→ **numBytes.** The number of bytes sent to the WWW browser.

Using Log Analysis Tools

Staring at log files might not give you the information you need. For example, the raw data in the log files might hide trends in the data that only programs that process the log data can elucidate. For example, it might not be clear, just from looking at the raw data, how the number of service users has varied over time.

Several log analysis tools are available for garnering more information from your log files, including getstats, wusage, and wwwstat.

Using getstats

getstats enables you to analyze your log files by various groupings; for example, you can analyze the data on a monthly basis, an hourly basis, by request, by domain, or by directory.

Kevin Hughes, `kevinh@eit.com`, wrote getstats (see fig. 19.1). It's available from the following URL:

`http://www.eit.com/software/getstats/getstats.html`

Figure 19.1

getstats.

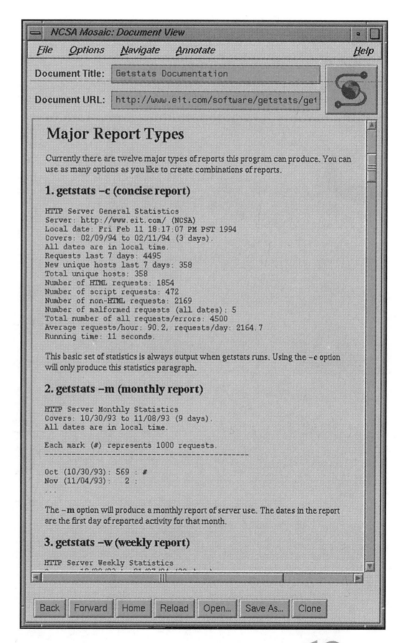

Using wusage

wusage creates statistics, graphs, and pie charts on a weekly basis and shows such things as the number of users that access the service and the location of users.

Thomas Boutell, `boutell@netcom.com`, wrote wusage (see fig. 19.2). It's available from the following URL:

`http://siva.cshl.org/wusage.html`

Using wwwstat

wwwstat, and its companion tool, gwstat, can provide graphical analysis of such things as the number of users accessing the service on an hourly basis.

Roy Fielding, `fielding@ics.uci.edu`, wrote wwwstat and gwstat (see fig. 19.3). They're available from the following URL:

`http://www.ics.uci.edu/Admin/wwwstats.html`

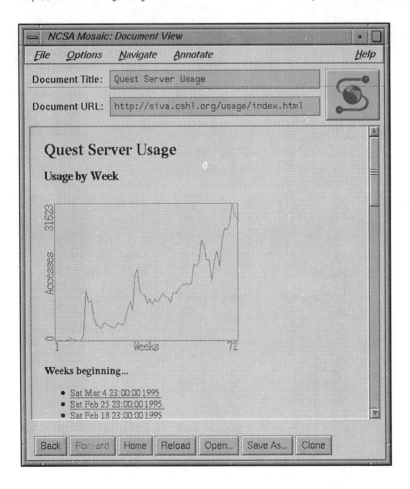

Figure 19.2

wusage.

Figure 19.3

wwwstats.

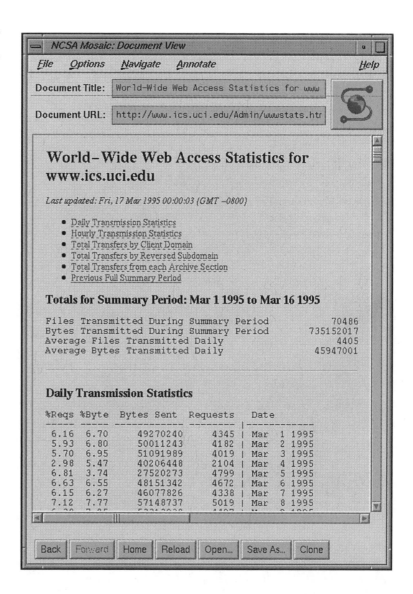

Archiving Log Files

Log files grow forever. Inevitably, you must archive, move, or delete them. Generally, you should write a cron job that does this task automatically. You can vary the parameters of the cron job according to the specifics of your service. For example, you might archive the log files to a separate directory at midnight every night, and delete the current files in the archive, or perhaps completing the same task on a weekly basis would be more appropriate. The problem you must solve is how to move the log files without disturbing the service. (You don't want to disturb the service every 24 hours.)

Running Under inetd

If httpd is running under inetd, you can just use the mv command to move the access_log files without affecting the overall service, owing to the fact that the next service request automatically starts a new access_log file.

Running httpd as a Standalone

When httpd runs in standalone mode, it keeps the log files open continuously (until it terminates). To move the log files to a new location, complete the following steps:

1. Use mv to move the log file to the archive file; httpd keeps writing to it anyway.

2. Restart httpd by issuing the following command, where *pid* stands for the process ID of the httpd service:

   ```
   kill -HUP pid
   ```

   When the service restarts, it opens a new log file as specified by the TransferLog directive in the http.conf configuration file.

Adding New Drives

Perhaps you're in the enviable position of having new Web documents from your company flooding onto the system to the extent that your disk space is filling up all too quickly. Now your problem is how to mount an additional drive without changing the path name to the moved files.

Let's say your new drive is mounted as /anatomy /upper and your current file system looks like the following:

```
% ls /usr/resources/WWW/plastic_surgery
noses/
```

```
chins/
tummies/
```

You decide, because the noses directory has grown beyond expectations, to move it to the new drive. Follow these steps:

1. Use mkdir to create a noses/ directory on /anatomy/upper.

2. Use mv to move the files and directories under noses/ to the new drive under /anatomy/upper /noses.

3. Create an alias for the moved directory by using the Alias directive to construct an entry in srm.conf similar to the following:

   ```
   Alias /noses/ /anatomy/upper/noses/
   ```

   When a user makes a request from the noses/ directory, httpd automatically substitutes a document from the /anatomy/upper/noses/ directory. Although the user is entering the same path for the desired document, the user is actually retrieving the information from the mounted drive.

4. Restart the httpd service using the following:

   ```
   % kill -HUP pid
   ```

5. Use rmdir to remove the noses/ directory on the old drive.

Using the preceding procedure makes the new drive transparent to your service users.

Advanced Web Management

Although httpd can routinely handle about thirty different kinds of file types, others exist that it cannot handle. One set of types it cannot handle, for example, is called the MIME types. This section shows you how to handle MIME types.

One area in which WWW browsers are weak is in searching for documents. One way to help the browser is to put an index.html file (which you write) that describes the layout of the document tree, at the top of the tree. If you don't use such a file, httpd can automatically index the directories so the browser can see what is available.

The following section explores how to handle MIME types, and how to have httpd automatically index and present your document offerings.

Handling More File Types

As more and more file types get thrown into the pot of Web documents, it is very possible that your WWW service does not recognize some existing file types. For example, if you have a Word document that you want your WWW service to distribute, you must define the new type.

Version 1.0 of HTTP adds MIME (Multipurpose Internet Mail Extension) information to the header file of all documents sent between the service and the browser to define the file type being sent.

The syntax of the information sent by the service is as follows:

→ First, the header information describing the file is sent.

→ Second, a blank line is sent to delimit the file description information from the actual document.

→ Third, the requested document is sent.

To send a TIFF file, for example, the service first passes the MIME type "image" and the subtype "tiff" in the header information, as shown here:

```
image/tiff
```

Having this file description information up front lets the browser decide how to display the document the service sends. Many file types require the browser to spawn an external display. If the MIME types are text/html or text/plain, the browser displays the data file. If the service sends other MIME types, the browser spawns external viewers. For example, if the MIME type sent is image/tiff, an X browser would spawn an xv window.

 n o t e When a WWW browser receives something other than an HTML or plain text file, it caches the document, and then looks in the mailcap file for the correct type of viewer to spawn for the given document (MIME) type.

Every time a WWW browser makes a request, the browser passes to the service all of the MIME types it can use. The service makes sure it sends only one of those MIME types to the browser.

The configuration file, mime.types, defines the standard MIME types that browsers and services can use. This file contains a very complete set of standards. If, however, you find that you want to define a new MIME type, you can use the following three directives in srm.conf (server resource map) to do so:

→ **AddEncoding.** Adds MIME types that can be passed

→ **AddType.** Defines a new file extension as representative of an existing MIME type

→ **DefaultType.** Defines default MIME type

The AddEncoding directive has the following format, in which *fileType* is the type of file being passed, and *extension* is the extension to the file name that identifies the *fileType*:

```
AddEncoding  fileType  extension
```

If, for example, documents on your service use a new compressed-file format, you would add the following line to mime.types, so that any file with the .X extension would be identified as a "compress" file:

```
AddEncoding  compress  X
```

None of this works, of course, if the browser does not know what to do with an .X file, which is why it lets the service know beforehand what MIME types it can handle.

The AddType directive lets you add a new file extension to an existing MIME type. If, for example, you want to define type .tif to be the same as type .tiff (because a PC cannot use more than three characters in the extension), you would put the following line in srm.conf:

```
AddType  image/tiff  tif
```

The DefaultType directive defines the type of MIME type to send to the browser if the document has an extension that the service does not recognize. The default DefaultType is text/html.

Using these directives enables you to offer the latest file types to the Internet community.

Enabling Automatic Directory Indexing

When a user uses an URL that is a directory name rather than a file name, the WWW service automatically tries to return the index.html file for that directory. You are responsible for creating the index.html file. If you do not include one, you can use the Indexes option for the Option directive in access.conf to return an automatically generated directory index, or an error. To allow users to see an index of the file system, you would include the following line in access.conf:

```
Options Indexes
```

If, for some reason, perhaps pertaining to security, you do not want users to see the contents of a directory, use the NONE value for the Option directive:

```
Options NONE
```

Otherwise, leave the indexing option enabled.

The two styles of indexing are *fancy* and *drab*. (Actually, drab is not a value; Fancy indexing is turned on or off.) You control that using two directives in srm.conf: FancyIndexing and IndexOptions. FancyIndexing is a toggle switch used for backward compatibility for HTTP 1.0. The default is ON.

The IndexOptions directive has a FancyIndexing option which, when included, turns on fancy indexing. The line in the access.conf file looks like the following:

```
IndexOptions FancyIndexing
```

FancyIndexing adds an icon before a file name and a file description after the file name.

You can use the following directives in srm.conf to customize the icons and descriptions associated with each file name:

→ **Add Description.** Associates a brief file description with a file extension

→ **AddIcon.** Defines the type of icon to display according to file name

→ **AddIconType.** Defines the type of icon to display according to file type

→ **DefaultIcon.** Default icon to display when FancyIndexing is on and an icon has not been associated with a file type

→ **IndexOptions.** Controls fancy indexing display

The syntax of AddDescription is simple, as follows, where *description* is a brief description of the file type (note the quote marks), and *fileExtension* is the file extension to which the description pertains:

```
AddDescription "description" *.fileExtension
```

For example:

```
AddDescription "TIFF image" *.tiff
```

The description (must be in quotes) appears to the right of the file name in the directory listing for any files that have the .tiff extension.

Both AddIcon and AddIconType have the same syntax, where *pathName* is the path name to the icon to be displayed, *fileName* is the name of a file, or kinds of listings (like the preceding *.tiff example), and *MIME_type* is a MIME type/subtype listing:

```
AddIcon pathName fileName
```

```
AddIconType pathName MIME_type
```

Rather than specify icons for specific directories, you can use wild cards with AddIcon to specify icons to use with different kinds of listings, including ^^DIRECTORY^^ for a directory, and ^^BLANKICON^^ for any blank lines.

You should make sure that you define an icon for every file type in your system. Mistakes do happen,

of course, so it's a good idea to define a DefaultIcon, using the following syntax, where *pathName* is the path name of an icon:

```
DefaultIcon pathName
```

For example:

```
DefaultIcon /usr/WWW/icons/whoKnows.rgb
```

The IndexOptions directive determines whether fancy indexing is turned on or off and what information is contained in the fancy indexing. The directive uses the following syntax:

```
IndexOptions option1 option2 option3
```

The possible *options* are as follows:

→ **FancyIndexing.** Turns on fancy indexing

→ **IconsAreLinks.** Makes the icons hyperlinks to their associated file names

→ **ScanHTMLTitles.** Displays, in the *description* field, the information between the <TITLE> HTML tags for HTML files without defined descriptions

→ **SuppresslastModified.** Prevents the display of the last date the files was modified in the directory index

→ **SuppressSize.** Prevents display of the file size in the directory index

→ **SuppressDescription.** Prevents display of the description field for all files

Fancy indexing also lets you add header and footer information to an index. Header and footer information can be plain text or HTML. You specify the header information in the HEADER file. You can use the Headername directive in srm.conf to change the name of the file you want to be the header.

You define the footer information in the README file. You can use the ReadmeName directive in srm.conf to change the name of the file you want to be the footer file. For example, the following defines that the contents of the bottom file be used as footer information:

```
ReadmeName /usr/resources/bottom
```

You use the IndexIgnore directive in srm.conf to enable or disable displaying the header and footer. The default is not to display the header and footer in an automatic directory listing, as shown here:

```
IndexIgnore */HEADER* */README*
```

You can eliminate that restriction for the entire service or for specific directories.

The following listing shows the defaults for directory listings:

```
AddIconType (TXT,/icons/text.xbm) text/*
AddIconType (IMG, /icons/image.xbm) image/*
AddIconType (SND,/icons/sound.xbm) audio/*
AddIcon /icons/movie.xbm .mpg .qt
AddIcon /icons/binary.xbm .bin
AddIcon /icons/back.xbm ..
AddIcon /icons/menu.xbm ^^DIRECTORY^^
AddIcon /icons/blank.xbm ^^BLANKICON^^
DefaultIcon /Icons/unknown.xbm
ReadmeName README
Geadername HEADER
IndexIgnore */.??* *~ *# */HEADER* */README*
```

The ".." indicates a partial file name.

Extending WWW Resources

You have seen that WWW browsers can access Gopher and FTP services, in addition to accessing WWW services. Other services, however, are not supported. Many WWW browsers, for example, cannot access WAIS services.

Not all information types are supported by WWW services either. Information can be derived from a table lookup in a database created dynamically at run time, for example. Most services expect information to remain dormant in source files.

The way to get around these restrictions is to use gateways. *Gateways* are programs or scripts written in a variety of programming languages—such as PERL, C, C++, C Shell, or the Bourne shell—that run external programs under the direction of a WWW service. The external program might pass user input to a WAIS service and return, to the WWW service, either HTML documentation, or an URL pointing to HTML documentation. The WWW service then passes that information on to the WWW client.

You can write your own gateways, use gateways written by others that are available either on the Internet or in your favorite software store, or use the gateways that come with your httpd service in the cgi-bin directory. Let's look at some of the included gateways.

Using Gateways in cgi-bin

Which gateway software is in cgi-bin depends on the WWW service software that you installed. This discussion covers the software distributed in the NCSA version of httpd.

cgi-bin includes the following gateways:

→ **archie.** Provides a gateway to Archie services using HTML <ISINDEX> tags

- **calendar.** Provides access to Unix's cal executable using HTML <ISINDEX> tags

- **date.** Displays today's date

- **finger.** Provides a gateway to Finger services using HTML <ISINDEX> tags

- **fortune.** Provides a connection to a fortune teller

Also included are some sample CGI test scripts, including the following:

- nph-test-cgi

- test-cgi

- test-cgi.tcl

The directory also includes miscellaneous HTML form examples, including jj, a submarine sandwich ordering form, and query, a generic form.

Service and CGI Script Interaction

There are two parts to the puzzle of service and CGI interaction:

- Getting input to the gateway script

- Getting information out of the gateway

Getting Input to the Gateway Script

Because you access a gateway script through a service, you might wonder how your gateway script can get any input. You cannot send your script information through switches on the command line. Instead, a gateway receives information in one of three ways:

- Environment variables

- Command line

- Standard input

Using Environment Variables

When a WWW service needs to pass a request made by a WWW client to a gateway, the service sets the following environment parameters as it executes the gateway program.

The following variables are set for all requests:

- **GATEWAY_INTERFACE.** The version number of the CGI specification supported by the WWW service

- **SERVER_NAME.** The name, IP address, or DNS alias, of the WWW server

- **SERVER_SOFTWARE.** The name and version number of the service

The following variables are set according to request:

- **AUTH_TYPE.** Used to authenticate the user ID, if the client host supports authentication

- **CONTENT_LENGTH.** The length of request as specified by WWW client

- **CONTENT_TYPE.** The type of data

- **PATH_INFO.** The input for the gateway script located at the end of the gateway's virtual path name

- **PATH_TRANSLATED.** Provides the absolute path name for PATH_INFO

- **QUERY_STRING.** The query information following the question mark (?) in the URL that specifies the gateway script

- **REMOTE_ADDR.** IP address of the client's host

- **REMOTE_HOST.** The name of the client's host

- **REMOTE_USER.** If the client host supports authentication, and the gateway script is protected, this is the user ID running the WWW client

- **REQUEST METHOD.** The method of the request; for example, GET, POST, and HEAD

- **SCRIPT_NAME.** The virtual path to gateway script

- **SERVER_PORT.** The port number of the client request

- **SERVER_PROTOCOL.** The name and version number of information protocol of the request

In addition to these variables, if the WWW client includes header lines in its request, the header names, with the prefix HTTP_ added, are set in the environment. The service, however, can ignore these variables if they have already been set, or if they conflict with other variables. Two such header names are ACCEPT and USER-AGENT. They become the following:

- **HTTP_ACCEPT.** Defines the MIME types the WWW client can handle

- **HTTP_USER_AGENT.** The name of the client's WWW browser

The two environment variables that mostly provide data for the gateway script are PATH_INFO and QUERY_STRiNG.

You can access a gateway script using its virtual path names. The PATH_INFO variable is set to any information beyond the virtual path name of the gateway script.

The QUERY_STRING is any information beyond a question mark in your URL. The WWW client, for example, requests the following URL:

```
http://www.corp.company.com
➡ /pathName?ask+about+something
```

Notice that you use the plus sign (+) to fill in blank spaces between words in the query. When the WWW service starts the gateway script, it sets QUERY_STRING to "ask+about+something."

Passing data after question marks to gateway scripts is called the GET method of accessing a script. All gateway scripts using this method must read the QUERY_STRING variable and parse the request. Generally, you use the GET method when the gateway script requires only one argument. The meaning of the script depends on the gateway script.

You can check to see in what way your gateway script is being accessed by examining the REQUEST_METHOD environment variable.

Using Standard Input
If your gateway script requires more input, you can enter it using the standard input. This method of input is called the POST method. The POST method is generally used with HTML forms. An *HTML form* is a page with several fill-in-the-blank fields. Each field could be input data to pass to the gateway script. The length of the queries is contained in the CONTENT_LENGTH variable.

Using the Command Line
A third way to pass user input to the gateway script is by using an <ISINDEX> tag in an HTML document. When a browser finds such a tag, it displays the following message:

This is a searchable index. Enter search keywords:

The input is then sent to the gateway script using the GET method.

Using CGI Test Scripts

The cgi-bin directory contains three test scripts you can use to see how the environment variables are set according to the information sent to the gateway script. The URL

```
http://hoohoo.ncsa.uiuc.edu/cgi-bin/test-cgi?
➡\ask+something+interesting
```

generates a test script report similar to the following:

```
CGI/1.0 test script report:

argc is 0. argv is .

SERVER_SOFTWARE = NCSA/1.4B
SERVER_NAME = hoohoo.ncsa.uiut.edu
GATEWAY_INTERFACE = CGI/1.1
SERVER_PROTOCOL = HTTP/1.0
SERVER_PORT = 80
REQUEST_METHOD = GET
HTTP_ACCEPT = text/plain, application/x-html,   \
     application/html, text/x-html, text/html
PATH_INFO =
PATH_TRANSLATED =
SCRIPT_NAME = /cgi-bin/test-cgi
QUERY_STRING = ask+something+interesting
REMOTE_HOST = companyGate.company.com
REMOTE_ADDR = 203.14.975.3
REMOTE_USER =
AUTH_TYPE =
CONTENT_TYPE =
CONTENT_LENGTH =
```

Getting Information from the Gateway Script

The only trick in getting documents returned properly to WWW browsers is adding a header to the returned document that defines the type of document that is returning. Documents can be almost any type, including audio clips, text, or images.

The first line of the header specifies the MIME type, for example, text/html, or text/plain. The second line of the header is blank. The blank line tells the browser that the following lines are from the document that was retrieved.

Instead of returning documents, a gateway script can also return a pointer to another document on the same or a different service. To return a pointer to another document, use the Location: directive. To point the WWW browser at a document in a different part of the service, for example, you return the virtual path name to the file:

```
Location: /pathName/fileName.html
```

If the document your reply points to is on a different service, perhaps your Gopher service, you would use an absolute path name, for example:

```
Location: gopher://furnace.engr.sgi.com/0
```

In each case, the WWW browser makes another request automatically to the file specified by the Location: directive.

Guidelines for Writing Gateway Scripts

This section contains only the broadest guidelines. For specific examples, look at the gateway scripts provided in the cgi-bin directory, or at the gateways available on the Internet listed in the following section.

It is a good idea to create a gateway script that can work both with and without information added to an URL. If the information is not added to the URL, your script must:

1. Get the input using the <ISINDEX> tag.

2. Send the request to stdout.

If the URL does have the query information following a question mark, your script must:

1. Retrieve the query from the QUERY_STRING environment variable.

2. Parse the query to rid it of the plus signs (+).

3. Carry out the query request.

4. Send the reply to stdout.

Gateway Security

Having your WWW service use gateways can open a Pandora's box of trouble. Receiving input from a WWW browser can waylay even the most innocent scripts. This section offers a simple checklist of areas of concern.

Consider the eval Statement

If the language that you write a gateway script in has an eval statement, such as PERL and the Bourne shell, be very careful how it can be misused. The eval statement allows the interpreter to execute a command, constructed using eval, outside of the gateway. Inputting metacharacters into eval statements can sometimes cause the

execution of arbitrary commands on your service's server. PERL actually has a CGI library to detect the dangerous use of metacharacters at the following URL:

```
ftp://ftp.ncsa.uiuc.edu/Web/httpd/Unix/ncsa_httpd
➥/cgi/cgi-lib.pl.Z
```

In short, do not trust the WWW client to behave responsibly.

Eliminate Server-Side Includes

Server-side includes should not be used at all on services. If they are on your service, however, at least disable them for the gateway script directories.

Avoid popen() and system()

Place backslashes in front of all characters if they have special meaning in the Bourne shell if you can use WWW client data to create a command line that calls popen() or system().

Free Gateways on the Internet

There are a number of gateway scripts available on the Internet that are of terrific value for your WWW service. The following sections describe those offerings.

Genera

Stanley Letovsky (letovsky@cs.jhu.edu) wrote the Genera gateway to integrate the use of Sybase databases with WWW services. The script can use an existing Sybase database or create a new one, and use a WWW front end. For example, it can use HTML forms for querying the database.

You can retrieve the gateway at the following URL:

```
http://cgsc.biology.yale.edu/genera.html
```

Hytelnet

Earl Fogel (`earl.fogel@usask.ca`) wrote the Hytelnet gateway to provide WWW access to telnet sites accessible on the Internet.

You can retrieve the gateway at the following URL:

```
http://info.cern.ch/hypertext/WWW/HytelnetGate/
Overview.html
```

man2html

Earl Hood (`ehood@convex.com`) wrote the man2html gateway to convert nroff manpages to HTML. The conversion is done on the fly. The advantage of this gateway is that you can be assured of receiving the latest version of the manpages. The disadvantage of converting documents on the fly is that they use CPU time.

You can retrieve the gateway at the following URL:

```
ftp://ftp.uci.edu/pub/dtd2html
```

Oracle

This gateway provides a WWW view of an Oracle database. The gateway turns the URL into a SQL SELECT directive and replies with an Oracle table.

You can retrieve the gateway at the following URL:

```
http://info.cern.ch/hypertext/WWW/RDBGate/   \
    Implementation.html
```

Making a WAIS Service Available to WWW Browsers

WAIS services are particularly powerful search engines. Searching for documents is one of a WWW browser's weakest aspects. One way around the problem is using a gateway to a WAIS service. This section describes how you can provide that.

You have the following options if you want to create a gateway to a WAIS service:

→ Do nothing, because Mosaic can already access WAIS services

→ Use a WAIS-to-WWW gateway available for free on the Internet

→ Create your own WAIS-to-WWW gateway

→ Buy a WAIS-to-WWW gateway

The Do Nothing Option

By "do nothing," I mean that all you provide the user through your WWW service is a hyperlink to a WAIS service. At the outset, this seems like an attractive solution. It costs nothing and it takes no time, and yet people with Mosaic can access a WAIS service.

Other WWW browsers may follow suit and also offer automatic access to WAIS services, but right now, that is not the case. All other WWW browsers receive that nasty message that says the WAIS service refuses to send its documents to you. This message makes your hyperlink look broken, which it is not, and it casts doubt on how well your WWW service is maintained. And if the WAIS service is valuable for one set of browsers, it must be valuable to all sets. Consequently, a "do nothing" solution is more of a step backward than forward.

Using WAIS-to-WWW Gateway Freeware

There are several sources on the Internet of free WAIS-to-WWW gateways. Use the following URLs to retrieve them:

```
http://www.ncsa.uiuc.edu:8001
➥/WAISServerName:portNumber/databaseName?
```

```
http://info.cern.ch:8001/WAISServerName:portNumber
➥/databaseName?
```

Actually, these services hide their true natures. They are really WWW services with WAIS gateways of their own. Your WWW service starts the gateway script that accesses one of these WWW services, that, in turn, uses its WAIS gateway to carry out the WWW browser's request. When the WWW service receives the WAIS reply, it changes it into HTML, and hands it over to your WWW service, which, in turn, hands it over to the WWW browser. This seems like a roundabout way of conducting business, but it is free and it works—most of the time.

Creating Your Own Gateway

As you learned previously, gateways are programs or scripts that run external programs under the direction of a WWW service. The external program might pass user input to a WAIS service and return, to the WWW service, either HTML documentation, or an URL pointing to HTML documentation. The WWW service then passes that information onto the WWW client. The Common Gateway Interface (CGI) provides a standard protocol for gateways that any WWW browser can use.

Gateway programs can be written in a variety of programming languages, including PERL, C, C++, and the Bourne and C Shell. The basic parts of the program include the following:

→ User input

→ CGI implementation

→ A search engine

→ HTML reply

To look at some gateway example code, look at the source files located at the URLs for the freeware WAIS-to-WWW gateways mentioned in the previous section, and look in the cgi-bin directory for wais.pl.

Buying Gateway Software

As the Internet matures, more and more software for it will be for sale. Freeware may continue to be a major attraction on the Internet, but it will become hard for programmers to resist selling people tools that they need.

WAISgate, a gateway software that you can buy, works with WWW browsers that support forms. WAISgate uses forms to create user queries.

You can get more information about WAISgate from the following URL:

```
http://www.wais.com/directory-of-servers.html
```

Choosing a Gateway

The most troublesome option is to create your own gateway software. Not only do you have to develop it, you have to maintain it. On the other hand, it probably offers you the best results. You can customize the interaction between the WWW and WAIS services.

WAISgate offers good results without having to develop the software. Its real downside, however, is that it does not support WWW browsers that cannot handle forms.

The freeware on the Internet is a good place to start while you are either buying or writing gateway software. The freeware, however, is not bullet-proof.

Managing WWW Security

I know I don't have to make a case for being careful about what you let users touch. This section describes WWW-specific security measures you can take to restrict access to your service by virtue of the domain name of the browser's host, or the identification of the user.

Restricting Access by Domain Name

You can deny or allow a host to access your service across the entire service or on a per-directory basis. You specify global restrictions in the access.conf file; you place per-directory restriction specifications in each directory in a file called, by default, .htaccess. You can alter the AccessFileName directive in the srm.conf configuration file if you want to change the name from .htaccess.

The directives you use to accomplish this are defined in access.conf and are shown as follows.

➜ **allow.** Permits the specified host access to the service

➜ **AllowOverride.** Defines whether per-directory access overrides global access restrictions

➜ **deny.** Restricts specified hosts from accessing the service

➜ **<Directory>.** Marker that has beginning and ending points within which all access directives apply to specified hosts

➜ **<Limit>.** Marker that has beginning and ending points within which the hosts are defined that can access a directory

➜ **order.** Describes the order in which the allow and deny directives are evaluated within a <Limit> section

The allow directive has the following syntax:

```
allow from host1  host2 ...
```

The *hosts* can define a host in one of the following ways:

all	Nobody gets in; all hosts are denied access
domain name	Only hosts from a domain name, for example, sgi.com, are granted service access
host name	Full name of the host, for example, warp.engr.sgi.com
IP address	Full IP address of the host, for example, 151.23.345.13
partial IP address	Up to the first three bytes of the IP address in case you want to make subnet access restrictions

The AllowOverride directive has the following syntax:

```
AllowOverride option1  option2 ...
```

The possible values for *option* include the following:

All	Everyone can override any global restrictions in this directory
AuthConfig	Enables use of AuthName, AuthType, TuthUserFile, AuthGroupFile directives
FileInfo	Enables use of AddType and AddEncoding directives
Limit	Enables the use of the Limit directive
None	Prevents anyone from overriding any global restrictions in this directory
Options	Enables use of the Options directive

The default is AllowOverride All.

The deny directive uses the following syntax:

```
deny from hostName1 hostName2 ...
```

The possible values for *hostName* include the following:

domain name	Only hosts from a domain name, for example, sgi.com, are granted service access
host name	Full name of the host, for example, warp.engr.sgi.com
IP address	Full IP address of the host, for example, 151.23.345.13
partial IP address	Up to the first three bytes of the IP address in case you want to make subnet access restrictions
all	Nobody gets in; all hosts are denied access

The <Directory> directive specifies a directory; for example,

```
<Directory /usr/local/etc/hosts>
```

The directive also marks the beginning of a block of directives that all pertain to the specified directory. The </Directory> marks the end of the block of directives for the specified directory.

The <Limit> directive marks the beginning of a block of directives that define the users that have access to a directory, or at the global level, access to the service. The </Limit> directive marks the end of the block of directives that defines (limits) user access.

The <Limit> directive uses the following syntax:

```
<Limit option1 option2 ...>
```

The possible values for *option* include the following:

GET	Enables browsers to run scripts and receive WWW documents
POST	Enables browsers to use POST scripts

The only directives allowed between <Limit> directives are allow, deny, order, and require.

The order directive uses the following syntax:

```
order ordering
```

in which *ordering* has one of the following values:

allow,deny	Considers allow directives before deny directives
deny,allow	Considers deny directives before allow directives

Let's take a look at some examples.

Restricting Service Access to Internal Use

If you want to give employees, but not Internet users, access to your WWW service, you can put the following lines in the access.conf (at the highest level of your document tree):

```
<Directory  /usr/resources/WWW/rockets>
    AllowOverride None
    Options Indexes
    <Limit GET>
        order deny,allow
        deny from all
        allow from yourCompany.com
    </Limit>
</Directory>
```

In the preceding example, no one can override the global access restrictions (Override None). Within the <Limit> descriptors, the deny descriptor is read first (order deny,allow), which allows no one to use the service. The allow descriptor makes an exception for people in your company (*yourCompany.com*). If you want to allow access by people within a subdomain of your company, you would supply the subdomain, for example, engr.sgi.com, rather than the domain, sgi.com.

If you wanted to make the same restriction true for only one of the directories in your service, you would put the same <Limit> section in that directory's .htaccess file.

```
<Limit GET>
    order deny,allow
    deny from all
    allow from yourCompany.com
</Limit>
```

Look for directories in your service that require such protection.

Restricting Access to Several Companies

When your company works in concert with several others, you might want to create a common ground of documents available to each company but not to outside Internet users.

The implementation of this idea is parallel to the previous example, except that you need to name each company in the <Limit> directive:

```
<Directory  /usr/resources/WWW/rockets>
    AllowOverride None
    Options Indexes
    <Limit GET>
        order deny,allow
        deny from all
        allow from yourCompany.com
theirCompany.com
    </Limit>
</Directory>
```

You could limit only specified directories by putting the following lines in the .htaccess file:

```
<Limit GET>
    order deny,allow
    deny from all
    allow from yourCompany.com theirCompany.com
</Limit>
```

You cannot restrict access to specific files unless you put a file in a directory by itself, which makes for unwieldy file structures—but if necessary, however, is easy enough to implement.

Requiring Passwords

If you want to use password access to directories in your service, you need the program included in the support/ directory called htpasswd.c. This program is not included in the prebuilt versions of httpd. Consequently, if you want to use the program, you have to download the entire source code and build it according to the instructions in Chapter 18, in the section, "Compiling the Generic WWW Service Binary."

To add or edit a user's password, you use the htpasswd program with the following syntax:

```
% htpasswd [-c] .htpasswdUserName
```

UserName is the name of the user file that you want to edit or add. The -c option specifies that the file be created (not edited). If you create a new *UserName* file, and htpasswd does not find a duplicate name, it prompts you for the user's password. If htpasswd finds the name, it asks you to change the password. You simply type it twice (to make sure you make no mistake) and the user's password changes. These user names and passwords need not correspond to the system level user names and passwords.

The user name-password combination can provide individual access permissions to the entire service, or to specific directories. When users come upon WWW pages protected in this way, they are prompted for the correct user name and password. If correct, they can get the WWW page along with all protected directories in a similar manner; the user does not have to reenter the user name and password every time.

To give individuals permission to access the service and specified directories, you need to use, in addition to .htpasswd, the following four directives:

AuthGroupFile *path*	Specifies the absolute path name to the file that lists user groups
AuthName *name*	Sets the authorization name for a directory; the name is descriptive and can contain white spaces
AuthType *type*	Sets the type of permission a user has in the directory; currently, only Basic is implemented
AuthUserFile *path*	Specifies the absolute path name, created using htpasswd, to the file that lists users and their passwords

All four directives work in concert; you cannot have one without the other three for the user authentication to work properly. They work at the service level and at the per-directory level.

Individual Permissions

Now, the idea is to put all these directives together so that only people who know a secret password can gain access to certain files.

In the access.conf file, add lines similar to the following:

```
<Directory /usr/resources/WWW/rockets>
    AllowOverride None
    Options Indexes
    AuthName secretPassword
    AuthType Basic
    AuthUserFile /usr/WWW/security/.htpasswd
    AuthGroupFile /usr/WWW/security/NULL
    <Limit GET>
```

```
        require user userName
    </Limit>
</Directory>
```

This all works, assuming that you did use htpasswd to define passwords for users.

The NULL value in AuthGroupFile just means that the user does not have to belong to a system administrator-defined group to gain access to the service.

If you want to accomplish the same task on a per-directory basis, put lines similar to the following in the .htaccess file in the directory:

```
AuthName secretPassword
AuthType Basic
AuthUserFile /usr/WWW/security/.htpasswd
AuthGroupFile /usr/WWW/security/.group1
<Limit GET>
    require user userName
</Limit>
```

Group Permissions

Rather than grant access to your service on a per-person basis, you might just put people into groups and grant group access, which you might find easier.

The entries to access.conf are similar to the previous example, with one exception.

```
<Directory /usr/resources/WWW/rockets>
    AllowOverride None
    Options Indexes
    AuthName secretPassword
    AuthType Basic
    AuthUserFile /usr/WWW/security/.htpasswd
    AuthGroupFile /usr/WWW/security/.group1
    <Limit GET>
        require group groupName
    </Limit>
</Directory>
```

Now the requirement for access to the service is membership in .group1, as indicated by the require statement.

Now, you use your favorite text editor to create the file, .group1. Place the file in the same directory as .htpasswd. The syntax of the entries is as follows, where *userName* is the user ID of each member of the group:

group1: *userName1 userName2 userName3 ...*

For every name you add to the group, you must use the htpasswd program to create a password for each one, for example:

% htpasswd /usr/people/.htpasswd *userName1*

Because you changed the access.conf configuration file, you have to reboot the system before the changes take effect. After you do so, only people who belong to the specified group can access your system.

Using Individual, Domain, and Group Permissions

Now that you've seen how to implement individual, domain, and group access, let's look at a combination of all three:

```
<Directory /usr/resources/WWW/rockets>
    AllowOverride None
    Options Indexes
    AuthName secretPassword
    AuthType Basic
    AuthUserFile /usr/WWW/security/.htpasswd
    AuthGroupFile /usr/WWW/security/groups
    <Limit GET>
        order deny,allow
        deny from all
        allow from company.com
        require group groupName
```

```
    </Limit>
</Directory>
```

The preceding example allows access to members of *company.com* that belong to *groupName*. If you wanted to allow access to only a subset of the people belonging to *groupName*, you would use the following within the <Limit> section:

```
require user userName
```

These restrictions, however, are more commonly used at the per-directory level. You would put the same <Limit> section in that directory's .htaccess file.

Compromising Security

Restricting user access to only those who belong to a specific domain is trustworthy unless you cannot trust DNS (Domain Name Server).

Restricting user access using user IDs is only 90 percent safe. UserIDs and passwords are sent over the Internet unencoded. Unscrupulous people who use sniffer programs sometimes can detect user names and passwords and use them to accomplish unscrupulous deeds.

A WWW browser can follow links from files in the resource tree to outside the tree, which poses a problem if, for example, one of the files in the directory is a symbolic link that takes the user to another directory. To prevent users from planting symbolic links that can take them all over, disable the followsymlink option in the Options directive (in access.conf).

Finally, use the None option with the AllowOverride directive whenever possible.

Misusing Personal HTML Directories

The Userdir directive in the srm.conf file permits users to make personal files available for public access. The default of the directive is as follows:

```
Userdir public_html
```

This means that under everyone's personal directory, they can access public_html. This all sounds fine, except for those people who plant their CGI (Common Gateway Interface scripts and symbolic links to other parts of the file system. (Remember, HTTP does not protect against user access to the root directory with the chroot() function the way FTP and Gopher do.) To guard against possible misuse of these files, put the following entries in access.conf, where */home* is the location of all user's home directories:

```
<Directory /home>
    AllowOverride None
    Options Indexes
</Directory>
```

If the user's home directories are more spread out, you need to use wild cards creatively; for example, substitute the following (or whatever works in your file structure) for the first line above:

```
<Directory /*/public_html*>
```

Limiting the Options directive to only Indexes prevents the use of symbolic links and CGI scripts (because the ExecCGI option in the Options directive is not set).

If you have to compromise this position to give users the opportunity to create symbolic links, use the SymLinksIfOwnerMatch option in the Options directive. This directive allows the service to follow a symbolic link if the owner of the link matches the owner of the target file.

You might find CGI scripts in one of three places, as follows:

→ cgi-bin

→ cgi-bin subdirectories you use the ScriptAlias directive to create

→ Personal HTML subdirectories

All of these are potential problem spots. Make sure that in all of these places, the Options directive does not include the ExecCGI or FollowSymLinks options.

Server-Side Includes

Server-side includes are pieces of information automatically added to documents sent to browsers. Examples include the date, author, and other metacharacter variables.

I have not discussed server-side includes very much for two reasons:

→ They degrade system performance.

→ They present a potential security breach.

The problem is that you can write anything in a server-side include. If someone were to write a bogus include, your server would infect all browsers that accessed it.

To prevent server-side includes, make sure not to use the All or Includes options in the Options directive. Or, if you find that you need to allow includes, use the IncludesNoExec option in the Options directive so that at least executable CGI scripts cannot be included in HTML documents.

Summary

This chapter introduced you to a variety of advanced service management issues including all the options available in the configuration directives. You saw, for example, how to move, update, and analyze log files, move directory structures, enable more document (MIME) types, and automate directory indexing.

This chapter continued with a discussion of gateways, which enable you to extend the usefulness of your Web service.

The security measures discussed in this chapter are designed to protect your service and all users who access it. The security measures in this chapter are HTTP-specific. More extensive security measures are presented in Chapter 8, "Making Your LAN Secure."

part

. . . .

Appendixes

Gopher Services

T he following is a list of Gopher services. The list

was prepared and distributed on the Internet by

David Riggins of Austin, Texas.

Riggins_dw@dir.texas.gov

Unless otherwise indicated, you can assume the

following values: Type=1, Port=70, Path=none.

Gopher Sites

Table A.1 lists some of the more interesting Gopher services you can find.

Table A.1

Service	Location
Australian Defence Force Academy (Canberra, Australia)/	Host=gopher.adfa.oz.au
Baylor College of Medicine/	Host=gopher.bcm.tmc.edu
Department of Information Resources (State of Texas [experimental])	Host=ocs.dir.texas.gov
Go M-Link/	Host=vienna.hh.lib.umich.edu
Internet Wiretap/	Host=wiretap.spies.com
InterNIC: Internet Network Information Center/	Host=rs.internic.net
Library of Congress (LC MARVEL)/	Host=marvel.loc.gov
North Carolina State University Library gopher/	Host=dewey.lib.ncsu.edu
PeachNet Information Service/	Host=Gopher.PeachNet.edu
South African Bibliographic and Information Network/	Host=info2.sabinet.co.za
Texas A&M/	Host=gopher.tamu.edu
The World (Public Access UNIX)/	Host=world.std.com
University of California-Irvine/	Host=gopherserver.cwis.uci.edu
University of California-Santa Barbara Library/	Port=3001 Host=ucsbuxa.ucsb.edu
University of Illinois at Chicago/	Host=gopher.uic.edu
University of Michigan Libraries/	Host=gopher.lib.umich.edu

Service	Location
University of Nevada/	Host=gopher.unr.edu
Whole Earth 'Lectronic Magazine-The WELL's Gopherspace/	Host=gopher.well.sf.ca.us
Yale University/	Host=yaleinfo.yale.edu

Gopher Sites by Technical Area

The following Gopher site listings are grouped by subject matter.

Agriculture

Table A.2 lists Gopher sites related to agriculture.

Table A.2

Service	Location
Australian Defence Force Academy (Canberra, Australia)/	Host=gopher.adfa.oz.au
CYFER-net USDA ES Gopher Server/	Host=cyfer.esusda.gov
Dendrome: Forest Tree Genome Mapping Database/	Host=s27w007.pswfs.gov
Extension Service USDA Information/	Host=zeus.esusda.gov
GRIN, National Genetic Resources Program, USDA-ARS/	Host=gopher.ars-grin.gov
GrainGenes, the Triticeae Genome Gopher/	Host=greengenes.cit.cornell.edu
Library of Congress (LC MARVEL)/	Host=marvel.loc.gov
Maize Genome Database Gopher/	Host=teosinte.agron.missouri.edu

continues

Table A.2, Continued

Service	Location
North Carolina State University Library gopher/	Host=dewey.lib.ncsu.edu
Soybean Data/	Host=mendel.agron.iastate.edu
Texas A&M/	Host=gopher.tamu.edu
University of California-Santa Barbara Library/	Port=3001 Host=ucsbuxa.ucsb.edu
University of Illinois at Chicago/	Host=gopher.uic.edu
University of Minnesota Soil Science Gopher Information Service/	Host=gopher.soils.umn.edu
University of Nevada/	Host=gopher.unr.edu

Astronomy and Astrophysics

Table A.3 lists Gopher sites related to astronomy and astrophysics.

Table A.3

Service	Location
Australian Defence Force Academy (Canberra, Australia)/	Host=gopher.adfa.oz.au
Library of Congress (LC MARVEL)/	Host=marvel.loc.gov
North Carolina State University Library gopher/	Host=dewey.lib.ncsu.edu
South African Bibliographic and Information Network/	Host=info2.sabinet.co.za
Space Telescope Electronic Information System (STEIS)/	Host=stsci.edu
Texas A&M/	Host=gopher.tamu.edu

Service	Location
University of California-Santa Barbara Library/	Port=3001 Host=ucsbuxa.ucsb.edu
University of Illinois at Chicago/	Host=gopher.uic.edu

Biology and Biosciences

Table A.4 lists Gopher sites related to biology and biosciences.

Table A.4

Service	Location
Arabidopsis Research Companion, Mass Gen Hospital/Harvard/	Host=weeds.mgh.harvard.edu
Biodiversity and Biological Collections Gopher/	Host=huh.harvard.edu
bioftp EMBnet, (CH)/	Host=bioftp.unibas.ch
BioInformatics gopher at ANU/	Host=life.anu.edu.au
Brookhaven National Laboratory Protein Data Bank/	Path=1/ Host=pdb.pdb.bnl.gov
CAMIS (Center for Advanced Medical Informatics at Stanford)/	Host=camis.stanford.edu
CWRU Medical School-Department of Biochemistry/	Host=biochemistry.cwru.edu
Computational Biology (Welchlab-Johns Hopkins University)/	Host=merlot.welch.jhu.edu
Dana-Farber Cancer Institute, Boston, MA/	Host=gopher.dfci.harvard.edu
Dendrome: Forest Tree Genome Mapping Database/	Host=s27w007.pswfs.gov

continues

Table A.4, Continued

Service	Location
DNA Data Bank of Japan, Natl. Inst. of Genetics, Mishima/	Host=gopher.nig.ac.jp
EMBnet BioInformation Resource EMBL, (DE)/	Path=1/ Host=ftp.embl-heidelberg.de
EMBnet Bioinformation Resource, (FR)/	Path=1/ Host=coli.polytechnique.fr
EMBnet Bioinformation Resource, (UK)/	Path=1/ Host=s-crim1.daresbury.ac.uk
Genethon (Human Genome Res. Center, Paris), (FR)/	Host=gopher.genethon.fr
GRIN, National Genetic Resources Program, USDA-ARS/	Host=gopher.ars-grin.gov
GrainGenes, the Triticeae Genome Gopher/	Host=greengenes.cit.cornell.edu
Human Genome Mapping Project Gopher Service (UK)/	Host=menu.crc.ac.uk
ICGEBnet, Int.Center for Genetic Eng. & Biotech, (IT)/	Host=genes.icgeb.trieste.it
INN, Weizmann Institute of Science (Israel)/	Host=sunbcd.weizmann.ac.il
IUBio Biology Archive, Indiana University (experimental)/	Host=ftp.bio.indiana.edu
JvNCnet/	Host=gopher.jvnc.net
Library of Congress (LC MARVEL)/	Host=marvel.loc.gov
MegaGopher (Universite de Montreal)/	Host=megasun.bch.umontreal.ca
Microbial Germplasm Database/	Path=1./mgd Host=ava.bcc.orst.edu

Service	Location
National Cancer Center, Tokyo, JAPAN/	Host=gopher.ncc.go.jp
National Institute of Health (NIH) Gopher/	Host=gopher.nih.gov
North Carolina State University Library gopher/	Host=dewey.lib.ncsu.edu
NSF Center for Biological Timing/	Path=1/departments/biotimin
Host=gopher.virginia.edu	
Oregon State University Biological Computing (BCC)/	Host=gopher.bcc.orst.edu
PIR Archive, University of Houston/	Host=ftp.bchs.uh.edu
State University of New York (SUNY)-Brooklyn Health Science Center/	Host=gopher1.medlib.hscbklyn.edu
State University of New York (SUNY)-Syracuse Health Science Center/	Host=micro.ec.hscsyr.edu
TECHNET, Singapore/	Host=solomon.technet.sg
Texas A&M/	Host=gopher.tamu.edu
USCgopher (University of Southern California)/	Host=cwis.usc.edu
University of California-Santa Barbara Library/	Port=3001
	Host=ucsbuxa.ucsb.edu
University of Houston Protein Information Resource/	Host=ftp.bchs.uh.edu
University of Illinois at Chicago/	Host=gopher.uic.edu
University of Nevada/	Host=gopher.unr.edu
University of New Mexico/	Host=peterpan.unm.edu
University of Notre Dame/	Host=gopher.nd.edu

continues

Table A.4, Continued

Service	Location
University of Wisconsin-Madison, Medical School/	Host=msd.medsch.wisc.edu
Vertebrate World Server at Colorado State University/	Host=neptune.rrb.colostate.edu
Worcester Foundation for Experimental Biology/	Host=sci.wfeb.edu
World Data Center on Microorganisms (WDC), RIKEN, Japan/	Host=fragrans.riken.go.jp

Botany

Table A.5 lists Gopher sites related to botany.

Table A.5

Service	Location
Australian National Botanical Gardens/	Host=155.187.10.12
Missouri Botanical Gardens/	Host=gopher.mobot.org
Texas A&M/	Host=gopher.tamu.edu
University of Georgia/	Host=gopher.uga.edu

Chemistry

Table A.6 lists Gopher sites related to chemistry.

Table A.6

Service	Location
Australian Defence Force Academy (Canberra, Australia)/	Host=gopher.adfa.oz.au
Centre for Scientific Computing, (FI)/	Host=gopher.csc.fi
Library of Congress (LC MARVEL)/	Host=marvel.loc.gov
North Carolina State University Library gopher/	Host=dewey.lib.ncsu.edu
University of California-Santa Barbara Library/	Port=3001 Host=ucsbuxa.ucsb.edu
University of Illinois at Chicago/	Host=gopher.uic.edu

Computers

Table A.7 lists Gopher services that offer information related to computing.

Table A.7

Service	Location
CPSR (Computer Professionals for Social Responsibility)	Host=gopher.cpsr.org
CREN/Educom/	Host=info.educom.edu
Computer Solutions by Hawkinson/	Host=csbh.com
HENSA micros (National software archive, Lancaster Univ.), (UK)/	Host=micros.hensa.ac.uk
Info Mac Archives (sumex-aim)/	Host=SUMEX-AIM.Stanford.EDU

continues

Table A.7, Continued

Service	Location
International Federation for Information Processing (IFIP)/	Path=1/International Federation for Information Processing Host=IETF.CNRI.Reston.Va.US
Library of Congress (LC MARVEL)/	Host=marvel.loc.gov
Liverpool University, Dept of Computer Science, (UK)/	Host=gopher.csc.liv.ac.uk
McGill Research Centre for Intelligent Machines, Montreal, Canada/	Host=lightning.mcrcim.mcgill.edu
National Center for Supercomputing Applications/	Host=gopher.ncsa.uiuc.edu
North Carolina State University Library gopher/	Host=dewey.lib.ncsu.edu
Novell Netwire Archives/	Host=ns.novell.com
Texas A&M/	Host=gopher.tamu.edu
University of California-Santa Barbara Library/	Port=3001 Host=ucsbuxa.ucsb.edu

Environment

Table A.8 lists Gopher sites related to the environment.

Table A.8

Service	Location
Australian Environmental Resources Information Network (ERIN)/	Host=kaos.erin.gov.au
CIESIN Global Change Information Gateway/	Host=gopher.ciesin.org

Service	Location
EcoGopher at the University of Virginia/	Host=ecosys.drdr.virginia.edu
EnviroGopher (at CMU)/	Host=envirolink.hss.cmu.edu
Go M-Link/	Host=vienna.hh.lib.umich.edu
GreenGopher at University of Virginia in Charlottesville/	Path=1/information/uva/greens@uva/greengopher Host=ecosys.drdr.Virginia.EDU
Library of Congress (LC MARVEL)/	Host=marvel.loc.gov
North Carolina State University Library gopher/	Host=dewey.lib.ncsu.edu
University of California-Santa Barbara Library/	Port=3001 Host=ucsbuxa.ucsb.edu
University of Nevada/	Host=gopher.unr.edu
Vertebrate World server at Colorado State University/	Host=neptune.rrb.colostate.edu

Geology and Oceanography

Table A.9 lists Gopher sites related to geology and oceanography.

Table A.9

Service	Location
Bedford Institute of Oceanography (Canada)/	Host=biome.bio.dfo.ca
Library of Congress (LC MARVEL)/	Host=marvel.loc.gov
North Carolina State University Library gopher/	Host=dewey.lib.ncsu.edu

continues

Table A.9, Continued

Service	Location
Northwestern University, Department of Geological Sciences/	Path=1/ Host=gopher.earth.nwu.edu
University of California-Davis/	Host=gopher.ucdavis.edu
University of California-Santa Barbara Library/	Port=3001 Host=ucsbuxa.ucsb.edu
University of California-Santa Barbara Geological Sciences Gopher/	Host=gopher.geol.ucsb.edu
University of Illinois at Chicago/	Host=gopher.uic.edu
University of Texas at El Paso, Geological Sciences Dept./	Host=dillon.geo.ep.utexas.edu
US Geological Survey (USGS)/	Host=info.er.usgs.gov
USGS Atlantic Marine Geology/	Host=bramble.er.usgs.gov

Medical

Table A.10 lists Gopher sites related to the medical field.

Table A.10

Service	Location
Australian Defence Force Academy (Canberra, Australia)/	Host=gopher.adfa.oz.au
Anesthesiology Gopher /	Host=eja.anes.hscsyr.edu
Austin Hospital, Melbourne, Australia/	Host=pet1.austin.unimelb.edu.au
Baylor College of Medicine/	Host=gopher.bcm.tmc.edu
CAMIS (Center for Advanced Medical Informatics at Stanford)/	Host=camis.stanford.edu

Service	Location
Cornell Medical College/	Host=gopher.med.cornell.edu
Dana-Farber Cancer Institute, Boston, MA/	Host=gopher.dfci.harvard.edu
Gustavus Adolphus College/	Host=gopher.gac.edu
ISU College of Pharmacy/	Host=pharmacy.isu.edu
JvNCnet/	Host=gopher.jvnc.net
Library of Congress (LC MARVEL)/	Host=marvel.loc.gov
National Cancer Center, Tokyo, JAPAN/	Host=gopher.ncc.go.jp
National Institute of Allergy and Infectious Disease (NIAID)/	Host=gopher.niaid.nih.gov
National Institute of Health (NIH) Gopher/	Host=gopher.nih.gov
North Carolina State University Library gopher/	Host=dewey.lib.ncsu.edu
Stanford University Medical Center/	Host=med-gopher.stanford.edu
State University of New York (SUNY)-Brooklyn Health Science Center/	Host=gopher1.medlib.hscbklyn.edu
State University of New York (SUNY)-Syracuse Health Science Center/	Host=micro.ec.hscsyr.edu
Texas A&M/	Host=gopher.tamu.edu
USCgopher (University of Southern California)/	Host=cwis.usc.edu
University of California-Santa Barbara Library/	Port=3001 Host=ucsbuxa.ucsb.edu
University of Illinois at Chicago/	Host=gopher.uic.edu

continues

Table A.10, Continued

Service	Location
University of Illinois at Urbana-Champaign/	Host=gopher.uiuc.edu
University of Nevada/	Host=gopher.unr.edu
University of New Mexico/	Host=peterpan.unm.edu
University of Texas Health Science Center at Houston/	Host=gopher.uth.tmc.edu
University of Texas M. D. Anderson Cancer Center/	Host=utmdacc.uth.tmc.edu
University of Texas Medical Branch/	Host=phil.utmb.edu
University of Washington, Pathology Department/	Host=larry.pathology.washington.edu
University of Wisconsin-Madison, Medical School/	Host=msd.medsch.wisc.edu
World Health Organization (WHO)/	Host=gopher.who.ch

Physics

Table A.11 lists Gopher sites related to physics.

Table A.11

Service	Location
Australian Defence Force Academy (Canberra, Australia)/	Host=gopher.adfa.oz.au
Centre for Scientific Computing, (FI)/	Host=gopher.csc.fi
ICTP, International Centre for Theoretical Physics, Trieste, (IT)/	Host=gopher.ictp.trieste.it

Service	Location
Institute of Physics, University of Zagreb, (HR)/	Host=gopher.ifs.hr
LANL Physics Information Service/	Host=mentor.lanl.gov
Library of Congress (LC MARVEL)/	Host=marvel.loc.gov
North Carolina State University Library gopher/	Host=dewey.lib.ncsu.edu
Physics Resources (Experimental)/	Host=granta.uchicago.edu
Presbyterian College (Clinton, SC)/	Host=cs1.presby.edu
Texas A&M/	Host=gopher.tamu.edu
University of California-Santa Barbara Library/	Port=3001 Host=ucsbuxa.ucsb.edu
University of Illinois at Chicago/	Host=gopher.uic.edu

Nontechnical Categories

This section lists Gopher sites of a nontechnical nature.

Art

Table A.12 lists Gopher sites related to art.

Table A.12

Service	Location
Library of Congress (LC MARVEL)/	Host=marvel.loc.gov
University of California-Santa Barbara Library/	Port=3001 Host=ucsbuxa.ucsb.edu
University of Illinois at Chicago/	Host=gopher.uic.edu

Books and Magazines

Table A.13 lists Gopher sites related to books and magazines (electronic and for sale).

Table A.13

Service	Location
ACADEME THIS WEEK (Chronicle of Higher Education)/	Host=chronicle.merit.edu
Internet Wiretap/	Host=wiretap.spies.com
Michigan State University/	Host=gopher.msu.edu
Nova Scotia Technology Network, N.S., Canada/	Host=nstn.ns.ca
O'Reilly & Associates (computer book publisher)/	Host=ora.com
The Electronic Newsstand(tm)/	Port=2100 Host=gopher.netsys.com
The New Republic Magazine/	Port=2101 Host=gopher.netsys.com
The World (Public Access UNIX)/	Host=world.std.com
University of California-Santa Barbara Library/	Port=3001 Host=ucsbuxa.ucsb.edu
University of Illinois at Chicago/	Host=gopher.uic.edu
University of Nevada/	Host=gopher.unr.edu

Education and Research

Table A.14 lists Gopher sites related to education and research.

Table A.14

Service	Location
Apple Computer Higher Education Gopher Server/	Host=info.hed.apple.com
AskERIC-(Educational Resources Information Center)/	Host=ericir.syr.edu
Centre for Scientific Computing, (FI)/	Host=gopher.csc.fi
Consortium for School Networking (CoSN)/	Host=cosn.org
Go M-Link/	Host=vienna.hh.lib.umich.edu
Library of Congress (LC MARVEL)/	Host=marvel.loc.gov
National Center on Adult Literacy/	Host=litserver.literacy.upenn.edu
National Science Foundation Gopher (STIS)/	Host=stis.nsf.gov

Employment Opportunities and Resume Postings

Table A.15 lists Gopher sites related to employment opportunities.

Table A.15

Service	Location
ACADEME THIS WEEK (Chronicle of Higher Education)/	Host=chronicle.merit.edu
Academic Position Network/	Port=11111 Host=wcni.cis.umn.edu
American Physiological Society/	Port=3300 Path=1/ Host=gopher.uth.tmc.edu

continues

Table A.15, Continued

Service	Location
IUPUI Integrated Technologies/	Host=INDYCMS.IUPUI.EDU
Online Career Center (at Msen)/	Port=9062 Host=garnet.msen.com
Virginia Coast Reserve Information System (VCRIS)/	Host=atlantic.evsc.Virginia.edu

Federal Government

Table A.16 lists Gopher sites related to the federal government.

Table A.16

Service	Location
Counterpoint Publishing/	Port=2001 Host=gopher.netsys.com
Federal Info. Exchange (FEDIX) (Under Construction-experimental)/	Host=fedix.fie.com
InterCon Systems Corporation/	Host=vector.intercon.com

Federal Laboratories

Table A.17 lists Gopher sites related to federal laboratories.

Table A.17

Service	Location
Brookhaven National Laboratory Protein Data Bank/	Path=1/ Host=pdb.pdb.bnl.gov
Federal Info. Exchange (FEDIX) (Under Construction - experimental)/	Host=fedix.fie.com

Service	Location
Library X at Johnson Space Center/	Host=krakatoa.jsc.nasa.gov
Los Alamos National Laboratory/	Host=gopher.lanl.gov
Michigan State University/	Host=gopher.msu.edu
NASA Goddard Space Flight Center/	Host=gopher.gsfc.nasa.gov
NASA Mid-Continent Technology Transfer Center/	Host=technology.com
NASA Network Applications and Information Center (NAIC)/	Host=naic.nasa.gov
NASA Shuttle Small Payloads Info/	Host=vx740.gsfc.nasa.gov
National Institute of Standards and Technology (NIST)/	Host=gopher-server.nist.gov
Oak Ridge National Laboratory ESD Gopher/	Host=jupiter.esd.ornl.gov

General Reference Resources

Table A.18 lists Gopher sites offered as general reference resources.

Table A.18

Service	Location
Australian Defence Force Academy (Canberra, Australia)/	Host=gopher.adfa.oz.au
Department of Information Resources (State of Texas)[experimental]/	Host=ocs.dir.texas.gov
Internet Wiretap/	Host=wiretap.spies.com
Library of Congress (LC MARVEL)/	Host=marvel.loc.gov
McGill Research Centre for Intelligent Machines, Montreal, Canada/	Host=lightning.mcrcim.mcgill.edu

continues

Table A.18, Continued

Service	Location
University of California-Santa Barbara Library/	Port=3001 Host=ucsbuxa.ucsb.edu
University of Illinois at Chicago/	Host=gopher.uic.edu
University of Michigan Libraries/	Host=gopher.lib.umich.edu
University of Nevada/	Host=gopher.unr.edu

Internet/Cyberspace

Table A.19 lists Gopher sites related to the Internet and cyberspace.

Table A.19

Service	Location
CPSR (Computer Professionals for Social Responsibility)	Host=gopher.cpsr.org
CREN/Educom/	Host=info.educom.edu
Electronic Frontier Foundation/	Host=gopher.eff.org
EFF-Austin/	Path=1/eff-austin Host=gopher.tic.com
Internet Society (includes IETF)/	Path=1/Internet Society (includes IETF) Host=ietf.CNRI.Reston.Va.US
Internet Wiretap/	Host=wiretap.spies.com
InterNIC: Internet Network Information Center/	Host=rs.internic.net
Matrix Information and Directory Services, Inc. (MIDS), Austin, Texas	Path=1/matrix Host=gopher.tic.com
Merit Network/	Host=nic.merit.edu
McGill Research Centre for Intelligent Machines, Montreal, Canada/	Host=lightning.mcrcim.mcgill.edu

Service	Location
Michigan State University/	Host=gopher.msu.edu
ONENET Networking Information/	Host=nic.onenet.net
PSGnet/RAINet: low-cost and international networking/	Host=gopher.psg.com
Sprintlink Gopher Server, Virginia USA/	Host=ftp.sprintlink.net
Texas Internet Consulting (TIC), Austin, Texas/	Host=gopher.tic.com
University of Nevada/	Host=gopher.unr.edu
Yale University/	Host=yaleinfo.yale.edu

Legal or Law-Related

Table A.20 lists Gopher sites about the law and legal issues.

Table A.20

Service	Location
Cleveland State University Law Library/	Host=gopher.law.csuohio.edu
Cornell Law School (experimental)/	Host=fatty.law.cornell.edu
Library of Congress (LC MARVEL)/	Host=marvel.loc.gov
Saint Louis University/	Host=sluava.slu.edu
University of California-Santa Barbara Library/	Port=3001 Host=ucsbuxa.ucsb.edu
University of Chicago Law School/	Host=lawnext.uchicago.edu.
University of Illinois at Chicago/	Host=gopher.uic.edu
Washington & Lee University/	Path=1/ Host=liberty.uc.wlu.edu

Music

Table A.21 lists music-related Gopher sites.

Table A.21

Service	Location
Internet Wiretap/	Host=wiretap.spies.com
Library of Congress (LC MARVEL)/	Host=marvel.loc.gov
Master Gopher Server @ Univ. of Minnesota/	Host=gopher.umn.edu
Texas A&M/	Host=gopher.tamu.edu
University of California-Santa Barbara Library/	Port=3001 Host=ucsbuxa.ucsb.edu
University of Michigan Libraries/	Host=gopher.lib.umich.edu

Technical Reports, Publications, Journals, and Newsletters

Table A.22 lists Gopher sites that contain technical reports, publications, journals, and newsletters.

Table A.22

Service	Location
Australian Defence Force Academy (Canberra, Australia)/	Host=gopher.adfa.oz.au
CICNET gopher server/	Host=nic.cic.net
CREN/Educom/	Host=info.educom.edu
EDUCOM Documents and News/	Host=educom.edu
Go M-Link/	Host=vienna.hh.lib.umich.edu
Michigan State University/	Host=gopher.msu.edu

Service	Location
Scholarly Communications Project Electronic Journals/	Host=borg.lib.vt.edu
University of California-Santa Barbara Library/	Port=3001 Host=ucsbuxa.ucsb.edu
University of Illinois at Chicago/	Host=gopher.uic.edu
Vortex Technology/	Host=gopher.vortex.com

Free Software on the Internet

There are scads of freeware on the Internet. This appendix offers a small sampling of applications of interest to Internet service sponsors.

Table B.1 Software Available on the Internet

Access	Directory	Description
boombox.micro.umn.edu	gttp://www.eit.com/software/getstats/getstats.html	getstats is a statistics package for WWW services
boombox.micro.umn.edu	/pub/gopher	Gopher helps you find information in the Internet
boombox.micro.umn.edu	pub/gopher/Unix/GopherTools	gla is one of the better log analyzer scripts
boombox.micro.umn.edu	pub/gopher/Unix/GopherTools	GLASS produces 22 reports
boombox.micro.umn.edu	/pub/gopher/Unix/gopher-gateway	Gopher2FTP is a Gopher to FTP gateway
boombox.micro.umn.edu	/pub/gopher/Unix/gopher-gateway	GopherSQL accepts Gopher requests and translates them into SQL requests
boombox.micro.umn.edu	pub/gopher/Unix/GopherTools	Logger is an older log analyzer
boombox.micro.umn.edu in	pub/gopher/Unix/GopherTools /glog directory	glog is a log analyzer that came with Gopher 1.x
feenix.metronet.com at	/pub/perl/scripts/gopher/tools	Fwgstat writes a usage report for Gopher services
ftp.funet.fi	/pub/networking/management/NeTraMet	NeTraMet is the first implementation of the Internet Accounting Architecture (RFC 1272); it is a tool for analyzing network traffic flow, and helps in network monitoring, capacity planning, and performance measurement
ftp.ncsa.uiuc.edu	/Web/mosaic	Mosaic is a multi-media browser for Internet information
ftp://austin.bedi.com/plexus/2.2.1/dist/Plexus-2.2.1.tar.Z		Plexus' WWW service software

Access	Directory	Description
ftp://ftp.ncsa.uiuc.edu	/Web/ncsa.httpd	httpd is the WWW server code developed by NCSA
ftp://info.cern.ch/pub/www/bin		CERN's WWW service software
Gophreport	feenix.metronet.com in /pub/perl/scripts/gopher/tools	reports Gopher Usage based on days, time, files, hosts, errors
http://bsdi.com/server/doc/plexus.html		is the code, written in the Perl scripting language, for a WWW server
http://info.cern.ch/hypertext/WWW/Daemon/Status.html		is the code for CERN's version of a WWW server
http://nearnet.gnn.com/mkt/travel/center.html		htget is a tool you can use to duplicate (mirror) all or part of the directory tree of another host
http://siva.cshl.org/wusage.html		wusage is a statistics package for WWW services
http://www.ics.uci.edu/WebSoft/wwwstat		wwwstat is a statistics package for WWW services
httpd://hopf.math.nwu.edu		is the code for the GN server which can serve both as a Gopher and WWW server
wuarchive.wustl.edu	/packages/wuarchive-ftpd/wu-ftpd-2.4.tar.Z	Washington University's version of FTP

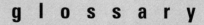

anchor   A hypertext link in the form of text or a graphic that, when clicked upon, takes you to the linked file

annotation   A Mosaic feature that enables you to add a comment to a viewed document

anonymous FTP   Enables you to log in to an FTP service using the login name anonymous

Archie   A search engine that finds file names on anonymous FTP services

ARPAnet   The first network of computers funded by the US Department of Defense Advanced Projects Agency

au   Extension for audio files

backbone   Generally very high-speed, T3 telephone lines that connect remote ends of networks and networks to one another; only service providers are connected to the Internet in this way

browser   A graphical software interface that enables you to look at information on the WWW

CERN   Home of WWW

checksumming   A service performed by UDP that checks to see if packets were changed during transmission

client   An application that makes a request of a service on a (sometimes) remote computer; the request can be, for example, a function call

database An organization of data into one or more tables of related data that is used to answer questions

dial up A connection to the Internet through a modem and telephone line that allows (only) e-mail and running processes on a remote computer

direct connection A connection to the Internet through a dedicated line, such as ISDN

Directory of Servers A service that describes what is available on servers throughout the world

Doc-ID In WAIS, an ID that identifies a specific document in a database

Eudora The most widely used e-mail system

FAQ Acronym for Frequently Asked Question; a document organized in a question and answer format

FTP Acronym for File Transfer Protocol; a popular mechanism for transferring files over the Internet

ftp The Unix command that runs the FTP client

gif An image format (Graphics Interchange Format)

Gopher An Internet service that provides menu descriptions of files on Internet servers; used primarily to find Internet information

Gopherspace Connected Gopher services

home page A document that serves as the entry way for all the information contained in a company's WWW service

host A server connected to the Internet

HTML Acronym for Hypertext Markup Language; the protocol used to define various text styles in a hypertext document, including emphasis and bulleted lists

html The extension for HTML files

HTTP Acronym for Hypertext Transfer Protocol; the protocol used by WWW services

hypertext A highlighted word that, when clicked on, opens another document

index files Files created by waisindex that make up the WAIS source database

ISDN A dedicated telephone line connection that transmits digital data at the rate of 56 Kbps

JPEG A compression standard (Joint Photographic Expert Group)

leased connection A connection to the Internet through a local phone company that allows your company to set up, for example, FTP, WWW, and Gopher services on the Internet

local area network (LAN) A group of computers linked by hardware and protocols such as Ethernet or Token-Ring

login The process of entering your user ID and password at a prompt to gain access to a service

MIME A protocol that describes the format of Internet messages (Multipurpose Internet Mail Extension)

Mosaic A graphical interface for the World Wide

Web that employs hypertext, images, video clips, and sound

news reader A tool that enables you to read about one of the thousands of special interest groups on the Internet

proxy A connection through a modem and telephone line to the Internet that enables you to use full-screen programs, such as Mosaic and Netscape, to browse the Internet

relevance feedback In WAIS, a score, between 0 and 1,000, that represents how closely a document satisfies search criteria

server A computer that runs services

service An application that processes requests by client applications, such as storing data, or executing an algorithm

SGML Acronym for Standard Generalized Markup Language; a language that describes the structure of a document

source In WAIS, describes a database and how to reach it

T1 A dedicated telephone line connection that transfers data at the rate of 1.4 Mbps

T3 A dedicated telephone line that transfers data at the rate of 45 Mbps

tags Annotations used by HTML, such as <H2>, </H2>

TCP/IP Acronym for Transmission Control Protocol/Internet Protocol; a communications protocol that allows computers of any make to communicate when running TCP/IP software

telnet An Internet service that enables you to log on to a computer over telephone lines

tiff A graphics format (Tag Image File Format)

URL Acronym for Uniform Resource Locator; a means of specifying the location of information on the Internet for WWW clients

Usenet An online news and bulletin board system accommodating over 7,000 interest groups

Veronica A tool that helps you find files on Gopher servers

viewer applications Software that gives you access to the images, video, and sounds stored on Internet servers

WAIS Acronym for Wide Area Information Server; a tool that helps you search for documents using keywords or selections of text as search criteria

WAIS client An application that formats user-defined search criteria to be used by waisserver; the goal is to find matches between search criteria and data files (of all types)

WAIS sources Databases created by waisindex that include, for example, a table of all unique words contained in a document

waisindex A mechanism that extracts data from raw data files (of most types) to put into databases, called WAIS sources, which allow waisserver to match search criteria to data files quickly

waisserver A mechanism that compares search criteria, supplied by a WAIS client, to WAIS sources

Web Short for World Wide Web (WWW)

wide area networks (WAN) Connecting computers over long distances using high-speed dedicated telephone lines or microwave transmissions

World Wide Web (WWW) A hypertext-based, multimedia system that enables you to browse and access information on the Internet

xbm A graphics format (X bitmapped)

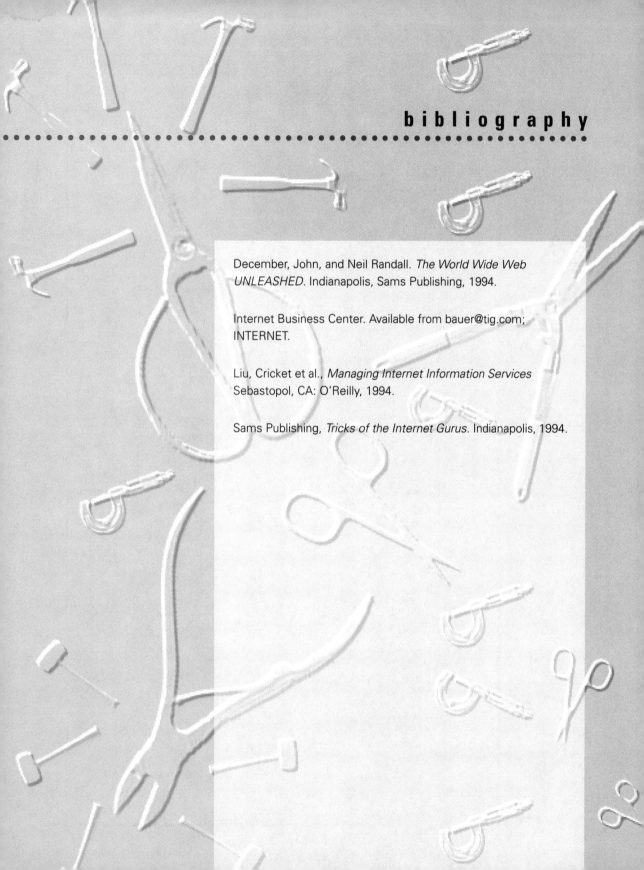

bibliography

December, John, and Neil Randall. *The World Wide Web UNLEASHED*. Indianapolis, Sams Publishing, 1994.

Internet Business Center. Available from bauer@tig.com; INTERNET.

Liu, Cricket et al., *Managing Internet Information Services* Sebastopol, CA: O'Reilly, 1994.

Sams Publishing, *Tricks of the Internet Gurus*. Indianapolis, 1994.

E

F

freeWAIS, 161-176

asterisk (*) wild card, 179
clients, 163
    building, 168-172
    customizing, 175
    finding documents, 173
compilers, setting options, 168
databases, 179-181
directories, 166-168
indexer, 162
libraries, setting variables, 168
Makefile, editing, 167-168
managing, 177-191
memory and disk space, freeing, 190
searches, 164
security issues, 178-180
services, managing, 172-175
software, attaining, 164-172
source file options, specifying, 189-190
synonyms, 188-189
users, changing, 178
waisindex, 181-184
    index files, 182
    indexing files, 182-188
    linking files, 188
    logging messages during indexing, 190
    making data files available to WWW
        browsers, 187-190
    source match algorithm, 184-185
waisserver, 174-175
Z39.50-1992 protocol, 194
see also WAIS (Wide Area Information
    Server); ZDIST
FTP (File Transfer Protocol), 59-62,
131-139, 318
administrative tools, 159-160
aliases, 144
Archie, 62, 146-147
archive files, organizing, 142-143
client/server relationship, 55
firewalls, 61

ftpadmin e-mail, checking, 148
Gopher, linking to, 237
ls-lR files, creating, 146
navigating aids, 143-147
README files, 143-144
search paths, defining, 145
services
    aliases, setting up, 120
    anonymous users, setting up, 122-123
    appearance of, 127-128
    configuring, 121-122
    IDs, 120
    inline configuration, 96
    naming, 120-121
    setting up, 119-129
    testing, 127
shutting down, 156-157
symbolic links, 145
syslog files, checking, 147-148
users
    format checks, 151
    groups, 153-154
    logging events, 157-158
    password checks, 152
    restricting access, 149-153
    restricting actions, 153
    restricting uploading files, 158-160
    sending messages to, 154-157
    see also WU (Washington University) FTP
ftp files, waisindex, 186
ftpcount command (WU FTP), 160
ftpd commands, 121
ftpshut command (WU FTP), 160
ftpwho command (WU FTP), 160
functions
    chroot(), 123
    popen(), 276
    system(), 276
Fwgstat program, 203, 314

G

H

J - L

W

X-Z

PLUG YOURSELF INTO...

THE MACMILLAN INFORMATION SUPERLIBRARY™

Free information and vast computer resources from the world's leading computer book publisher—online!

FIND THE BOOKS THAT ARE RIGHT FOR YOU!

A complete online catalog, plus sample chapters and tables of contents give you an in-depth look at *all* of our books, including hard-to-find titles. It's the best way to find the books you need!

- **STAY INFORMED** with the latest computer industry news through our online newsletter, press releases, and customized Information SuperLibrary Reports.

- **GET FAST ANSWERS** to your questions about MCP books and software.

- **VISIT** our online bookstore for the latest information and editions!

- **COMMUNICATE** with our expert authors through e-mail and conferences.

- **DOWNLOAD SOFTWARE** from the immense MCP library:
    - Source code and files from MCP books
    - The best shareware, freeware, and demos

- **DISCOVER HOT SPOTS** on other parts of the Internet.

- **WIN BOOKS** in ongoing contests and giveaways!

TO PLUG INTO MCP: ➤ WORLD WIDE WEB: **http://www.mcp.com**

GOPHER: gopher.mcp.com

FTP: ftp.mcp.com

WANT MORE INFORMATION?

CHECK OUT THESE RELATED TOPICS OR SEE YOUR LOCAL BOOKSTORE

CAD and 3D Studio

As the number one CAD publisher in the world, and as a Registered Publisher of Autodesk, New Riders Publishing provides unequaled content on this complex topic. Industry-leading products include AutoCAD and 3D Studio.

Networking

As the leading Novell NetWare publisher, New Riders Publishing delivers cutting-edge products for network professionals. We publish books for all levels of users, from those wanting to gain NetWare Certification, to those administering or installing a network. Leading books in this category include *Inside NetWare 3.12, CNE Training Guide: Managing NetWare Systems, Inside TCP/IP,* and *NetWare: The Professional Reference.*

Graphics

New Riders provides readers with the most comprehensive product tutorials and references available for the graphics market. Best-sellers include *Inside CorelDRAW! 5, Inside Photoshop 3,* and *Adobe Photoshop NOW!*

Internet and Communications

As one of the fastest growing publishers in the communications market, New Riders provides unparalleled information and detail on this ever-changing topic area. We publish international best-sellers such as *New Riders' Official Internet Yellow Pages, 2nd Edition,* a directory of over 10,000 listings of Internet sites and resources from around the world, and *Riding the Internet Highway, Deluxe Edition.*

Operating Systems

Expanding off our expertise in technical markets, and driven by the needs of the computing and business professional, New Riders offers comprehensive references for experienced and advanced users of today's most popular operating systems, including *Understanding Windows 95, Inside Unix, Inside Windows 3.11 Platinum Edition, Inside OS/2 Warp Version 3,* and *Inside MS-DOS 6.22.*

Other Markets

Professionals looking to increase productivity and maximize the potential of their software and hardware should spend time discovering our line of products for Word, Excel, and Lotus 1-2-3. These titles include *Inside Word 6 for Windows, Inside Excel 5 for Windows, Inside 1-2-3 Release 5,* and *Inside WordPerfect for Windows.*

Orders/Customer Service   **1-800-653-6156**   Source Code   **NRP95**

New Riders Publishing   201 West 103rd Street ◆ Indianapolis, Indiana 46290 USA

REGISTRATION CARD

Building a Linux Internet Server

Name _____ Title _____

Company _____ Type of business _____

Address _____

City/State/ZIP _____

Have you used these types of books before? ☐ yes ☐ no

If yes, which ones? _____

_____

How many computer books do you purchase each year? ☐ 1–5 ☐ 6 or more

How did you learn about this book? _____

Where did you purchase this book? _____

Which applications do you currently use? _____

_____

Which computer magazines do you subscribe to? _____

_____

What trade shows do you attend? _____

_____

Comments: _____

_____

_____

Would you like to be placed on our preferred mailing list? ☐ yes ☐ no

☐ **I would like to see my name in print!** You may use my name and quote me in future New Riders products and promotions. My daytime phone number is: _____

New Riders Publishing   201 West 103rd Street ◆ Indianapolis, Indiana 46290 USA

Fax to ▮▮▮▮▮▮   Orders/Customer Service ▮▮▮▮▮▮   Source Code ▮▮▮▮▮▮

Fold Here

- -

BUSINESS REPLY MAIL
FIRST-CLASS MAIL PERMIT NO. 9918 INDIANAPOLIS IN

POSTAGE WILL BE PAID BY THE ADDRESSEE

**NEW RIDERS PUBLISHING
201 W 103RD ST
INDIANAPOLIS IN 46290-9058**